D1927665

The Great Flood

by

Nick Thom

Grosvenor House
Publishing Limited

This book is published by
Grosvenor House Publishing Ltd
28-30 High Street, Guildford, Surrey, GU1 3HY.
www.grosvenorhousepublishing.co.uk

A CIP record for this book
is available from the British Library

ISBN 978-1-906645-92-2

Preface

In a sceptical age where so many of the foundations of our various cultures are being questioned and then tossed aside, proof that Noah's flood – or indeed Manu's flood of Hindu tradition – was a real event would give even hardened sceptics reason to stop and think. Yet the sheer impossibility that any flood could ever have risen to cover mountains puts the idea of proving it into the realm of fantasy. To most scientists, even to most Biblical scholars, the story of Noah is obviously nothing more than the story of a really impressive river flood that has been blown out of all proportion over centuries of telling and retelling. How could it possibly be true? If the claims made in the Bible, the Koran and the Hindu Vedas are to be believed, the flood that Noah and Manu survived actually wiped the rest of mankind from the face of the earth. There is surely no way that a disaster of such magnitude could possibly have been missed by science – you would have thought.

I guess we could debate the magnitude of the disaster as it is described; for example whether the passages in the Bible and the Koran actually refer to the extinction of all life or whether perhaps they only refer to those living in a particular region, whether the 'mountains' that were covered were just local areas of high ground or whether Mount Everest should be included. But, whatever the finer details, the description we have of Noah's flood is of something quite different from anything the world has experienced in all of recorded history.

The Great Flood therefore represents a serious challenge, a point of conflict between science and religion, and the task I have taken on here is to answer a simple question: is it true or not? If not then Jews, Christians, Muslims and Hindus all need to rethink their faiths – or at least rethink the level of trust they have in their scriptures. But if it really is true then not only has the most awesome natural disaster in the history of mankind's occupation of the planet been missed by science but the scriptures have been subject to a great deal of undeserved criticism.

Whether you approach this subject as a sceptic or as a believer, whether your mind is open to persuasion or not, I hope that you enjoy reading this book as much as I enjoyed researching it and writing it. I believe I have a tale to tell, a surprising tale but a true tale, perhaps even a tale that will change your view of the planet you live on.

Nick Thom
University of Nottingham
February 2009

Other books by the same author:

The Origin of Tongues (2nd Edition), Grosvenor House Publishing, 2007

History Rewritten, Grosvenor House Publishing, 2008

Nick Thom is a member of:

New Writers UK
[www.newwritersuk.co.uk]

Contents

1

Introduction

This is a book about something truly mind-boggling. If there really ever was a 'Great Flood' then it was quite simply the most dramatic event in all of mankind's history. Ice Ages have come and gone, super-volcanoes have erupted; but these would pale into insignificance beside the truly catastrophic consequences of a worldwide flood. Yet this is the claim made in the Bible and repeated by the Koran, and it is believed by hundreds of millions of people today! We all know the story of Noah, who survived with his family and a multitude of animals in a large boat (referred to in the Bible as an 'ark') while the rest of mankind perished. If you've never read the original you have probably seen a film interpretation or read one of several slightly quirky books based on the story of Noah. But can we really believe it? As a rational human being I find myself questioning the traditional story no matter how much I may wish it to be true.

In the case of the Great Flood there is generally no trouble defining the line where myth and science meet; they don't meet at all! Myth says that waters covered the mountain tops – or at least some mountain tops – and that mankind (other than Noah and his family) was wiped out in a tremendous catastrophe; you can read about it in the Bible, in the book of Genesis chapters 6 to 8, and there are numerous references in the Koran. Science says that such a disaster could not possibly have happened. Or does it? Perhaps I simply mean that scientists are yet to dream up a rational explanation. Could myth and science possibly be reconciled one day? Could there really ever have been a Great Flood?

I remember the floods in south-east England in 1968. I remember gazing out over the mighty river that, only hours before, had been nothing more than a tranquil stream. To us in our village this was a Great Flood. Every road out of the village was flooded; an abandoned car lay half-submerged in several feet of water. Yet by evening it had all gone. Noah would hardly have been impressed.

Every year the people of Bangladesh experience flooding on a truly massive scale. The Jamuna River, the mighty waterway formed from the confluence of the great Indian rivers Ganges and Brahmaputra, bursts its banks during each monsoon season. There is no point trying to stop it. There is so much monsoon rainwater pouring off the land that it inundates much of the country, a country of well over a hundred million people. And these floods can last for many weeks, even months. Surely Bangladeshis have a right to talk in terms of a Great Flood? Yet the depth is only measured in feet. So long as you have a house on stilts you wouldn't even have to move. If Noah had constructed his ark in Bangladesh, I doubt whether the annual river flood would even have been deep enough to float it!

In August 2005 the Louisiana state and United States national authorities were caught completely off guard when the levees around the city of New Orleans failed under the onslaught of hurricane Katrina – despite the warnings of engineers. The authorities didn't expect it because they couldn't really imagine it; nor could the city's inhabitants. They couldn't imagine it because it was 21st Century America and things like that just didn't happen. But it did. Those nearest to the breaches suffered a devastating onrush of water and within minutes their houses were lying metres deep. By the time dawn broke most of the city lay beneath the flood. Around two thousand died; tens of thousands had their lives ruined; for them this truly was a Great Flood. Yet the area affected was only a few kilometres across. An ark would certainly have been useful – but its journey would have lasted no more than a few minutes.

On December 26th 2004 the calm of another Indian Ocean day by the seaside was shattered as the ocean itself suddenly rose by several metres, sending giant waves crashing hundreds of metres inland. This was something far outside anyone's experience, something those who saw it could never have imagined in their worst nightmares. Yet it happened. The physical effects of a magnitude 9.1 earthquake not far beneath the seabed were suddenly clear to all as tsunamis zipped at hundreds of miles per hour right across the Indian Ocean. Within minutes two hundred thousand had died on the west coast of Sumatra; within hours they had been joined by tens of thousands more from Thailand, India, Sri Lanka and even from the coast of Africa. As floods go this was about as dramatic as it gets. However, with a duration of little more than 10 minutes at any given location, does it really deserve to be called a Great Flood?

These are some of the most dramatic floods in human experience – and none of them comes even remotely close to matching the story told in the Bible.

CATASTROPHES OF LONG AGO

It is only a century and a half since Charles Darwin shocked the scientific world by providing good reason to believe that the planet we live on is actually very old indeed.[1] The religious establishment was more than shocked; it was traumatised. Darwin spoke in terms of millions of years, and that didn't sit at all comfortably with the then-current Christian view that creation itself had only taken place some 6000 years ago.[2] Regrettably for some the trauma is still very real.

Darwin had argued that the only way to understand the fossil record, not to mention the amazing variety of life present on the planet, was in terms of gradual changes taking place from generation to generation, changes which were so gradual that they would only be observed over thousands of generations. This was the 'Theory of Evolution' and evolution has now undeniably become a fundamental part of mainstream science. It is a theory that has stood the test of time better than most and, while modifications are constantly being made, the ideas expressed in *The Origin of Species* are very widely believed today. The change in scientific thinking has become unstoppable. Darwin's observations on the development of biological species no longer required any belief in ancient catastrophes, just countless millennia of continuing existence; this concept, known as 'uniformitarianism', is now widely accepted.

With the age of the Earth now counted in millions of years, geologists felt more confident in offering their own explanations for the way the world was. Geological strata had been on display all over the world of course, positively inviting speculation as to how they arrived in such a state, and geologists began to speak in terms of slow deposition of layers of sediment at the bottom of lakes and oceans, layers which had since been lifted, twisted, bent and broken by titanic forces. There was also plenty of evidence for volcanic activity and the formation of great masses of volcanic rock. And so earth science set out on the road which has since led to the discovery and then measurement of continental drift (more correctly 'plate tectonics') whereby, for example, America and Europe are separating by a few centimetres every year. Discovery after discovery has reinforced the view that the Earth has been changing steadily in response to conditions not unlike those operating today and that the same can be said for plant and animal life. Continents move, mountain ranges are born and are then eroded away, volcanoes spew out lava fields, the oceans wear away at the coasts and then deposit their sediments in layers; and so the whole process continues much as it has for countless eons of time. It is a comforting view of the world, if not a particularly exciting one – and it doesn't really seem to hold any place for the sort of Great Flood that the Bible and the Koran describe.

Uniformitarianism has not had it all its own way however. You cannot have avoided hearing something about the famous asteroid impact of about 65 million years ago, which many blame for the extinction of the dinosaurs, not to mention thousands of other plant and animal species. This was certainly not part of any gradual development plan! The horizon between the Cretaceous Era (before 65 million years ago) and the succeeding Palaeocene Era is extremely clear in the geological record and the sudden disappearance of so many fossil types is particularly shocking. Much earlier, about 220 million years ago, an even greater extinction of species marked the abrupt end of the Permian Era. On the other hand if a catastrophe on this sort of scale only strikes once every hundred million years or so, then it would seem we don't have too much to worry about. Our species will probably have disappeared through 'natural causes' (or perhaps more likely through self-destruction) long before the next one hits us.

Of much more immediate interest for our times are Ice Ages. Right across the north European plain lies a scattering of massive boulders, long thought to represent hard evidence of a Great Flood. Yet scientists are now in absolutely no doubt that the awesome power which ripped these great rocks from their points of origin (often tens of miles distant) was not that of water but of ice. Conventionally we speak of our current age, commencing at the end of the last Ice Age in about 9000BC, as the 'Holocene', but the reality is that we are still very much in the 'Pleistocene' Era, a 2-million-year-long age of alternating ice and warmth. Most fortunately for us at present we are currently enjoying an unusually stable warm period, but there is every reason to believe that the ice will return one day. My home in Nottingham, England, was at the edge of an ice sheet as little as 15000 years ago. Cities like Stockholm, Montreal and Winnipeg would have been under thicknesses of ice measured in kilometres.

We can look back at least 400000 years by taking cores through the Antarctic ice sheet[3] and it is possible to learn quite a lot about the temperature fluctuations that have occurred in the past from detailed analysis of the chemistry of the ice itself as well as the frozen dust particles it contains. And the message is very clear. The last so-called 'glacial maximum', the coldest part of the Ice Age, occurred in about 18000BC. Since that time the glaciers have been in retreat, liberating unimaginable volumes of water. Between about 18000BC and 4000BC ocean levels rose by over 100 metres worldwide.[4] The land bridge between Asia and America now lies beneath the icy waters of the Bering Strait. All around the world islands have been created, islands like Britain, Sri Lanka, Sumatra, Borneo, Taiwan and those of Japan; and islands which once existed have now been submerged deep beneath the waves. You could certainly call this a Great Flood. On the other hand you would have to be pretty slow-moving to be caught out by it! With a rise of about 2 centimetres per year at the height of the melt, you could hardly have been taken by surprise.

EXPLANATIONS OFFERED FOR THE GREAT FLOOD

So are the stories of a Great Flood simply the distant memory of the rise of the oceans after the Ice Age? I hardly think that could be possible given the almost imperceptibly gradual rate involved – which leaves us searching for alternatives. Here are three of the most commonly proposed.

Experts have long drawn attention to the vast glacial lakes that formed in both Canada and Siberia as the ice melted at the end of the Ice Age, and the fact that enormous volumes of water were released on occasions as particular ice barriers gave way. The most significant such event known to science was undoubtedly the sudden emptying of glacial lake Agassiz, stretching across a large part of central Canada. This event, datable to around 6250BC, is thought to have liberated approximately 163000 cubic kilometres of water[5] in a single outflow, causing about half a metre of sea level rise worldwide over a period that may have been as short as a few days. In comparison to normal geological timescales this was certainly pretty dramatic, and I guess there must have been people living on shores with little tidal range, for example in the Mediterranean, whose lives were drastically affected. Someone may even have died! It would certainly have led to tales being told for many a year – but could it really have been perceived as dramatic enough for those tales to survive over thousands of years to form the basis of Noah's flood?

A recent popular alternative is the so-called 'Black Sea flood', proposed by Bill Ryan and Walter Pitman in their book *Noah's Flood*. These two researchers became aware that the history of the Black Sea, the large body of water north of Turkey, was not all you might have expected it to be. They discovered mention in the scientific literature of the existence of an ancient shoreline over 100 metres beneath the current sea level, something they also proved by their own investigations. You may wonder why that should be a surprise since I have just referred to sea levels globally being over 100 metres lower in the past than they are now, but the point is that the waters of the Black Sea flow out to the Mediterranean through two narrow and relatively shallow straits. The depth of the northern one, the Bosphorus, where modern Istanbul is located, is no more than about 40 metres at its shallowest section, and this should therefore have been a minimum level for the Black Sea. However it seems that during the last phase of the Ice Age regional rainfall was so low that the whole sea began to evaporate faster than the rivers could keep the water supply coming in, leading to a drastic reduction in level. And the really interesting thing for Ryan and Pitman was the well-preserved form of the coastal dunes seen deep beneath the current surface which, they believed, indicated rapid rather than gradual submersion. Their explanation was that there had been a sudden flooding of the Black Sea basin from the Mediterranean, perhaps caused by an earthquake which opened up the Bosphorus strait, and they supported their case by evidence from cores through the sea bed showing that freshwater molluscs had suddenly been replaced by saltwater varieties. Their date for this event, based on Carbon 14 dating of the youngest saltwater molluscs, was about 5600BC.

If Ryan and Pitman are correct (and there is a powerful body of scientific opinion which disagrees with their explanation), then this flood would have been very dramatic indeed.[6] The area which would suddenly have been inundated is considerable, notably a 100-kilometre-wide coastal plain on the northern edge of the Black Sea, although the reality, even if Ryan and Pitman's explanation is accepted, is that the rate of water rise would only have been of the order of a foot or two per day; evacuation would not have been too difficult. So, traumatic though it would have been for those individuals involved, could it really have become the flood that covered mountains described in the pages of the Bible and the Koran?

Well, maybe; but undoubtedly the most commonly cited scientific explanation for the Great Flood story is a quite different event. The problem with the Black Sea flood is that it is in the wrong place! The early stories of the Bible are set in Iraq, the land through which two mighty rivers flow, the Tigris and the Euphrates, carrying rainfall run-off and snow melt from the mountains of eastern Turkey all the way to the Persian Gulf. It was here in 1929, whilst excavating the southern Iraqi city of Ur, that the famous archaeologist Leonard Woolley found evidence for a very substantial flood indeed.[7] He had dug down through the layers of Ur's royal history, the so-called Early Dynastic period (3rd Millennium BC), the period for which he would later unearth a stunning set of royal graves, then down through earlier pre-Dynastic layers, and he had now entered solid clay. It looked as though the earliest days of Ur's history had been reached. Woolley however was not convinced and he instructed his diggers to keep on going. Eight feet of clay they removed and then, suddenly, they found themselves entering another city layer. It was quite different in character (pottery types, building construction) from those above the clay and it suggested that Ur had been abandoned for a period and then rebuilt at a later date, possibly by quite different people.

To Woolley those eight feet of clay were a godsend. The clay could only have been deposited by water and it meant that the city of Ur had been engulfed by a very serious flood. Any suggestion of confirmation of the Bible story was good news for attracting funding and the story of Woolley's 'proof' of the Great Flood was soon headline news. The date of this flood according to modern understanding of archaeological dates would have been some time around 3800BC.[8]

But was this really the flood of Noah? Less widely publicised were Woolley's findings from elsewhere on the site of Ur, notably from the higher part of the city. Here, in contrast to lower down, there was absolutely no clay layer at all. The occupation layers simply followed one from another. And this could only mean that this particular flood, though it certainly deposited large quantities of silt and clay over the lower city, had a limited depth. Nevertheless, an inundation of the Euphrates flood-plain, whilst it may only have lasted some days, would have covered a very wide area indeed, to the extent that the entire land would have appeared, from the vantage point of Ur's citadel, to be covered with water. It is not hard to see how such a devastating flood could have led to tales of high drama and spectacular escape. Unlike the Black Sea flood it would have been a genuinely sudden event in which many people would certainly have lost their lives. Escape by boat would have been a logical and sensible course of action so it is not hard to see the story of Noah emerging from the flood waters. This seems a reasonably plausible explanation and my impression is that it has attracted widespread acceptance, from both religious and non-religious alike. Yet it can hardly be said to have covered mountains. If it was the source of the Noah story then that story has certainly grown in the telling!

THE FLOOD OF NOAH

The story of Noah is given in both the Bible and the Koran. However it is the Bible which gives us the details. The full story can be read in Chapters 6, 7 and 8 of the book of Genesis. The essential points are:

a) Noah was warned by God to build a boat (the ark) to escape a flood.
b) He took his family on board, together with representatives of different types of animal.
c) The flood came accompanied by rain and also by the sea rising.
d) Everyone on earth apart from Noah died.
e) The tops of the mountains were covered.
f) The flood lasted several months.
g) The ark grounded in the mountains of Ararat (eastern Turkey).

As I am sure you can see straight away, there are several features here which are quite different from any of the floods mentioned so far. That doesn't prove anything on its own since folk stories often tend to be embroidered by those telling them, but it should probably make us pause for thought. The exaggeration seems to be so large, taking the story so far outside the bounds of normal imagination, that one wonders how the key writings of three of our greatest religions (Judaism, Christianity and Islam) should have swallowed it. How, for example, could anyone imagine that Noah could have run aground amongst mountains to the north of the Iraqi plain when the rivers flow the other way? What should we understand by the statement that the sea rose, as well as rain falling?

Let me immediately start to annoy those who have convinced themselves that nothing less than a flood in which every creature on the planet died (except Noah and those with him) is acceptable. I am quite prepared to accept less! I have no fixed agenda; I simply want to know the truth. I am not of the view that God dies if my own understanding of the Bible or the Koran is wrong. If my understanding is wrong then I must change it; it's as simple as that. I am therefore not even going to consider what might be termed the Creationist agenda, in which all of the planet's geology has to be fitted into a few thousand years. Scientists are far from infallible – that's obvious enough – but the weight of evidence that the geological processes of erosion, sedimentation, volcanism and plate tectonics have been proceeding for millions of years is simply overwhelming. I will not, therefore, be seeking a joint explanation for the flood and the end of the dinosaurs!

I am also not of the view that the right approach to solving the mystery of the Great Flood is to head off to the slopes of Mount Ararat in eastern Turkey and look for the remains of a large wooden ship. I may not be a Biblical scholar but I know enough to realise that the text speaks of *mountains* not *one mountain*, and that the name *Ararat* comes from *Urartu*, the land which is now Kurdistan. The description of Noah's landing place, whether true or false, could therefore refer to anywhere among the hills to the north and north-east of the Iraqi plain.

No; the approach which I wish to take here is, I hope, rather more scientific. If there really was a Great Flood then there will be evidence, genuine scientific evidence. For a start one would expect there to be signals in the geological record; if freshwater lakes were inundated that would surely leave its mark; if animal and plant life suffered some sort of catastrophe then we should still be able to see signs of it today; and if human life was extinguished over large areas of the planet then the effects should certainly still be visible. Perhaps I am over-optimistic in some of my expectations, but these are the areas where I shall be looking for answers. As in any investigation the trick is to look at the totality of the evidence rather than to be swayed unduly by any one item. In a murder investigation the detective looks for means, motive and opportunity. In this investigation I shall be doing something similar. I need to find a possible time window, clues that something big happened and also a possible mechanism by which it might have happened. Without all three the case will fall apart and I will have to admit that the Great Flood is a fabrication – or at best a wild exaggeration.

SUMMARY

Three perfectly rational explanations are already on offer, all of which have a sound scientific basis. These are: a sudden half-metre global sea level rise due to the emptying of a glacial lake in Canada; a rapid inundation of the Black Sea; and a massive river flood in Iraq. In complete contrast to all three I have a story of a flood that covered mountains and in which vast numbers of people died.

But that isn't quite the whole picture. In fact we have a great deal more than just a single story. The story in the Bible and the Koran may be the best known, but it is actually but one of a myriad of tales that stem from the deepest folk memories (real or imagined) of peoples right across the planet. This, therefore, is the logical place to start. In Part 1 of this book I shall be examining the evidence from different branches of human knowledge, searching for clues which might help to track down the true origin of the Great Flood story, but before consulting archaeologists, geologists and the like we would be well advised to seek the input of a historian. There's an awful lot of folk history out there and some of it might just help us to get a better idea of what we are looking for.

I trust you will find this journey of discovery an interesting one, perhaps even a bit of an eye-opener. It concerns the very distant past, but it also concerns the trustworthiness of the Bible – and by extension the Koran, which clearly supports the Bible story. The world deserves to know the truth, whatever that truth may be.

PART 1

THE EVIDENCE

2

Legend and Myth

Let me start this chapter with a question: just how much credence should we give to stories from long, long ago, even stories which are scientifically rather more believable than that of Noah and the Great Flood?

There was a time when no respectable academic would be caught believing such fanciful accounts as Homer's description of the Trojan War found in the *Iliad*, or the legends of King Arthur of England, set down in writing by Walter Map in the 12th Century. But times have changed. In the late 19th Century, Heinrich Schliemann, a wealthy German industrialist, decided to pursue his childhood dream and look for the site of Troy itself – and he found it. We now know that the city described by Homer was real. Its citadel emerged from a small hill in the extreme north-west corner of Turkey and the site has since yielded abundant evidence of its importance through a period of around three thousand years. There is continuing debate as to exactly which archaeological level (if any) might relate to the Trojan War, but there are few ancient historians today who would dismiss the idea that such a war ever took place. Indeed, if the Level VI city is to be identified with Homer's Troy, it was a truly vast city – and it certainly suffered violent destruction towards the end of the 2nd Millennium BC, at the end of the Late Bronze Age.[1] Admittedly the *Iliad* is a tale of gods and goddesses, of miracles and heroic deeds, but woven into the text is a highly believable undercurrent of real events. It was written down several hundred years after the events it describes and so must have relied on oral transmission during the intervening centuries, something which is also evident from the metre of the verse and the way phrases are repeated, but the fact remains that significant truth is to be found interspersed with much artistic exaggeration.

In the case of King Arthur there is, I must concede, no unassailable evidence that there really was a king of that name. However we can now be quite sure that Walter Map didn't just make him up! The writings of a 9th Century Welsh Monk named Nennius refer to an epic poem telling of the twelve battles fought by Arthur, a Celtic warrior king, against invading Saxon forces, a poem written in Celtic and certainly dating from before Nennius' time. Another text found among Nennius' works but actually added at a later date refers to Arthur's victory at the battle of Mount Badon in the year 518 and his death at the battle of Camlann in 539.[2] The 6th Century Celtic writer Gildas, although he doesn't mention the name

Arthur, tells us that the advance of the Saxons was stemmed (by someone he calls Ambrosius Aurelianus) for a few decades during the first half of the 6th Century, and he also includes mention of the battle of Mount Badon.[3] So, whether the name *Arthur* is correct or not, the context of the Arthur legends was certainly real enough, namely the struggle between Celts and Saxons for control of Britain. Of course the tales of knights in shining armour come straight from the time in which the legends were written down, some six and a half centuries after the events themselves, but the fact is that there is an underlying truth behind the legend.

Now for something really impressive! The 'Vedas' comprise a group of stories from India, only committed to writing in the late 18th and early 19th Centuries. They tell of events from literally thousands of years ago, having been transmitted orally through the generations by the Hindu priestly caste. It was a matter of considerable pride to achieve word-for-word perfection despite the archaic form of the language, which meant that the learner had little idea of the meaning. The Rigveda, the oldest Veda of all, tells of battles between peoples in the land now known as the Punjab and, extraordinary though it may seem, it is pretty clear that many of the tales relate to events that took place over 3000 years before they were written down! Surely we have no right to expect any real truth to remain across so wide a chasm of time? Yet the warfare described in the Rigveda ties in plausibly enough with archaeology. In the early 2nd Millennium BC the successful and long-lasting city-based civilisation of the Indus Valley began to decline, to be replaced by the Indo-European-speaking civilisation which dominates today. From archaeology we can see that this coincided with the introduction of horse culture into India, while in the Rigveda the invading people known as Aryans make extensive use of horses and chariots. Furthermore, one of the cities mentioned in the Rigveda, Harayupiya, can plausibly be identified as Harappa, one of the two largest centres of the Indus Valley culture.[4] The point is that, while nothing can be proved regarding the specifics of the tales, it seems certain that there is a genuine kernel of truth embedded within them, even after three and a half millennia of oral transmission – passed down through some 140 generations. To call this 'remarkable' would be a serious understatement.

NOAH

None of this proves Noah's flood of course – but it does mean that we shouldn't rush to dismiss a story just because it has been transmitted by word of mouth for thousands of years.

So just how did the story of Noah originate? And when?

Back in the 19th Century much of archaeology was aimed directly at supporting – or at least illuminating – the pages of the Bible, so, when the story broke that one of the clay tablets covered with cuneiform writing found in the ruins of the great northern Iraqi city of Nineveh actually described a great flood, public excitement could hardly be contained. We now know that the tablet concerned actually contained a part of the Bronze Age classic, the *Epic of Gilgamesh*,[5] the most famous tale to emerge from ancient Iraq. It was a best-seller throughout the 2nd Millennium BC, as evidenced by the sheer number of copies or part-copies that have turned up in excavations from Egypt to Turkey, as well as in Iraq itself. It clearly had a similar status to the writings of Homer in later Greek society. The whole story is fascinating and delightful and Gilgamesh is portrayed as a character with whom we can still identify today, but it is a single episode that is of principal interest here, namely a meeting that took place between Gilgamesh and a very old man called 'Utanapishtim'. Gilgamesh had had a roller-coaster of a life and, following the death of his close friend Enkidu, his roller-coaster had just about left the tracks. Once he had been young, brash and confident, without a care in the world. He was, after all, king of the powerful southern Iraqi city of Uruk, and he had been successful in securing the supremacy of Uruk over the rival city of Kish in central Iraq. But now, following Enkidu's death, he had to come face to face with his own mortality and it frightened him out of his wits! He simply had to know the answer to life, the universe and everything, and there was only one man on earth who could possibly help, namely Utanapishtim who, according to the story, had actually survived the Great Flood. So Gilgamesh set out on his long, hard and geographically uncertain journey, and eventually found him. Utanapishtim then tells the story of the flood from his perspective and the essentials are as follows:

a) The gods told him to build a ship.
b) He took his family, some selected craftsmen and representatives of the animal kingdom.
c) The flood came with a seven-day storm.
d) One or two islands were visible to Utanapishtim during his time on board.
e) Everyone apart from Utanapishtim and his companions died in the flood.
f) He eventually ran aground on Mount Nisir (location unknown but said to be in Kurdistan or Armenia[6]).

The parallels with the story of Noah are unmistakable – and I could have added others, notably the fact that both Noah and Utanapishtim are reported to have sent out birds to search for dry land (a raven and a dove in both stories, also a swallow in the case of Utanapishtim). There are differences of course but they in no way affect the main elements of the story. It seems almost inescapable that the two stories are essentially one. It is not possible to judge from the texts alone which is the more reliable version, but the two stories are almost certainly derived from the same original, whatever the truth of that original may have been.

So the question arises: can we date the *Epic of Gilgamesh*? The texts currently in our possession were written in the Akkadian language, the number-one language of Iraq over a period of 2000 years, and they date from the mid 2nd Millennium BC onwards. However the tale itself is set in much earlier times. The city of Uruk had a long and distinguished history and almost all of it dates from well before the mid 2nd Millennium BC. In fact Uruk was the leading city in all Iraq for almost a thousand years, through most of the 4th Millennium BC and into the early centuries of the 3rd Millennium BC. This we know from archaeology.

However the detailed picture given in the Gilgamesh epic is not that of the so-called 'Uruk period', the period when Uruk reigned supreme; the picture painted is of a time when Uruk was rivalled by the city of Kish, lying some 100 miles to the north-west, up the river Euphrates, and this brings us forward to the beginning of the archaeological phase known as 'Early Dynastic I', with a date somewhere in the 2800-2500BC range.[7]

Help is also available from another remarkable document, the so-called *Sumerian king list*, which is a list of the rulers of southern Iraq, the land known in earliest times as 'Sumer'.[8] Admittedly the early parts of the list are not exactly 100% trustworthy, as can be deduced from the rather unlikely reign lengths attributed to some of the early kings. It is also true that the list of dynasties given in the king list, from numerous different cities in Iraq, can hardly be sequential; that is to say many reigned in parallel with each other. Nevertheless, specialists believe that the *Sumerian king list*'s '1st Dynasty of Uruk', the fifth ruler of which bears the name *Gilgamesh*, most probably ruled during the Early Dynastic I phase.

Gilgamesh was therefore almost certainly a real character from southern Iraq who lived very roughly in 2600BC. Utanapishtim however is quite another matter. The *Epic of Gilgamesh* is slightly confusing in that it speaks of Gilgamesh himself rebuilding the walls of Uruk "after the flood", which would suggest that only a few years had passed since that earth-shattering event. On the other hand there is archaeological evidence for a rather less than earth-shattering flood at about that time in the form of silt and mud deposits at the city of Shuruppak, located a little north of Uruk, quite possibly a large enough flood to have caused serious damage to the mud-brick walls of Uruk but not exactly a mountain-covering event. So was this what Utanapishtim and his crew had survived, alone among mankind? Utanapishtim's home city was indeed Shuruppak, the very city in which this flood evidence was discovered; yet the picture of Utanapishtim's flood given in the epic is of something much, much bigger. Utanapishtim is also portrayed as a very old man indeed, a man whose life had been unnaturally extended by the gift of immortality (it was the immortality that Gilgamesh was really after), which sounds as though Utanapishtim's flood was actually much more distant in time.

So, given the parallels between the floods of Utanapishtim and Noah, and given the archaeological period in which Gilgamesh reigned, it would appear practically certain that the Bible and the Koran speak of a story which, whether true or not, can be traced back at least to the first half of the 3rd Millennium BC. Incidentally, although the flood story contained in the *Epic of Gilgamesh* is much the most complete version from Iraq, we also possess significant extracts from two other versions. One, in which the flood survivor is named 'Ziusudra', was written in the Sumerian language, the first written language of Iraq and the language which would have been in common use in Gilgamesh's day. The other is the Old Babylonian tale of *Atrahasis and the flood*, which again includes many of the same themes.[9]

There is no doubt that Noah's flood represents a serious mystery. The tale is old, very old indeed, much older than all the written texts we now possess including the *Epic of Gilgamesh*. And the type of flood which is described is quite unlike any that we experience today, in its duration (months in the case of the Bible story), depth (mountains covered), and also in the puzzling claim that the survivor grounded his ship on a mountain! It could be a complete fabrication of course, but it is not a Jewish, Christian or Muslim fabrication; whether true or false, the origin of the story predates all these religions.

DATING NOAH'S FLOOD

The only serious textual evidence available here is the Bible. The Koran includes many stories of Noah but none which give any detail regarding date. So the question is: does the Bible give enough detail for us to actually assign a date?

The Bible record is known to be historically trustworthy, at least approximately, back to about the 9th Century BC, when kings like Jehoshaphat and Ahab reigned; this we know from references in well-dated records from the kingdom of Assyria, now northern Iraq, the world superpower of the day.[10] I would argue that there is sufficient correlation between Bible history and the history of surrounding lands to suggest that it is probably trustworthy, at least in terms of its historical setting, as far back as the days of Abraham, and in *History Rewritten* I suggest that Abraham was probably born in the late 20th Century BC.[11] However, it would be a brave person who expressed confidence in the dates of any Bible characters earlier than Abraham.

If you look at a modern Bible translation and turn to the book of Genesis, chapter 11, you will see a list of Abraham's ancestors back through just 10 generations to Noah – with detailed dating information. If you add the numbers up you will find that Abraham was born just 290 years after the Great Flood, giving a flood date of around 2200BC, the time of the Egyptian 'Old Kingdom' and a time of known kings and empires in Iraq. There is plenty of evidence for unbroken cultural continuity in both lands, no sign of any mass extinction of human life and, in my opinion at least, absolutely no question of any worldwide flood having occurred at that time. So where does that leave the Bible? Well the place to look is in the footnotes – if you have a Bible with footnotes – where you may read that dating information has been taken from the oldest Hebrew text currently in our possession, the 'Masoretic' Bible, but that other sources give differing numbers. In particular the Greek translation known as the 'Septuagint', made in Egypt during the last three centuries BC, gives 1150 years from Noah to Abraham rather than 290; the Samaritan Pentateuch gives 940 years. And source texts for the Septuagint are much older than those of the Masoretic Bible.[12] Furthermore, with three different numbers on offer the only honest position to take is that the truth may not lie in any of them!

I would even go further and suggest that the Bible itself gives good reason to question whether any of these figures is actually intended to cover the whole period from Noah to Abraham. In Genesis chapter 10 we read a full list of Noah's descendants, and it is principally a list of the lands and peoples of the Middle East. Noah's son Shem is said to have fathered five sons named as Elam, Ashur, Arphaxad, Lud and Aram. If you know your ancient Middle East geography, you will recognise some or all of these. Elam was a country just east of ancient Sumer, now in south-western Iran. Ashur was a famous city on the banks of the Tigris River in northern Iraq, the capital of the kingdom of Assyria. Arpaxhad can be identified with the ancient city of Arrapha, modern Kirkuk. Lud, most believe, meant Lydia in western Turkey. And Aram was a land now distributed between Syria and Jordan, south-west of the river Euphrates; Aramaic was the common language of the Middle East in Jesus' day. So according to this passage Shem fathered five individuals who gave their names to five different nations or cities – or at least that seems to be the literal meaning. But the truth is that the key expression translated here as *became the father of* is sometimes used in the Bible for *became the ancestor of*, and in this case the latter meaning looks much the more plausible. What the Bible appears to be saying is that the nations of Elam, Ashur, Arpaxhad, Lud and Aram are all descended from Shem's blood-line. Similarly we read that Shem's brother Ham fathered four more nations, namely Kush (Sudan), Mizraim (Egypt), Put (Libya) and Canaan (Palestine), and that his other brother, Japheth, fathered Gomer and Magog (both in northern Turkey), Madai (western Iran), Javan (Greece),

Tubal (south-central Turkey), Meshech (central Turkey) and Tiras (north-west Turkey).

Now it seems a little irrational to me to believe that these 16 grandsons of Noah headed straight off to various corners of the world giving their individual names to the lands they settled in. The perfectly valid meaning *became the ancestor of* allows the suggestion that, as the descendants of Noah multiplied on the Earth, they gradually spread out and reached the 16 lands mentioned. The process should logically have taken many centuries, probably millennia – certainly not the mere blink of an eye implied by most modern Bible translations.

The upshot of all this seems to be that it is quite impossible to be definite about the dates for the story of Noah and the Great Flood just by studying the pages of the Bible, although there is reason enough to believe that the period of time between Noah and Abraham should be measured in thousands rather than hundreds of years. We clearly need more evidence.

Fortunately there is abundant evidence!

The story of Noah (and his *alter egos* Utanapishtim, Ziusudra and Atrahasis) is certainly the most famous flood tale we have – but it is far from alone. The truth is that the Middle East stories are matched by large numbers of other tales right across the face of the planet. They may not be so well known; in the main they are stories which have been handed down orally and have become part of tribal folklore. They therefore inevitably contain much that is the product of generations of fertile imagination. However the stories are real enough; and an absolutely consistent theme right across the world is that one day, a very long time ago, the oceans rose to cover the land. Let me give you some examples.[13]

THE GREAT INDIAN FLOOD

The Middle East is known as a great centre of early civilisation, but it was far from alone. To the east lay the lands of Pakistan and India, the seat of a literate civilisation since the early 3rd Millennium BC. That civilisation, the Indus Valley civilisation, has given much to modern Hindu culture and one of the tales which can be traced back to truly ancient times is the story of Manu, the first human according to Hindu mythology.[14] The story appears in many slightly differing forms and Manu himself can be found in sculpture both modern and extremely ancient. Here is a typical version.

> *Manu, the first human, found a small fish in his washwater. The fish begged protection from the larger fishes, in return for which it would save Manu. Manu kept the fish safe, transferring it to larger and larger reservoirs as it grew, eventually taking it to the ocean. The fish warned Manu of a coming deluge and told him to build a ship. When the flood rose, the*

fish came and Manu tied the craft to its horn. The fish led him to a northern mountain and told Manu to tie the ship's rope to a tree to prevent it from drifting. Manu alone of all creatures survived.[15]

The story is admittedly short on scientific detail and long on mythology. However you will recognise a tale of a flood not unlike that of Noah in the Bible. Manu built a ship; he landed on a mountainside; all other creatures perished in the flood. Have a look at another version of the Hindu tale in which Manu goes under his earlier name, Satyavrata.

One day when Satyavrata was bathing in a river, he was visited by a fish which craved protection and which he transferred to successively larger vessels as it grew. At last Satyavrata recognised it as the god Vishnu, the Lord of the Universe. Vishnu told him that in seven days all the corrupt creatures will be destroyed by a deluge, but Satyavrata would be saved in a large vessel. He was told to take aboard the miraculous vessel all kinds of medicinal herbs, grain, the seven 'Nishis' and their wives, and pairs of brute animals. After seven days the oceans began to overflow the coasts and constant rain began flooding the earth. A large vessel floated in on the rising waters and Satyavrata and the Nishis entered with their wives and cargo. During the deluge, Vishnu preserved the vessel by again taking the form of a giant fish and tying it to himself with a huge sea serpent.[16]

The role of the fish ties these two stories firmly together, but there is additional detail in the second tale. Here it is clearly stated that the oceans rose to cover the land. As in the story of Noah, the description is certainly not that of a river flood.

Now I suppose it would be possible to argue that these are simply versions of the Noah story that have been taken to India and adopted into Indus Valley and then Hindu culture – or indeed that the story travelled the other way. It is quite true that there is evidence of trade links dating back to the 3rd Millennium BC, so this cannot be ruled out. But what about the next three tales, all from the southern fringes of the Himalaya mountain range?

A flood once covered the whole world and drowned everyone except for one couple, who climbed up a tree on the highest peak of Leng hill.[17]

A couple escaped a great flood on the top of a mountain called Tedong, near Darjeeling.[18]

Tibet was almost totally inundated until the god Gya took compassion on the survivors, drew off the waters through Bengal, and sent teachers to civilise the people.[19]

It is hard to deny that these last three tales are entirely independent of Noah or any Middle Eastern flood story. Yet they all speak of a similarly devastating flood.

THE GREAT FLOODS OF SOUTH-EAST ASIA

As we move east, we find large numbers of flood stories scattered across all the lands from India to the South China Sea. The mythical elements are always strong; but could they possibly contain kernels of truth from the very distant past? Let me quote you an extract from a Vietnamese tale.

> *A kite once quarrelled with a crab and pecked a hole in its skull. In revenge, the crab caused the sea and rivers to swell until the waters reached the sky. The only survivors were a brother and sister who took a pair of all kinds of animals with them in a huge chest. They floated for seven days and nights. Then the brother heard a cock crowing outside, sent by the spirits to signal that the flood had abated. All disembarked, birds first, then the animals, then the two people.*[20]

As it happens there are several of these brother-sister stories, all different yet all with common themes, and most include the point that the brother and sister, being the only two people left in all the world, had to marry each other in order for the human race to survive. Here are two more brother-sister stories, one from the Burma-China border region and the other from Taiwan.

> *After death came into the world as a result of a macaque's curse, sky and earth longed for human souls and bones. That is how the flood began. An orphaned brother and sister lived in squalor in a village. A pair of golden birds flew down to them one day, warned them that a huge wave would flood the earth, and told them to take shelter in a gourd and not to come out until they heard the birds again. The two children warned their neighbours but the people didn't believe them. The children sawed off the top of a gourd and went inside. For ninety-nine days there was no wind or rain and the earth became parched. Then torrents of rain fell and the resulting flood washed everything away. The brother and sister occasionally could hear the gourd bump against the bottom of heaven. After long waiting, they heard the birds calling, left the gourd and found they had landed atop a mountain, and the flood had receded. .... Brother and sister then went in search of other people, exploring north and south respectively. They found nobody else, and the golden birds appeared again and urged them to marry. They refused .... they consented. They had six sons and six daughters.*[21]

> *The four sea gods .... told Kabitt and Aka that in five days, when the moon was full, the sea will make a booming sound and they should escape to a mountain where there are stars. On the fifth day the two gods fled to a mountain, and when they reached the summit the sea began booming and rising. Kakumodan's house was flooded but he and his wife escaped by climbing a ladder to the sky. In their haste, though, they forgot the children and, upon reaching safety, they futilely called for them. Sura and Nakao, however, had climbed into a wooden mortar and had floated to safety to Ragasan mountain. The brother and sister, now alone in the world, feared to offend the ancestral gods, but of necessity they became man and wife.*[22]

You could certainly argue that these three brother-sister stories, and others scattered from central India to the Philippines, are all one and the same in their underlying content despite the quite different mythologies which appear, but it is surely not possible to argue that they have any direct link to the story of Noah. You may dismiss them entirely of course – but these tales represent descriptions of a flood, obviously not a river flood, in a quite different part of the world from that of Noah. The mention of a giant wave and of the sea booming might indicate a tsunami, but the duration appears to be a lot longer than the few minutes of raised sea levels that a tsunami can generate (12 years in the case of an Indian version of the story!). And if these tales really do represent a genuine flood in which the sea rose to cover the land over a significant percentage of the planet then we might expect to find similar evidence on other continents too – and indeed we do.

ABORIGINAL FLOODS OF AUSTRALIA

At this stage I should state that I am most whole-heartedly indebted to Mark Isaak, whose website presents a collation of flood stories from around the world. In all he presents some 374 stories (date March 2004), of which I have discarded almost 50%, either as being simply too mythical and hard to interpret for use as real evidence, or because they seem to relate to a fairly local event (a river flood or a tsunami), or because two or more stories are so close as to be almost identical. The remaining 189 flood myths are all human tales of large-scale flooding. They may involve intervention by a god or gods; they may include miraculous occurrences; but at root they are all human tales and concern the lives of seemingly real people.

Turning to the continent of Australia, the tales are as mysterious and mythical as ever – but nearly all speak of waters rising rather than merely rain falling. Let me quote you a selection of three of the saner-sounding examples, from Queensland, South Australia and Victoria:

> *A great flood drowned most of the people. A few escaped to the top of the tall mountain Bibbiringda, which is inland of the northern bay of Cape Cleveland.*[23]

> *A man's two wives ran away from him. He pursued them to Encounter Bay, saw them at a distance, and angrily cried out for the waters to rise and drown them. A terrible flood washed over the hills and killed the two women. The waters rose so high that a man named Nepelle, who lived at Rauwoke, had to drag his canoe up to the top of the hill now called Point Macleay. The dense part of the Milky Way shows his canoe floating in the sky.*[24]

> *Bunjil, the creator, was angry with people because of the evil they did so he caused the ocean to flood by urinating into it. All people were destroyed*

> *except those whom Bunjil loved and fixed as stars in the sky, and a man and a woman who climbed a tall tree on a mountain, and from whom the present human race is descended.*[25]

Now whatever you think of tribal myths and legends, it is clear that here we have traditions which most definitely speak of a Great Flood and which equally definitely owe nothing to Noah. Flood stories are found in all parts of Australia, from peoples of differing languages and cultures. The stories are easy to dismiss – but should we? Just to help you think about the issue, here is a tale from the island of New Guinea, just north of Australia.

> *People made the lizards angry, first by making a lot of noise and then by teasing them. Finally, the people incurred the wrath of the Lizard Man, who caused it to rain for days, and the water rose. People climbed to the highest mountain, but still the rain came and the water rose higher. People were drowning. Two brothers built a small raft and climbed aboard. Others tried to climb on with them but the raft only held two. The two brothers floated off, and only they survived the flood.*[26]

But the ultimate test of a global flood is whether the same types of tale can be found in the New World as well as in the Old.

FLOOD STORIES FROM AMERICA

Anthropologists believe that there was minimal contact between Old and New Worlds, between Asia and America, from the time the rising waters closed the land bridge to Alaska (about 11000BC[27]) to the arrival of Christopher Columbus in 1492AD. Admittedly the Eskimos of the far north made the crossing[28] but there is no way that any story they brought with them could possibly have spread far into the continent. If the flood was just an Old World myth, then American mythology should be virtually flood-free.[29]

But nothing could be further from the truth. Native American memories are as rich a source of flood tales as those of any other people on earth. Of course America has known all about Noah since the 16th Century, when the Spanish conquistadors brought their religion to the American colonies, and it is evident that some of the Native American tales have been profoundly influenced by the Bible story. I have therefore tried to ignore these and to concentrate only on flood stories which are clearly of independent origin. And there are many. Let me quote you a selection. The first is told by the Skokomish people of Washington State.

> *Once a big flood came. People made ropes of twisted cedar limbs and used them to fasten their canoes to the mountains. The flood covered the Olympic Mountains* [which peak at around 2500 metres!]. *Some of the ropes*

> *broke and the canoes drifted to the country of the Flatheads. That is why the Skokomish and the Flatheads speak the same language.*[30]

And from the Maidu tribes of Central California:

> *As the Indians of old lived tranquilly in the Sacramento Valley, a mighty rushing of waters came suddenly so that the whole valley became like an ocean. Many Indians were overtaken by the waters, and the frogs and the salmon overtook and ate many others. Only two escaped to the hills, but the Great Man made them fruitful so the world was soon repopulated with many tribes.*[31]

Moving across the continent, let's hear from the Chippewa people who live in the region around Lake Superior on the Canada-United States border.

> *In the beginning of time, in September, there was a great snow. A mouse nibbled a hole in a leather bag which contained the sun's heat and the heat escaped and melted all the snow in an instant. The waters rose to cover even the highest mountains. One old man had foreseen the flood and warned everybody, but the others had thought to escape to the hills; they drowned in the flood. The old man had prepared a canoe and survived, rescuing animals he came across. After a while he sent in turn the beaver, otter, muskrat and duck to find land. Only the duck returned, with some mud in its bill. The old man cast the mud on the water and blew on it, making solid land.*[32]

In other similar tales from Canada and the northern United States it is one of the other animals that finds the mud. But the point is not the obviously mythical embroidery which surrounds the story, nor the attempt to find a scientific reason for the appearance of all the water; it is the underlying theme which is found in dozens of tales from the west coast of Canada down to Mexico, across to the lands of the Cree and down to the Mississippi basin, the theme of a seemingly impossibly large flood. This next story gives the view as recalled by the Kwakiutl people who live on Vancouver Island.

> *Very long ago a flood covered everything but three mountains, one near Bella-Bella, one north-east of there, and a hill called Ko-Kwus on Don Island which rose with the flood to stay above the water. Nearly all people floated on logs and trees in different directions. Some people had small canoes with anchors and managed to land near their homes when the waters subsided. Of the Hailtzuk, only two men, a woman and a dog survived.*[33]

And here is an example from the large number of flood stories found in Mexico, this one from the Tlapanec people who live in the south of the country.

> *A buzzard told a man working in the fields not to work any more and caused all the trees that had been cut to rise again. The buzzard told the man to make a box for himself and take along in it a dog and a chicken.*

> *The man survived the flood in this box. When the waters lowered, the chicken turned into a buzzard and the man lived with the dog* [who later conveniently turned into a woman].[34]

In fact many of the Mexican stories include the themes of a buzzard and escape in a box, although other details vary considerably.

Moving to the continent of South America, here too we find abundant and extremely varied myths, all recalling a momentous flood. This first example comes courtesy of the tribes of the Purus River in central Amazonia.

> *Once upon a time, people heard a rumbling above and below the ground; the sun and moon turned red, blue and yellow, and wild beasts mingled fearlessly with man. A month later they saw darkness ascending from the earth to the sky, accompanied by a roar and by thunder and heavy rain. Everything was in dreadful confusion. Some people lost themselves. Some people died without knowing why. The water rose to cover the earth, and people took refuge in the highest trees. There they perished from cold and hunger, for it continued to be dark and rainy. Only Uassu and his wife survived. When they came down after the flood they could not find even a sign of a single corpse.*[35]

In western Amazonia, the Jívaro people are famous as the legendary headhunters, the people who used to shrink the heads of their enemies and wear them around their necks. They too have many tales to tell of the day the flood struck. This one is about two boys, one of whom had just been turned into a snake!

> *...... the lake began to overflow. The snake told his brother that the lake would continue to grow and all the people would perish unless they made their escape. The snake told him to take a calabash and flee to a palm tree on the highest mountain. The brother told his people what was happening, but they didn't believe him. He fled to the top of a palm tree on the top of a mountain and returned many days later when the waters had subsided. Vultures were eating the dead people in the valley.*[36]

And here are three quite different tales, from Peru, Bolivia and eastern Brazil.

> *Long ago, before there were any Incas, the country was populous, but the ocean broke out of its bounds, the land was covered and the people perished. Some say that a few people survived in caves on the highest mountains. Others say that only six people survived on a float.*[37]

> *The evil supernatural being Aguara-Tunpa declared war against the god Tunpaete, creator of the Chiriguanos. He set fire to the prairies in autumn, destroying all the plants and the land animals. The people, who had not then begun farming, nearly died of hunger, but they retreated to the banks of the rivers and survived on fish. Seeing people still surviving, Aguara-Tunpa caused a torrential rain. Acting on a hint given them by*

> *Tunpaete, the Chiriguanos placed two sibling babies, a boy and a girl, on a large mate leaf and set it afloat on the water. The flood rose, covering the earth and killing the rest of the Chiriguanos, but the two babies survived and eventually landed on solid ground when the flood sank.*[38]

> *The great god Tupi warned a medicine man named Tamanduare of a coming great flood that would cover the earth, and he told Tamanduare to seek refuge on a lofty peak with a palm tree at its top. Tamanduare and his family went there immediately and when they arrived it began to rain. It continued to rain until the whole earth was flooded. The water covered even the summit of the mountain and Tamanduare and his family climbed into the palm tree and lived there, eating its fruit, until the water subsided. Then they descended and repopulated the devastated world.*[39]

Again we see the same familiar themes of mountains being covered and people having to flee to higher ground or to escape in a boat. One particular point in the Bolivian tale, from the Chiriguano people, is that the story is set in pre-agricultural times, which means before about 1500BC in that part of the world.

Finally in this section, to emphasise the near-worldwide spread of flood myths, let me take you right down to the very southern tip of South America, the land of Tierra del Fuego.

> *Léxuwakipa, the rusty brown speckled ibis, felt offended by the people, so she let it snow so much that ice came to cover the entire earth. This happened at the time of Yáiaasága, when men seized power from the women. When the ice melted, it rapidly flooded all the earth. People hurried to their canoes but many didn't make it, and more perished when they couldn't find sheltered places. Some people reached the five mountain tops which stayed above the flood. These mountains were Usláka, Wémarwaia, Auwáratuléra, Welalánux and Piatuléra. The water stayed at its high mark for two days and then rapidly lowered.*[40]

A WORLD VIEW

I hope you have found these stories thought-provoking. Each one on its own is just a myth, like so many myths around the world. You can't help suspecting that the fertile imagination of generations of story-tellers has been at work. But on the other hand there are an awful lot of them, many from people who would never normally have set eyes on any expanse of water larger than a medium-sized river! The next map shows the locations of the 189 stories reported by Mark Isaak which seem to me to be sufficiently intelligible (and sufficiently different from other stories) to be taken seriously, together with a couple more from other sources. I have to admit that although I say "sufficiently different", this in no way implies that they are all of separate origin. The Noah-type stories have already been highlighted as almost certainly having a common original. The same is true of several clusters of stories with common themes such as escape in a box (central Mexico) or canoes tethered to a mountain by ropes (Washington State region).

It is astonishing just how widespread these flood stories are. There are obvious concentrations, notably America, South-East Asia and Australia; and there are also obvious gaps, notably much of Africa (there are none hidden by the key) and Europe. However, the overwhelming impression is that either the concept of a Great Flood is so firmly embedded in the human psyche that it naturally springs up all over the world or else there actually was some real and nearly worldwide event which triggered the various stories still told today. I am no psychologist, but the first of these options doesn't seem all that likely to me. On the other hand the second option is frankly almost inconceivable.

With such a mass of evidence, however debatable its reliability, it makes sense to analyse it as far as we can. If there were no common theme then we might be prepared to accept that humans are in some way predisposed to imagining floods; however one recurrent theme has certainly emerged and that is the phenomenon of the oceans rising to cover the land. Over the next few sections I will see if I can track down further clues.

FLOOD DURATION

This is a tricky issue. For a start, most of the stories give no figures at all. Next, it is clear that stories with a common origin sometimes have wildly differing durations (for example, several months for Noah, seven days for Atrahasis and Ziusudra). One understandable source of confusion over a hundred or more generations of oral tradition is the distinction between

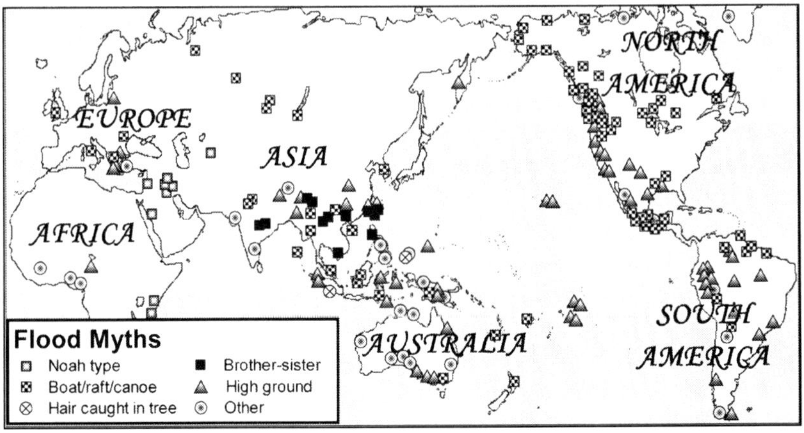

the duration of an initial rainstorm and the total duration of the flood. To some extent this was visible in the stories of Ziusudra and Utanapishtim. Although the two stories are clearly one, the seven days are simply those during which rain fell in the case of Utanapishtim, while the flood continued afterwards for an undisclosed period. In the Ziusudra story (and that of Atrahasis) seven days is the total flood duration. With this possible problem in mind, it is perhaps not too surprising that several stories give a length in days (four, five, seven, nine, ten, twenty), while about the same number measure the length in months (three, five, six, eight, twelve). Many others simply speak of *a long time* or *several months*, and, as I noted earlier, some even extend to years.

Now clearly the reason for all this disagreement may be that none of the tales is actually based on a real event! However, it is worth bearing in mind that periods of several months are commonly stated and, of course, if the oceans really had risen to cover the land, the durations would have been different in different locations since high ground would have been submerged for less time than low-lying land.

FLOOD DEPTH

This is another very difficult matter to gauge from the flood myths alone, and it is something which could easily have changed in the telling in many instances. The only real indication possible is where it is stated that people survived by climbing a mountain. A story from the Greek island of Samothrace, for example, would appear to put an upper limit of about 1000 metres. But even this is fraught with uncertainty since in many cases you have to suspect that the story originated in a quite different location from the place where it is now told. For example, if the Lithuanian tale actually originated in Lithuania, then the flood could not have exceeded about 250 metres in that area, since we are told that people survived on the "highest mountain". But did it really originate there? Lithuanian language and culture only arrived in Lithuania about 2000 years ago.[41] Similarly, the story currently told on the island of Nias, west of Sumatra, would limit the maximum depth to under 100 metres – if it really originated on Nias itself. Conversely however, if we were to take seriously the stories told by several Native American tribes from Washington State we would have to conclude that the flood extended to the snow line on Mount Rainier, which is several thousand metres, and that it covered the 2500-metre-high Olympic range completely. Most impressive of all is the tradition from Tibet that all of Tibet was once under water!

Unfortunately, I think we have to admit that the issue of depth remains completely unresolved. The traditional interpretation (though not necessarily the real meaning) of the Noah story is that even Mount

Everest was covered. Set against this are tales which speak of survivors, sometimes in trees, and in many cases the stories read as though the depth were no more than a few hundred metres at most – although of course even a flood of 10 metres would be beyond our wildest imaginations based on modern-day experience. The storm surge associated with a cyclone that recently devastated swathes of Burma was only estimated at 3.5 metres for example.

WHEN DID THE TALES ORIGINATE?

Individual stories are virtually undatable. Only in a few cases are there any date-dependent facts, for example the South American tale that speaks of pre-agricultural times. And, of course, there is the general point that the deeply mythological nature of the stories suggests an oral transmission period measured in thousands rather than hundreds of years.

There are clues however. There are two quite distinct stories in which a woman got her hair caught in a tree. In one, from the island of Enggano, south of Sumatra, the woman was the sole survivor of a flood that totally covered the island and she survived when her hair was caught in a thorn tree, which presumably acted as a life jacket and allowed her to float long enough to reach land above the flood level.[42] In another story, from Palau Island in the Pacific, the woman escapes on a raft, which drifts until she gets her hair caught in a tree on the top of a mountain.[43] Now the stories are quite different with the exception of the woman's hair being caught in a tree, but this is not a line likely to occur too often just by chance. The locations from which these tales come are some 1300 miles apart. However there is a connection; both islands are inhabited by people who speak an Austronesian language, and it is known that these languages and the cultures that went with them originated in Taiwan in about 3500BC,[44] spreading south and west through the Philippines, Indonesia and, eventually, the Pacific. If these two stories had a common origin, that origin could hardly be dated later than the 3rd Millennium BC, the approximate date at which the languages must have separated.

And the evidence is much more powerful still in the case of the brother-sister stories. The common theme is that two young people, a brother and a sister, survived a great flood in a box, a casket, a giant gourd or a dug-out canoe. When they made land, they found they were the only people to have survived, so they had to marry each other to ensure the survival of the human race. Now this makes a good story and it would not be too surprising to see something like it arising independently in more than one location. But I count twelve – and that simply cannot be coincidence! The range of these tales is from Taiwan to central India, taking in communities in Vietnam, southern China and Burma; so how can this spread possibly be explained? There has certainly been no obvious recent population movement.

Chapter 4 will explore the clues to be gleaned from the current distribution of languages around the world, but here let me introduce what I feel is the only possible language family that could account for this particular tale. It is known as 'Austro-Asiatic', and its present-day range is from Vietnamese in the east to languages in central India. The following map illustrates my analysis of the history of the language family;[45] the method used to derive it will be outlined in Chapter 4.

The analysis is of course approximate, although I believe there are good reasons to think that the dates and routes of spread are quite tightly constrained. The only brother-sister flood myth that does not appear to lie on or close to a route of spread of the Austro-Asiatic language family is that shown in the Philippines. However this could easily have been brought by Austronesian speakers from Taiwan, since Austronesian language is known to have been profoundly influenced by contact with Austro-Asiatic; in fact many believe the two language families are directly related.

So much for the linguistics; the key point here is that if the brother-sister story really was carried across South-East Asia by Austro-Asiatic speakers, and if the dates shown on the map are approximately correct, then its date of origin is pushed right back to a remarkable 6500BC, with a location in eastern India. And you would have to think that a story that survives, albeit with various different mutations, for eight and a half millennia must either be a very good story indeed or else must contain a very important kernel of truth. At least, you might think that if we weren't talking about the surely impossible subject of a worldwide flood hundreds of metres deep!

SUMMARY

I trust you are now both illuminated by the wide range of flood stories of which the world can boast and also a little puzzled as to how there can possibly be a shred of truth in any of them. However, a clear conclusion from this chapter is that Noah no longer stands alone. If Noah is just a mythical figure then he is in excellent company on several continents. I would also say that our search for the Great Flood has now changed subtly. There does seem to be plenty of reason to doubt the theory that Mount Everest was ever covered (quite apart from scientific considerations) since many tales appear to refer to a flood of no more than a few hundred metres. On the other hand the evidence of the brother-sister stories is that the timeframe should be shunted some distance back into pre-history. If 6500BC really is a sensible estimate then we are dealing with times some three and a half millennia before the development of writing, at least two millennia

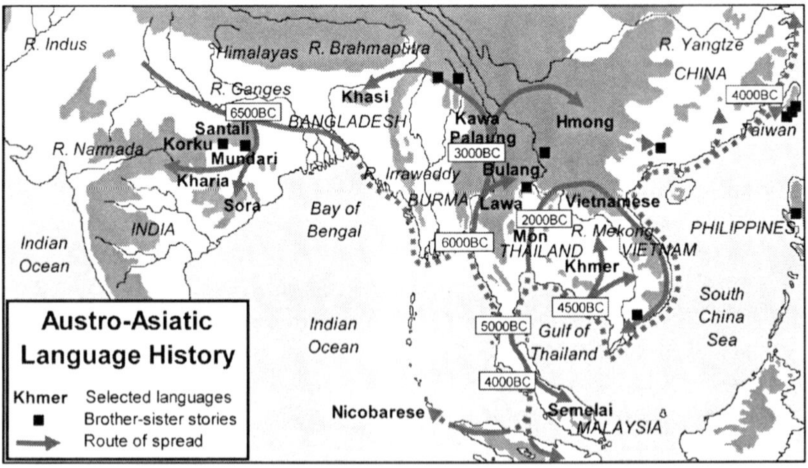

before the first letter-like signs, which certainly makes our search a little more difficult!

Basically this chapter has thrown down a challenge to science. Human myth speaks loud and clear; it states unequivocally that there really was a day when the oceans rose to cover the land. These myths come from coastal communities such as those who lived along the western seaboard of America, but they also come from communities who had never seen any significant expanse of water in their lives, such as those in central India. The challenge to science is: can it manage to 'debunk' these myths?

Over the course of the next few chapters I shall be asking this question of various different professions. If any branch of human knowledge can be found to prove that there was no possible time-window during which the Great Flood could have occurred, then it didn't occur – no argument. Similarly, if I find no positive evidence that anything catastrophic ever happened then I really have to doubt whether the tales are true; and perhaps most crucially of all, if there is no scientific explanation for the Great Flood then it remains no more than an unsupported and highly dubious myth.

The challenge has been thrown down; let's hear what the experts have to say on the matter.

3

The Archaeologist's Report

Much of what we know of ancient human history comes from archaeology. The written word can take us no further back than about 3000BC, and at that date it is limited to Egypt and Iraq. Even in the Middle East writing only became widespread in the 2nd Millennium BC. In 3rd Millennium BC India a form of writing was in use – but only to a limited extent and it has not yet been deciphered. In China it is only with the coming to power of the Chou dynasty in the late 2nd Millennium BC that significant written records become available, and these are very limited in number as a result of the First Emperor's book-burning edict of the late 3rd Century BC. And in the Americas all is in darkness until the earliest Mayan texts emerge in the first few centuries AD. Clearly if we need to look back as far as the 7th Millennium BC, as I suggested might be the case in the last chapter, then we will not get there by looking at written records alone.

Archaeology is the study of the physical remains of past peoples and civilisations. It will tell us nothing of names, of rulers, governments, laws etc., but it will at least tell us something about the physical condition of a people, the types of houses they inhabited, their towns and cities, their fashions (at least in the case of durable products like pottery), possibly even details such as their diet and their state of health. As far as this investigation goes, what we really need from archaeology is an overall picture of the development of society, principally so that we can check for 'anomalies', unexplained 'hiccoughs' in development which just might be related to some ancient disaster. It seems unlikely that we would actually find any direct evidence for a Great Flood through archaeology even if it did happen; after all, the disaster we are looking for is not one of turbulent waters carrying sediment but of a rise in sea level, possibly over a period of weeks or months, and it is hard to see what direct archaeological sign this would leave. Any evidence that emerges is therefore likely to be somewhat circumstantial. It might just be possible, if we were very lucky indeed, that the skeleton of a fish or other marine creature could be found where it shouldn't be – but this would be a massive stroke of luck, almost certainly ignored by any archaeologist as nothing more than an indication of the varied diet of the people of that time!

So where should we look? Well, it would obviously make sense to pay particular attention to low-lying parts of the world, since they would be the first to suffer in the event of a rise in sea level. It would also make sense to concentrate on regions where civilisation is known to have a long and archaeologically visible history. With these points in mind I suggest the place to start is with the great plain of the Tigris and Euphrates rivers, forming much of the modern state of Iraq, one of the flattest parts of the planet and a key early centre of advanced human culture.

ANCIENT IRAQ

Iraq is seen by many as the cradle of modern civilisation. It was one of the two locations where real writing first developed – the other being Egypt. The Garden of Eden where, according to Jews, Christians and Muslims, Adam and Eve were created by God, is generally placed in Iraq, since the Tigris and Euphrates are both said to have flowed from (or into) Eden. The word *Eden* is also the Sumerian word for *plain*, and the Sumerians were the most ancient inhabitants of the Iraqi plain of which we have direct (i.e. written) knowledge.

So what do we know?

We know that the development of writing was the culmination of a long period during which the city of Uruk dominated the land. So-called Uruk culture can be seen in cities right across Iraq and northern Syria and, by counting back the archaeological layers, each of which is distinguished by its own individual pottery forms, architectural techniques etc., as well as by use of Carbon 14 dating, it can be determined that Uruk culture originated in about 3800BC – plus or minus a century or two.

You may remember that this date, 3800BC, has already been mentioned in this book. It was the date of the flood deposits discovered at the city of Ur by Sir Leonard Woolley, deposits which separate the Uruk culture layers from an earlier culture that goes by the name of 'Ubaid'. It looks highly likely that this flood caused a major political change in Iraq, allowing the city of Uruk to rise to prominence. This is interesting. Until that time the principal city of the region had been Eridu, lying about 10 miles south of Ur, and one would assume that the flood which left such dramatic evidence at Ur had also brought disaster to nearby Eridu; yet it was less disastrous to Uruk for some reason. Let me speculate a little here. Eridu now lies about 140 miles from the Persian Gulf; in 3800BC it was right on the coast. Nearly 6000 years of silt deposition have caused an inexorable south-eastward growth of the Iraqi plain. Could it therefore be that the flood of 3800BC was actually associated with the sea rather than with the Euphrates river? The obvious cause would be a cyclone, bringing a storm surge and consequent flood of turbulent sea-water across the plain. This might just explain the quite exceptional depth of silty clay deposit found at Ur. The region is not subject to cyclones today, but it is hard to

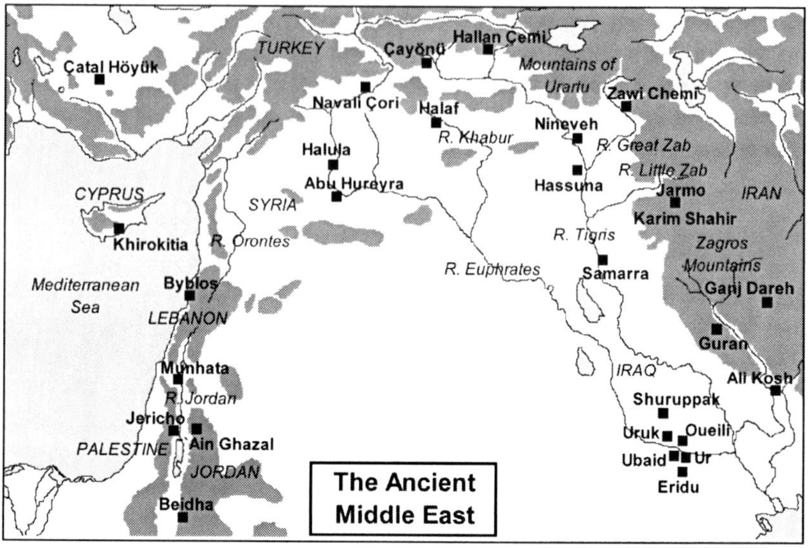

be certain how the climate may have operated at a time when so much was different. Arabia, for example, was a land of grass and moderate rainfall in those days, with lakes where now the dunes of the Empty Quarter stand.

And if this flood was associated with a rise in sea level due to a storm surge, together with the heavy rainfall associated with a cyclone, then it begins to match the story of Noah a little better than a river flood – but the problem is that it can't explain the hundreds of other flood stories from all over the world. The duration would also have been measured in days at most. So, dramatic though this flood must have been for those who witnessed it, and dramatic though archaeology reveals its political consequences to have been, it still doesn't appear to be what we are looking for. Political consequence: yes; annihilation of most of the Iraqi population: definitely not!

Never mind; if the 3800BC flood isn't the one we are looking for, we'd better push on. The Uruk period was preceded by the long-lasting culture known as Ubaid, named after a small settlement just outside Ur. Archaeologists have traditionally divided the Ubaid period into four phases, covering the centuries from about 5500BC through to 3800BC, the phases being distinguished mainly by the changing fashions in pottery. During this whole period Eridu was much the largest of the southern Iraqi settlements, and this ties in with Sumerian tradition, expressed in the first few lines of the *Sumerian king list*, namely that kingship descended first on Eridu. Given the continuity evident throughout the Ubaid period and the relatively modest change represented by the onset of Uruk culture in about 3800BC, together with the evidence of the *Sumerian king list*, it is logical to suggest that the Ubaid people were direct ancestors of the Sumerians, or at the very least that they contributed directly to later Sumerian culture.

But the founding of Eridu in the mid 6th Millennium BC is about as far back as we can go in southern Iraq. The settlement known as Tell Oueili seems to have predated Eridu by a century or two (a phase sometimes designated 'Ubaid 0'), but before this the whole Iraqi plain is an archaeological blank. The rather surprising conclusion drawn by archaeologists is that southern Iraq had no settled inhabitants before this time, no villages and no agriculture. Hunter-gatherer groups may have roamed the land, but their traces are almost impossible to find other than at regularly used shelters such as caves – and there are no caves on the southern Iraqi plain.

The lack of evidence before the 6th Millennium BC is surprising because agriculture was certainly being practised elsewhere in the Middle East and beyond. The culture of Tell Oueili was very similar to that known as 'Samarran', found along the middle reaches of the Tigris river, north of the modern city of Baghdad, and Samarran culture developed from that found at the settlement of Hassuna, south of modern Mosul. And Hassuna represents a key piece in the archaeological jigsaw of the Middle East. It was a small village site inhabited from about 6000BC, with decorated pottery evident right from the start, and it has parallels with the styles used at contemporary sites in northern Iraq, northern Syria and as far as Cilicia in southern Turkey. Samarran pottery is similar in style to that found in the later archaeological levels at Hassuna, from about 5500BC. The evidence such as it is therefore suggests that the Sumerian culture of southern Iraq must have spread south from the middle Tigris region during the first half of the 6th Millennium BC, while parallel movements of culture occurred westward into Syria and beyond.

OK; what was happening before 6000BC?

The culture that immediately preceded (and was probably related to) that of Hassuna is named after the settlement of Jarmo near the modern city of Suleimaniya in eastern Iraq, in the foothills of the Zagros Mountains. Jarmo was a permanently inhabited settlement where people were practising both arable farming (wheat and barley) and animal husbandry (sheep and goats) between about 7000BC and 5800BC. Pottery appeared about two thirds of the way through the period of occupation. Other related sites were Guran, also in the Zagros foothills, and Ali Kosh on the plains of south-west Iran, both with clear similarities to Jarmo from about 6500BC. Guran and Ali Kosh in their turn have similarities in the stone tools used during their earliest phases (about 7000BC) to those found at Ganj Dareh, high in the Zagros Mountains, and before that Karim Shahir, a seasonally occupied site near Jarmo dating between about

9000BC and 7000BC. And even earlier than Karim Shahir is the site of Zawi Chemi north of Mosul in Kurdistan. Here storage pits have been found, suggesting the presence of a sedentary population with the need to store grain of some sort, with dates of 10000-9000BC.[1]

It's an inevitably fragmented picture due to the hit-and-miss nature of archaeology and the immense stretch of time that has elapsed since these ancient villages were inhabited. Nevertheless there is now enough evidence to suggest that agricultural development was initiated in the hills of western Iran, northern Iraq and south-eastern Turkey (modern Kurdistan – the region where the wild versions of wheat and barley grew naturally) as far back as about 10000BC, with a continuous record of occupation and absolutely no sign of any unexplained disruption to progress. However, according to the data, it was only in about 6000BC that people took these ideas out onto the plain of the Tigris and Euphrates. From that time on there is a continuous record of occupation at low-level sites also. The implications are clear:

- The latest possible date for a Great Flood covering the Iraqi plain is 6000BC.
- If such an event took place between 10000BC and 6000BC then it could not have covered the settlements of the Zagros Mountain region and Kurdistan. Therefore its depth could not have been greater than a few hundred metres.

We are left pondering the mystery of the Iraqi plain. It does seem a little strange that there is no low-level evidence before 6000BC. There would not, so far as we can tell, have been anything unattractive about life out on the plain. There would have been plenty of fertility in the soil either side of the Tigris and Euphrates, and plenty of meat available in the form of wildfowl and animals. Of course it could be that the evidence has been obscured by subsequent layers of added silt; yet it is undeniable that if there ever had been settled agricultural life out on the plain before 6000BC, the culture of those times has since vanished entirely, to be replaced by that of the Sumerians, descending from the hills to the north.[2]

Looking around the rest of the Middle East there is an unfortunate lack of low-lying plains! Signs of early civilisation are everywhere, notably the sites marked on the previous map right across southern Turkey as far as the well known early Neolithic city of Çatal Höyük, which prospered between about 7500BC and 6000BC, but they all lie at a considerable elevation above the sea. Halaf is lower (about 400 metres above sea level) but was not occupied until around 5500BC. Halula, also at about 400 metres, does indeed show continuing occupation through the 7th and 6th Millennia BC, but also reveals a significant cultural change a little before 6000BC;

the same is true of Abu Hureyra.[3] And of course in the event that sea level rise really did reach settlements such as Halula and Abu Hureyra, a cultural change is as much as one would expect. The population would simply have escaped to the adjacent hills and returned to rebuild their homes and their lives when it was safe to do so. There would be no other sign that anything had happened at all – which makes this search for evidence very difficult indeed.

However there is one further Middle Eastern location which must definitely be investigated. It is not a particularly large area – the population would probably have escaped easily enough from any flood there might have been – but the thing that makes this particular location worth investigating is that it lies below sea level. If the sea ever flooded it, it would have remained flooded for a very long time. It is time to drop in on Jericho, arguably the oldest city in the world.

THE JORDAN VALLEY

If the Mediterranean were to rise by around 50 metres the entire valley of the river Jordan would be inundated – and the water would never drain away. Evaporation would slowly reduce the level since this would far exceed the relatively meagre inflow from the surrounding catchment area, but by my calculation it would be well over 100 years before the walls of Jericho finally emerged from their watery tomb. Here, surely, is the ultimate test; here you might expect to find real proof that there never was any Great Flood.

The city of Jericho has been excavated by various archaeologists over the years, but most famously by Kathleen Kenyon in the late 1950s,[4] and her findings shocked the academic world. This was largely due to her use of the newly-developed art of Carbon 14 dating, which revealed that the earliest city at Jericho had been founded in the 8th or possibly even the 9th Millennium BC which, at that time, pushed back the dawn of civilisation by thousands of years. She even found signs that people had been living in rudimentary shelters across the site for a thousand years before this. So the question arises: is there any evidence at all for a 100-year-long break in occupation at Jericho? And if so when?

The answer to the first question is a very clear 'yes'. The first phase of city life, usually designated 'Pre-pottery Neolithic A', lasted for several hundred years. It saw the construction of a large, thick city wall surrounding a town comprising well-built houses with rounded corners, and it represented a giant stride from semi-nomadic cave dwelling to fully settled life. Agriculture in the Jordan Valley was also well established.[5] However, this phase of city life came to an end for an unknown reason, probably some time in the 8th Millennium BC, and the site was abandoned for a considerable period. This is known from the extensive erosion that was found to have occurred along the side slopes of the site.

After an indeterminate time the site was occupied once more, this time by a quite different people bearing a quite different culture, usually known as 'Pre-pottery Neolithic B'. Based on the limited Carbon 14 dating information, this phase commenced some time before 7000BC and it lasted until the second half of the 7th Millennium BC. The inhabitants built solid rectangular houses using hand-made bricks and wooden frames; they kept pigs, sheep and cattle and they grew wheat and barley. For the times the society was a prosperous one and it was technically highly advanced. The town was surprisingly large, with a population measured in thousands. However, like its predecessor, this town also came to a sudden end and the site lay unoccupied for a further indeterminate period of time while erosion steadily transformed the city into an amorphous mound of rubble.[6]

This abandonment was followed by a very surprising change. The next inhabitants, known to archaeology as 'Pottery Neolithic A', were much more primitive. They lived in pits dug into the ground, which would presumably have been covered by some perishable superstructure (wood and skins for instance). The only significant advance they brought was the use of pottery.

There is no need to take you any further through the rich and varied history of Jericho since there is a continuous record of occupation from Pottery Neolithic A right through to the close of the Middle Bronze Age, some time in the 2nd Millennium BC, and so no possibility that the Jordan valley could have been flooded during that whole period. But we are still left with two long-lasting phases during which Jericho lay unoccupied; the first was some time around 8000BC, the second was in about 6250BC. In neither case is it possible to say anything definite about the duration, just that it was long enough to reduce the walls of the city to a natural angle of rest – which means several decades at least. The backward step taken by society between Pre-pottery Neolithic B and Pottery Neolithic A is particularly dramatic and therefore quite suggestive of a major disaster of some sort in that part of the world. To quote Kenyon's own words on the subject: "for some reason the light of progress seemed to flicker out".

At the time of Kenyon's excavations Jericho was unique; this is no longer the case. Parallel evidence has now been found at several other locations (shown on the previous map), including Byblos in Lebanon, Halula and Abu Hureyra in Syria, Munhata in the Jordan valley, and Beidha and Ain Ghazal, both in the modern state of Jordan. Until the site at Ain Ghazal was excavated a serious question confronted archaeologists as to what could be found to bridge the gap between the disappearance of Pre-pottery Neolithic B culture and the appearance some time later of the much less sophisticated Pottery Neolithic A. At Munhata, another site lying below sea level, the picture was similar to that at Jericho, with a clear break in occupation, although the culture that eventually resettled the site, known as 'Yarmukian', was not the same as Pottery Neolithic A. In Byblos, which was excavated before the Second World War, the picture is confused unfortunately, and modern archaeologists suspect that the relatively crude excavation techniques of the time have led to an obscuring of the transition from Pre-Pottery Neolithic B to Yarmukian. At Beidha, although the evidence is excellent, the site was abandoned during the Pre-pottery Neolithic B period and never re-occupied. At Halula and Abu Hureyra on the Euphrates the Pre-pottery Neolithic B culture came to a definite end and was replaced by another, termed 'Pre-Halaf' (Halaf culture paralleling that of Ubaid in Iraq from about 5500BC).[7] At Ain Ghazal however things were quite different. There the Pre-pottery Neolithic B levels gave way smoothly to a further development of the same culture, now termed 'Pre-pottery Neolithic C', and thence to the well-recognised Yarmukian phase.[8] The Pre-pottery Neolithic C period lasted some 500 years. Whatever it was that had caused destruction and a break in occupation at Jericho and Munhata, and the sudden end of Pre-pottery Neolithic B occupation elsewhere, for some reason it had not affected Ain Ghazal.

This is important. Apart from anything else it provides evidence for the length of the break at the end of the Pre-pottery Neolithic B period at Jericho and Munhata and it was considerably longer than 100 years. It also provides a limit to the disaster, whatever caused it. While lowland sites saw a marked change of culture and, perhaps coincidentally, sub-sea-level sites saw a long break in occupation, Ain Ghazal, sitting over 700 metres above sea level on the Jordanian plateau, saw no change at all, simply steady progress – which means that although the Jericho evidence had the potential to blow any idea of a Great Flood clean out of the water, it has actually done quite the opposite! There is no proof that the agent of destruction was a flood, but it does look very much as if a disaster of some sort brought Pre-pottery Neolithic B civilisation to an end over a very wide area, and there's no denying the fact that it was those perched well above sea level who survived. Not only so but we have a fairly tight date range for this disaster, some time around 6250BC.[9]

In fact it is well recognised by archaeologists that Pre-pottery Neolithic B culture was brought to an end by a disaster of some kind, and the culprit most commonly proposed is climate change. In the absence of a flood this seems the only way to explain such a complete extinction of culture across such a wide area. To give you an idea of the extent of this collapse of civilisation, let me take you to the island of Cyprus, where Khirokhitia is the best known site of many on the island with an advanced culture similar to Pre-pottery Neolithic B. Not only did it come to a sudden end at approximately the same time as Pre-pottery Neolithic B but it was followed by a millennium and a half during which the island was totally unoccupied by humans.[10] Once again, climate change is the only explanation experts can come up with.

To summarise the evidence thus far: we have a very clear time window, starting in about 6250BC, when it is theoretically possible for a flood many hundreds of metres deep to have occurred. However daft the idea, it matches the specific evidence from sub-sea-level sites in the Jordan valley as well as the collapse of Pre-pottery Neolithic B civilisation everywhere except on very high ground. It also fits well with the picture in Iraq, where the lack of human occupation evidence out on the plain of the Tigris and Euphrates before the 6th Millennium BC contrasts with the continuous development seen at sites in the Zagros Mountains. Interestingly, 6250BC is also close to the estimate given in the last chapter based on the distribution of brother-sister flood myths.

Middle Eastern archaeology also provides limits to the depth of any possible flood – if we really are talking of a flood. It would have to have been deeper than 50 metres or it wouldn't have flooded the Jordan valley, and it was certainly less than 700 metres or Ain Ghazal would never have survived. Admittedly the mountains of Cyprus are higher than 700 metres, but how long could refugees have survived up in the mountains? They may not have drowned, but could they have avoided death through starvation?

EGYPT

You may well have been expecting a visit to the famous land of the pharaohs, the seat of one of ancient history's best known and most advanced civilisations. But the simple truth is that Egypt was not at all advanced in 6250BC. There were no cities and there was no agriculture, which means there is very little evidence to go on. Before the times of the pharaohs, which means before 3000BC, we have no records to help us, just the clues left in the sand to be read by archaeologists. These clues tell us that during the 4th and 5th Millennia BC Egypt was divided between two quite different cultures, one around the Nile delta with strong similarities to Palestine, the other in southern Egypt.[11] In the Nile delta region arable farming arrived in about 4500BC and it clearly came from Palestine. That it arrived from Palestine is no surprise I guess – that's the only direction from which Middle Eastern crop types could have come – but the late arrival date certainly is. It's only about 250 miles from Jericho to the Nile, and agriculture had been practised in Jericho since the 9th Millennium BC.[12] How is it possible that the idea of farming took over 4000 years to travel just 250 miles? Did the ancient Egyptians simply not want to know? In contrast wheat and barley farming arrived in southern England in about 4300BC after a journey of more than 2000 miles from Turkey.

And what makes this even more perplexing is that there is real evidence from much earlier times for the practising of primitive agriculture actually in the Nile valley itself. The evidence comes from pollen analysis, which reveals the presence of both a wheat-like grass and wild barley, and also from the appearance of sickle gloss on what are thought to be stone sickle blades.[13] Admittedly if this really was agriculture it wasn't particularly advanced; it may only have consisted of the organised harvesting of naturally growing grasses. However, it is not the brilliance or otherwise of this development, which took place during the phase known as 'Qadan' in southern Egypt and northern Sudan, datable to as far back as the 10th Millennium BC, it is the fact that it disappeared without trace that seems so surprising. Even more disturbing, it may not only have been early farming experiments that disappeared but possibly the people themselves as well! In the opinion of some at least, there seems to have been a real 'population hiatus' between what is known as the Epipalaeolithic Period (Qadan culture) and the Neolithic.[14] The pastoralist society that went on to dominate southern Egypt from about 6000BC and eventually took over the whole country was quite different from what went before, and it emerged from the then grass-covered hills of the Sahara Desert.[15] Archaeologists have even found that the quintessentially Egyptian art of mummification was also practised by ancient Saharan societies.

This evidence is a little hard to explain. Whatever caused the disappearance of this relatively advanced Nile valley society, it must have been something pretty significant, something that stopped progress dead in its tracks. And although the evidence doesn't provide an accurate date, 6250BC sits comfortably enough within the possible time window.

All in all, as I leave the Middle East, the birthplace of modern agriculture, there is no avoiding the conclusion that something major really did take place very roughly in 6250BC, something that affected Iraq, Palestine and, possibly, Egypt as well. Not only that, but the effect seems to have been most pronounced in low-lying regions. But what about the rest of the world? Is there anything anywhere else to support these rather odd conclusions? Here I have to confess that this will be a very selective archaeologist's report – it's impossible to do more within sensible space limits – but I feel I should at least check out the two other principal regions where agriculture was already being practised in 6250BC. Wheat and barley are important crops in temperate climates, but in tropical and subtropical latitudes today's staple crop of choice is rice, and in China rice cultivation was already in full swing in 6250BC.

THE NORTH CHINA PLAIN

China is by no means entirely low-lying. However the greatest concentration of population today can be found across an extensive plain through which flow the lower reaches of the Yellow and Yangtze rivers, stretching from Beijing in the north to Nanjing and Shanghai in the south, and it is on this plain, where the Yangtze river spills out across the lowlands below the famous Yangtze gorges, that the first evidence for rice planting is found.

The modern, politically acceptable version of Chinese history emphasises continuity of culture throughout the course of the millennia. Written Chinese history is excellent, as far as it goes, and it tells us unequivocally of the coming to power of the First Emperor in 221BC. Before that there is enough evidence to piece together a confused phase known as the 'Warring States' period and, earlier still, the Chou dynasty, dating from the mid 11th Century BC. Archaeology then tells us something of the previous rulers, the Shang emperors, with their capital at Anyang in the middle of the north China plain, although written evidence is now nothing more than legend and myth.

Archaeologically, the Shang dynasty emerged from the culture named after the site of Lungshan, with settlements right across the plain and with origins in Shandong and Jiangsu provinces on the east coast. The continuity between Lungshan times and the Shang dynasty is visible in art, architecture and even in religious practice (as evidenced by the famous 'oracle bones' for instance[16]) and Lungshan culture can be traced back to about 3000BC – all based on Carbon 14 dating.

The culture that preceded Lungshan right across northern China, with origins in the middle reaches of the Yellow River and its tributary the Wei, and which then spread east across the plain, is known as 'Yangshao'. Lungshan and Yangshao cultures were quite different from each other and many sites show a very sharp change at the transition, often with evidence of destruction. The art and pottery of Yangshao culture bears similarities to those further west, in Central Asia, while Lungshan designs are much more 'Pacific' in nature, strongly resembling those of South-East Asia and Polynesia. However, these are mere details; the point is that there is continuous evidence of human occupation right across the north China plain back to the early days of Yangshao culture, some time around 5000BC.

The Yangshao people were agriculturalists – but they were not growers of rice. They had inherited agriculture based on millet from the previous inhabitants of the region, who are usually named after the site of Peiligang. The Peiligang people were the very first agriculturalists of northern China and they can be traced back to around 6500BC in the hills of Inner Mongolia.[17] As far as village life based on millet growing is concerned, there is no evidence out on the plains until the first low-level Peiligang sites in the 6th Millennium BC, and in this respect the evidence (or lack of it) is very similar to that in Iraq and the Nile delta. Admittedly the north China plain is known to have been a land of lakes and marsh in

these times and you could certainly argue that it may have been unsuitable for human habitation, or at least unsuitable for settled agriculture. In summary, therefore, we can do no more than remark that northern China provides no archaeological evidence against a flood having covered the plain some time in the late 7th Millennium BC – but that there is also nothing that directly supports it.

CENTRAL AND SOUTHERN CHINA

Meanwhile, on the middle Yangtze and the upper reaches of the Huai River, a quite different form of agriculture was being developed. The sites of Jia Lake and Pengtoushan date to around 7000BC and they reveal pretty firm evidence (in the form of grains and ancient paddy fields) that rice agriculture had begun.[18] In fact there has since been a concentration of finds in the Pengtoushan region, most rather later than Pengtoushan itself, suggesting that this was the principal early centre; Jia Lake may have been an offshoot – or they may both have derived from an original development elsewhere. Both sites sit near the western edge of the plain, but there is no evidence for any significant eastward spread of rice agriculture until the emergence of what is known as 'Hemudu' culture in the Shanghai region in about 5000BC. There is then an explosion of finds both from the area around Hemudu and also from the middle Yangtze, around Pengtoushan, but there is surprisingly little to cover the intervening 500 miles.[19]

So what does all this mean? There is still no consensus as to exactly where Chinese rice agriculture started, although the Pengtoushan region is most commonly proposed. But in fact there are several isolated southern Chinese sites (shown on the map) where cultivated rice remains have been found, all with similar or earlier start dates to those of Pengtoushan and Jia Lake,[20] which either means that the idea of rice growing sprang up independently in several locations or, much more plausibly, that it had been spreading across the land from well before 7000BC.[21] But the key question is whether there is any evidence for a break in continuity in low-lying locations in around 6250BC – and this is not an easy question to answer. The southern sites either show no evidence later than 6250BC, or, in the case of Zhenpiyan, are at a relatively high elevation. Pengtoushan itself comes to an end in about 6500BC. It's true that Jia Lake is both low-lying and appears to have been occupied continuously from 7000BC through to some time in the 5th Millennium BC, but then Jia Lake is only a few miles from land over 500 metres above sea level, so abandonment and reoccupation by the same people would have been quite feasible.

However, the key pointers that something might have disrupted life some time in the 7th Millennium BC are the indirect ones. Despite the fact that rice cultivation was in progress in various locations across central and southern China as far east as Xianrendong as early as 7000BC, development seems to have stalled for some reason. It apparently took some 2000 years for rice farming to catch on in Hemudu and the surrounding area even though the distance from Xianrendong is only 250 miles, which is a remarkably slow rate of progress compared to the way wheat and barley growing galloped across the Middle East and fanned out into Europe. It is also very surprising how 'patchy' later development was. It seems to have been concentrated in the coastal area around Shanghai and on the middle Yangtze, with only isolated sites elsewhere. Those in southern China seem to have given up on the idea completely for some reason. None of this necessarily implies a flood of course but it has to be admitted that widespread devastation and population loss would be one possible cause of this 'anomaly'. Even if there had been a flood there are enough hills for survival to have been possible everywhere apart from the north China plain – unless the flood level was very high indeed – but it might not have been so easy simply to pick up the threads of life again once the disaster was over. Seed stocks may have been wiped out, requiring cultivation from wild rice once more – and would anyone still have the know-how to do it? As in the Middle East, therefore, there are more than enough suspicious facts to make us wonder, but not nearly enough for us to be sure.

But I have not yet quite completed this review of low-lying regions where agriculture was practised. By 6250BC wheat and barley farming extended eastwards as far as Pakistan, and the Indus valley of Pakistan is as flat as southern Iraq; there is no high ground for hundreds of miles. It is to the Indian subcontinent therefore that we must now turn in the search for further clues.

THE VALLEY OF THE INDUS

The history of civilisation in the Indian subcontinent is almost as old as it is in China. When describing the evidence for oral transmission of the Rigveda I mentioned the Indus Valley civilisation, which covered all of Pakistan and parts of neighbouring India throughout the 3rd Millennium BC, an advanced society of town and city dwellers with a written script which we unfortunately do not yet understand. The Indus Valley civilisation sprang from the so-called Amri culture of the 4th Millennium BC, whose settlements can be found scattered across the Indus plain of southern Pakistan. While Amri civilisation dominated the plain, a series of not dissimilar cultures have been identified in the now-barren hills of Baluchistan (eastern Iran and western Pakistan),[22] hills which would then have seen much higher rainfall than today. There are parallels with the civilisations of Iraq to the west and there is plenty of evidence for trade with Iraq from very early times. For instance, the remains of towns and villages of the Quetta culture can be found near the Afghan border (in what today is no-go territory for foreigners) and strong connections are apparent with sites in southern Iran as far as the land of Elam on the border of ancient Sumer. The pottery parallels mean that this culture can be tied to the Ubaid phase in Iraq during the 5th Millennium BC. In fact it is clear that the Elamites of south-west Iran were trading widely in those days.[23]

However the origins of Quetta culture go much deeper than this. The site of Mehrgarh (and other neighbouring villages), not far from modern Quetta, is the oldest known centre of agriculture on the Indian subcontinent, and it lies right on the western edge of that subcontinent, on the plain beneath the Bolan pass, on the road from Quetta to the Indus valley. The earliest levels at Mehrgarh have been dated to the 7th Millennium BC, and they reveal that even in those pre-pottery days agriculture based on wheat, barley, sheep and cattle was already being practised.[24] This discovery came as a major surprise to most researchers; it meant that the agricultural know-how of western Iran, seen already at sites like Karim Shahir and Zawi Chemi, spread as quickly to the east as it did to the west. Just as was the case at sites such as Jarmo and Ali Kosh far to the west, pottery also appeared at Mehrgarh at the end of the 7th Millennium BC, not only in the utilitarian forms of dishes, jars etc., but also in the form of figurines, presumably reflecting part of the belief system of the people.

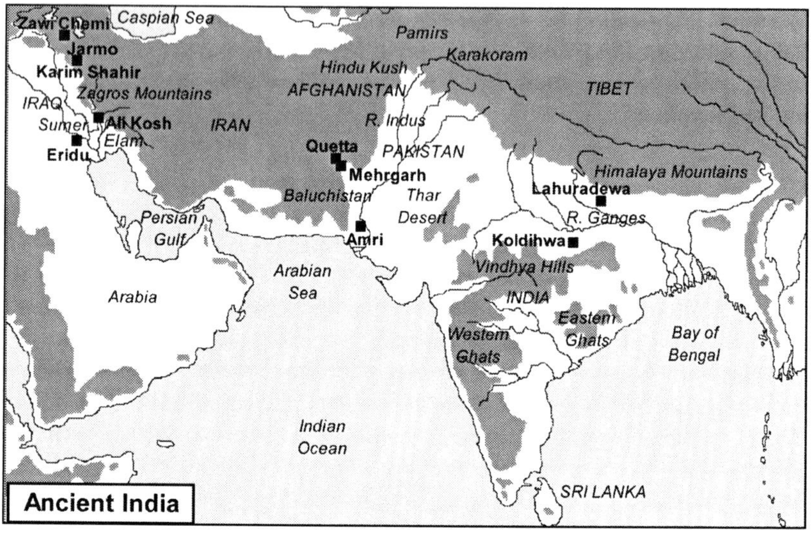

The question is: what stopped this culture from spreading steadily across the fertile plain of the Indus? There is a yawning 3000-year gap between the first signs of agriculture in Mehrgarh and the Amri cultures of the Indus Valley. In fact the only pre-Amri settlements that have been unearthed to date in the lower Indus region are clusters of hunter-gatherer communities near the coast and also in what is now the Thar Desert, dating from the 5th Millennium BC.[25] Despite over 2000 years of agricultural practice just 300 miles away at Mehrgarh, the people of the lower Indus seem to have remained blissfully ignorant of the art. In fact the culture of the Thar Desert people of the 5th Millennium BC was related much more closely to sites further east than to Mehrgarh, and much of the subsequent development of Indian agriculture stems from the Vindhya Hills area of central India and the adjacent Ganges valley (sites such as Koldihwa and Lahuradewa), where rice cultivation can be traced back at least as far as the 6th Millennium BC. It is quite a mystery why the achievements made at Mehrgarh failed to impact on the rest of the subcontinent.

And perhaps the greatest mystery of all is seen back at Mehrgarh itself. It consists of a massive thickness of alluvial silt which covered the site some time between the 7th Millennium BC pre-pottery phase and subsequent occupation periods, although dating discrepancies mean that it is impossible to be confident about the precise date at which this alluvium was deposited.[26] Nor is it at all clear why it is there, although I would have to doubt whether this alluvial layer represents direct evidence for a flood of the sort we are looking for here. Silt transport requires fast flowing water and that is not what a general rise in sea level would be expected to bring. It seems much more likely that something local, for example a landslide caused by an earthquake, may have dammed and/or diverted the waters of the Bolan river (a tributary of the Indus). On the other hand the date is close enough to 6250BC considering the uncertainty in dating information from Mehrgarh and, even if inundation by the sea cannot explain this silt deposit directly, it would certainly explain the occurrence of landslides. Floods always have the effect of changing the water regime in the ground, which leads to a temporary weakening of the soil.

The alluvial deposit at Mehrgarh remains an enigma, yet to be explained. Nevertheless, perhaps the more relevant issue in Pakistan as far as this investigation goes is still the inexplicable fact that the spread of agriculture came to sudden and grinding halt. Was it simply that the land was unsuitable until climate change produced drier conditions? Or is it possible that a whole community of early Indus valley farmers was suddenly wiped out by a catastrophe of mind-blowing proportions?

SUMMARY

As I said, this has been a highly selective report on the archaeological evidence and it has been limited to those parts of the world where agriculture was first to take hold. A significant amount of evidence from other places does of course exist, and some of it will be referred to in later chapters. But, for the moment, this report has served its purpose. The challenge was to produce evidence to contradict the claims of legend and myth that the world once drowned in a catastrophic flood. We have looked in all the most obvious places, the places where village life is known to have begun, and, in those places at least, archaeology has failed the challenge in some style. Not only has it done nothing to squash the idea of a Great Flood, but it has produced a date, 6250BC, the approximate date for the sudden and hard-to-explain end of the Middle Eastern agricultural society known as 'Pre-pottery Neolithic B'. At Jericho, 250 metres below sea level, there is a dramatic break in occupation followed by erosion of the site and reoccupation centuries later by a much more primitive people. Yet up on the Jordanian plateau, 700 metres above sea level, things just carried on as normal, Pre-pottery Neolithic B giving way to Pre-pottery Neolithic C as if nothing had happened. And as if that weren't enough, there seem to be 'anomalies' in the spread of agriculture wherever I look, in Iraq, Egypt, China and Pakistan, as if something had unaccountably interrupted progress at an indeterminate date which, in each case, could easily have been around 6250BC.

So, archaeology has failed to sink the idea of a Great Flood. It has, I think, proved beyond reasonable doubt that there could not have been a flood that actually covered the entire land surface of the planet; in fact the continuity of culture in the Zagros Mountains suggests a maximum elevation of just over 500 metres above sea level. Nevertheless, to most people a 500-metre rise in sea level would certainly be dramatic enough to be termed a 'Great' Flood – in which case archaeology has failed and we must therefore turn to other spheres of human knowledge.

Archaeology is the direct study of the human past; let's now take a look at a much less direct indicator, namely human language. If we can deduce something about the spread of language across the planet and even the point of origin of the various families of language spoken on the earth today, then that should give us information about the spread of human culture, just as surely as does archaeology. It is time for linguistics to take up the challenge where archaeology has failed.

4

The Linguist's Report

The power of language analysis has been tapped already, in Chapter 2, to derive an estimate for the date of the original brother-sister flood myth, the basis for a tale that is now told from the Philippines to India. In fact it was this evidence that first pointed towards a date as far back as the 7th Millennium BC. Since then, far from throwing any spanners in the works, archaeology has confirmed the likelihood that something pretty disastrous really did take place at about that time, and many of the signs relate to the unexpected disruption of cultural progress. And it is reasonable to expect that disruption to cultural progress would also be reflected in disruption to the spread of language. The task in this chapter therefore is to deduce the way that language has spread over the course of the millennia and to look for any unexplained events or interesting coincidences. After all, if there really ever had been a flood that covered the world's low-lying plains, we should see evidence of it in a subsequent spread of language from adjacent higher ground, refilling the empty land. That at least is the theory.

It is hard to say exactly how many different families of language there are in the world today. Some are sufficiently distinct to be recognised by all linguists; others are fiercely debated. Where two language families may be totally unrelated in the opinion of some, others see connections. The most disputed part of the world is undoubtedly the Americas, where the number of families present ranges from 3 to 25 or more depending on the belief of the individual linguist. And with this level of disagreement you will realise that there is also plenty of uncertainty in the time and place of origin of each family. Nevertheless, there is a hard core of language families where there is considerable agreement between experts, and it is with this hard core that I intend to begin this report into our linguistic past.

Before setting off let me say a few words about the link between language and culture since I am assuming that culture, as defined by archaeology, and language, deduced from linguistics, go hand in hand,[1] and I admit that this is not entirely true. English is a good example of this. The English language is listed as a 'Germanic' tongue, related to German, Dutch and the Scandinavian languages, and it is true that Anglo-Saxon culture first arrived in England via invaders from Germany, the Netherlands and Scandinavia. Yet in reality English culture is a composite, including ancient Celtic custom and Roman heritage as well as massive French influence from the time of the Norman Conquest in 1066, an influence which means that over half the words in a medium-sized English dictionary are of Norman French origin. It would be possible therefore to derive a system of language classification which implied that English was at least as close to French as it is to German. Yet the unanimous view of linguists is that English is a Germanic language; why? The point is that it's the root of a language, the part that really controls the grammar, which betrays its true origin; the rest is simply added on through later influence. That is why English is classed as a Germanic language. Its Germanic ancestry can be seen in its grammar and in the most common words; these are the elements linguists use to derive family relationship. Whether you could also say that English culture is Germanic at root is much more debatable.

OK; the relationship between language and culture is clearly not straightforward and it may therefore be that the pattern of language spread doesn't map perfectly onto the pattern of cultural spread. Never mind; let's see what the language evidence has to say for itself anyway, and I will start with the language family that has been studied more than any other on the planet. It is the family that includes English, German and French, as well as languages all the way to Bengali (spoken in eastern India and Bangladesh), and it is known as Indo-European.

INDO-EUROPEAN

The Indo-European language family includes almost all the languages of Europe, as well as most of those spoken in India and Pakistan, and the spread of Indo-European over the course of the millennia is one of the great stories of human history. It is not too difficult to look back two or three thousand years because of the considerable assistance available from written histories, and this means we can see reasonably clearly where and approximately when each individual branch of Indo-European originated. For example Germanic speakers are known from Roman history, when they inhabited modern Germany, the Czech Republic and Poland. Similarly the branch known as 'Italic', which includes French, Spanish, Portuguese, Italian, Romanian and a few minority tongues, is exclusively made up of those languages that have descended from Latin, the language of the Roman Empire. Celtic is another branch, now confined to the extreme west of Europe, but history lets us know that Celtic peoples once lived right across central Europe, and archaeology strongly suggests that the culture stemmed from Austria and Hungary about 3000 years ago. The other European branches of the Indo-European family are Greek, Albanian and the mighty Slavonic branch (Russian, Polish, Czech, Serbo-Croat, Bulgarian etc.). There is some disagreement about the origin of the Slavonic branch, but the most common suggestion is that Slavonic languages share an origin with ancient Thracian, which would place them in Romania and Bulgaria in the 1st Millennium BC.[2] As for Greek, all that is really known is that Greek culture arrived from the north during the 3rd Millennium BC,[3] while all we can say about Albanian is that it has been more or less where it is since the earliest records we have. Putting all this information together it is evident that the Indo-European languages of Europe stem from the eastern regions of the continent and that the date of origin was clearly much earlier than 1000BC, by which time the branches were already distinct from one another.

But this is only half the story. The greatest concentration of Indo-European speakers today is to be found in India and Pakistan, speaking languages of the so-called 'Indic' branch of the family, while an adjacent branch is known as 'Iranian' and includes Persian, Kurdish, Pashto and several more. So how do these languages come to be where they now are? Well, despite the objections of many Indian academics, the near-consensus these days is that they arrived from somewhere in Central Asia and that they were introduced into the north of Pakistan by invaders in the early 2nd Millennium BC. These are believed to be the people known in the Rigveda as 'Aryans', and archaeology supports the tales of the Rigveda in the sense that a very significant cultural change took place at that time and that many of the new elements (for example much increased use of the horse) can be traced back to Central Asia.[4] Similarly, the arrival of the Iranian people in Iran can be traced to the early 1st Millennium BC, again arriving from the north, from Central Asia.[5] The other member of the eastern side of the family is Armenian, which most would say shares an origin with Iranian.[6]

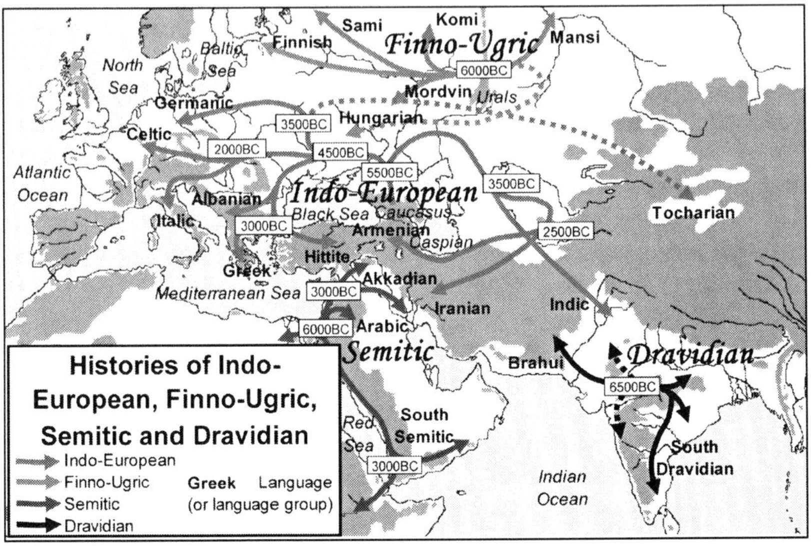

Histories of Indo-European, Finno-Ugric, Semitic and Dravidian

The difficult issue is how to bring the two halves of the family together. The discovery that ancient Hittite, spoken in what is now Turkey, was Indo-European complicates matters somewhat. Many linguists see Hittite as the closest we have to the original Indo-European tongue, which suggests that the family may have originated in Turkey, spreading east and west, perhaps as the languages of the first wheat and barley farmers; archaeologist Colin Renfrew is one of the best known proponents of this view.[7] On the other hand linguists generally put the origin of the family at 4000-7000BC, which is a little too recent if it really was the speech of the first farmers, and many archaeologists point to the 5th Millennium BC 'Kurgan' culture of southern Russia as the cultural ancestor of later Indo-European-speaking societies.[8] An origin in southern Russia also fits better with the evidence of Indic and Iranian, where archaeology suggests movement south from Central Asia, and indeed this is now much the most widely held view. It is a view with which I am in full agreement. The map shows my own interpretation of the evidence, and the dates and exact lines of language spread come from my own analysis,[9] but in most respects it is typical of majority opinion. The date I am proposing for the origin of the whole family, 5500BC, sits right in the middle of the range of views held by mainstream linguists.

This is all very well but does it provide evidence for or against a catastrophe having occurred in about 6250BC? Yes; it certainly does. Something was responsible for 'unleashing' Indo-European from its home in southern Russia and spreading it far and wide, and there are really only two possible types of cause. The first is that Indo-European speakers of 5500BC had made a technological or social advance that gave them a clear advantage over their rivals. This could have been agriculture – but it wasn't; that spread east and west from the Middle East. It could have been a military advance such as horse-riding – but it wasn't; the horse would not be domesticated until 4000BC. In fact I am not aware of anything that archaeologists can point to which would back up the view that the Indo-European speakers of 5500BC had made any significant stride forward. And this therefore implies that it was a different type of cause entirely that led to this impressive language expansion, and the only other possible type of cause that springs to mind is the destruction of all who stood in their path by agent or agents unknown!

I could go further based on my own language analysis and suggest that ancestral Indo-European had actually arrived in southern Russia from the south, from the adjacent Caucasus Mountains.[10] The Caucasus forms a bottleneck between the Black Sea and the Caspian and it is reasonable that a people moving north into Russia should see little language division until they arrived level with the northern shores of the Caspian and Black Seas, at which point different groups would naturally spread east and west, each group then seeing its own language develop separately. So, if 5500BC is correct for the initial split point, then it may well have been in around 6250BC that Indo-European speakers first moved out from the Caucasus onto the Russian plain. The support that Indo-European language history gives to the theory that a great disaster befell low-lying regions all over the world could therefore hardly be stronger.

Yet, if anything, the evidence of my second language example is actually more persuasive still.

FINNO-UGRIC

Finno-Ugric languages are much less widespread than Indo-European, the best known being Finnish and Hungarian. Most are distributed across the region either side of the Ural Mountains, stretching from the river Ob in the east to the Baltic Sea in the west, except in the case of Hungarian which is the end product of a long and relatively recent (9th Century AD) migration; its closest relatives are to be found east of the Ural Mountains. The historical evidence is more limited than is the case for Indo-European, but most would associate a form of pottery known as 'pit-comb ware' with Finno-Ugric speakers, and pit-comb pottery can be seen spreading west through Russia from the 4th Millennium BC. Its origins can be traced back to the so-called Ural-Kama culture from just west of the Ural Mountains.

The date shown on the map for the original Finno-Ugric tongue, 6000BC, is absolutely typical of the estimates made by linguists.[11] The location, the Ural Mountains, is almost dictated by the current language distribution, and in fact this language group is actually half of a larger language family which linguists know as 'Uralic', named after the Ural Mountains. The other half of the family, the 'Samoyedic' group, are located further north in the Ural Mountain region. Once again there is little disagreement amongst linguists.

However, while there is little disagreement there is plenty of discussion as to what it all means. The puzzle is just why this spread of language should have taken place. In the case of Indo-European there is some doubt about the precise point of origin and some suggestion that speakers may have had agricultural know-how to give them an edge over the competition. But in the case of Finno-Ugric languages there is no real doubt about the point of origin and no possibility that agriculture was involved. Neither does there seem to be evidence for any other technological advantage. The whole thing is utterly inexplicable. On the other hand, as far as this book goes, the fact that the language group originated in or near the only piece of high ground for hundreds of miles at a date which was certainly close to 6250BC is powerful evidence in support of a flood – however improbable this notion may still appear to you.[12]

DRAVIDIAN

Unfortunately it is hard to find such agreement amongst linguists for most other language families. The exception that springs to mind is the Austronesian family which, all agree, stems from Taiwan, but as it never left Taiwan until about 3500BC this is hardly relevant here. I have however found two further relatively non-controversial examples for you, the first of which is the Dravidian family.

Most Dravidian languages are spoken in southern India (Tamil for example) but some are scattered among remote areas further north, and a single representative, Brahui, is spoken in Pakistan and parts of Afghanistan. The majority of linguists would place the origin of the family somewhere in central or southern India, as I have shown it on the map. The date is rather more debatable, but 6500BC (which comes from my own analysis) is probably a typical estimate.[13] And, as with the Finno-Ugric languages, the point is that there seems no apparent reason why a significant language spread should have occurred in India at this time when the subcontinent had been filled with Stone Age hunter-gatherer tribes for so long. And in case you suspect the language analysis, it is well supported by archaeology. In the last chapter I made the point that agriculture seems to have been stopped dead in its tracks in the hills to the west of the Indus, and that the 5th Millennium BC cultures of the Indus plain actually came from the east, from the very area of central India shown as the source of Dravidian language. In agreement with this, the language analysis shows the ancestor of Brahui spreading westwards across the plain of the Indus to reach its current location. For some reason it seems to have travelled against the expected flow of culture, and it is very difficult to imagine how that could possibly have happened unless something had somehow got rid of the competition. Is it really a coincidence that the centre of Indian culture (including early agriculture) from the 6th Millennium BC matches the location shown for ancestral Dravidian and that the location was an area of high ground overlooking the plains of the Indus and the Ganges? It gives yet further reason to wonder whether some catastrophe may have befallen those living at insufficient elevation above sea level.

SEMITIC

My final relatively non-controversial language group is Semitic, which is actually part of a much larger family known as Afro-Asiatic, spoken right across the northern half of Africa as well as the Middle East. Most linguists would place the point of origin of the family as a whole somewhere in East Africa with a date well over 10000 years ago.[14] In the case of the Semitic group, however, we are fortunate to have very early written records (cuneiform tablets from various locations in both Syria and Iraq) and these show Semitic speech spreading across northern Syria and Iraq during the 3rd Millennium BC. These languages were of the northern Semitic subgroup, whose principal members today are Arabic and Hebrew. However there is also a southern Semitic subgroup with remnant languages in Yemen and Oman as well as widely spoken languages in Ethiopia, and we know from archaeology that the Ethiopian cultures associated with those languages descend from the culture of ancient Sheba (whose queen famously visited king Solomon of Israel). The land of Sheba is now the modern state of Yemen, lying right at the southern corner of Arabia, and Sheban culture can be traced back archaeologically to the 3rd Millennium BC.

Bearing in mind the difference between northern and southern Semitic tongues today, and bearing in mind the distance between Yemen and the Syria/Iraq region, my estimate for the date of the original Semitic language is 6000BC, admittedly a rather earlier figure than would be given by most linguists.[15]

Now, with an origin for the whole Afro-Asiatic family somewhere in East Africa and two Semitic subgroups located in Asia, it is obvious that Semitic language somehow either made the journey across the Red Sea or else it arrived directly from Egypt, and I am firmly of the view that the direct route was the one taken. If this is so and if my date for the original Semitic language is correct, then it arrived from Egypt in about 6000BC, divided and spread both north and south into Asia; but what happened to it in Egypt? For some reason it vanished. For some reason it was unable to stand up to the Egyptian language, which moved east from the Sahara and whose speakers appear from archaeology to have been less advanced than the Semites.[16] The date of origin of Semitic language, 6000BC, may mean nothing; the location may or may not have been on high ground; and it is true that subsequent spread was not across any significant expanse of low-lying plain. The puzzle is simply its fate in the low-lying country of Egypt.

So: four different language families; four different language expansions datable to the 5500-6500BC time window. In three cases the most likely location for the point of origin of the family was an area of high ground next door to extensive plains. I hope you can also remember the case of the Austro-Asiatic family presented in Chapter 2 whose common ancestor, I suggested, was spoken in eastern India, not too far from early Dravidian and also with a date of 6500BC. However, Austro-Asiatic takes me well beyond any region of consensus and depends on analysis which, though I believe it to be valid, is not yet (year 2008) widely accepted. Nevertheless, if I fail to make full use of this analysis then I am withholding what I believe to be important evidence. Many linguists would broadly agree with the locations and dates I have shown for Indo-European, Finno-Ugric, Dravidian and Semitic; from here on however we are stepping into disputed territory. Up until this point it has also been possible to refer to archaeology in support of many of the language spread patterns; from here on we will have to let the languages speak for themselves.

BREAKING NEW GROUND

There are basically two accepted techniques currently in vogue for the analysis of language history. The premier technique is known as the 'comparative method' and it consists of painstakingly comparing words and grammatical forms in different languages and tracing commonalities, i.e. repeated cases where the same sorts of difference occur (for example *light*, *might*, *right* in English; *licht*, *macht*, *recht* in German). This is a thorough approach and gives a very full understanding of language change. Unfortunately, however, it fails to generate any measure of the degree of difference between languages.

The second technique is the one most commonly used to measure language change and is known as 'lexicostatistical glottochronology' (five 'o's in one word; is that a record?). It works by comparing 100 different words in two languages and calculating the percentage where the two are clearly related. The developers of the technique then made a calibration between the percentage of related words (from their selected list of 100) and the language change time that had elapsed. In the case of English and German for example, this implies that the common ancestor was spoken some time in the mid 1st Millennium AD. This is a pretty good system and has given some very useful results, but it also has some very serious drawbacks, not least reliance on vocabulary alone with no reference to grammar.

It was to address these issues that I felt the need to formulate a new method of measurement; you can read the details in *The Origin of Tongues* if you are interested. It combines measurements of vocabulary, grammar and sound, and uses a different mathematical equation to produce a measure of 'difference' between languages. It is also accompanied by a new technique for constructing a language family tree, leading to a means of interpreting such family trees in terms of both the passage of time and the physical movement of languages. It is still an approximate analysis of course – linguistics can never be a precise science – but it is, in my view, a considerable improvement on what has gone before. In the cases of Indo-European and Finno-Ugric, the analysis did nothing more than produce agreement with current majority opinion. For both Semitic and Dravidian it allowed me to be a little more definite about the point of origin and to firm up on the date, although in neither case did the analysis challenge currently accepted wisdom to any significant degree. Austro-Asiatic however is quite another matter.

AUSTRO-ASIATIC

There is absolutely no currently accepted history for this family, and the language spread map presented in Chapter 2 relies totally on the analysis method in *The Origin of Tongues*. And, besides providing a likely source for the brother-sister flood myth and yet another example of a sudden spread of language across a low-lying plain – in this case the Ganges valley, this analysis also throws up a further remarkable fact. The Austro-Asiatic language family suffers from a unique problem; there is a seemingly inexplicable difference in grammar between the Austro-Asiatic languages of central India and those of the rest of the family, a much greater difference than would be expected based on a comparison of vocabulary alone. In fact the difference is so great that it is as if one side of the family or the other sat down one day and completely redesigned the structure of their language – and they decided to model it on that of their neighbours, who spoke languages of the family known as Sino-Tibetan!

Yet, fascinatingly, this sort of thing can actually occur. It happens when two peoples are thrust together and are forced to communicate, and the resulting language is known as a 'pidgin'. Pidgins arose all over the world as a result of the slave trade, as slaves from different tribes were forced to work together. Their children then continued to use the somewhat artificial form of language their parents had resorted to. But why should an Austro-Asiatic-speaking group have felt such pressing need to communicate with a Sino-Tibetan group at a date which, according to the map of Austro-Asiatic development presented in Chapter 2, fell some time between 6500 and 6000BC? What sort of emergency could have caused it? And how was it that this particular community were the ones that then spread their culture like wildfire across the lower Ganges and far beyond? They could hardly have been slaves. If the whole idea wasn't so ridiculous you would have to think that they were the sole survivors of some terrible disaster, a disaster that forced two peoples to share the same refuge, for example an ever-shrinking patch of high ground surrounded by rising flood waters. The language evidence as it stands so far seems to be making a pretty poor job of disproving the Great Flood!

I don't wish to bore you with too many more examples at this stage, although I very much hope you will want to read *The Origin of Tongues* and see for yourself just how language study enables hidden elements of our cultural past to be reconstructed. I will therefore pick out just two more language families, both of which provide important evidence datable to around 6250BC.

PAMA-NYUNGAN

The Pama-Nyungan language family is spoken by aboriginal peoples in Australia, and before the arrival of European settlers it covered around 80% of the land surface of the continent. It was spoken right down the eastern half of Australia and across the south as far as the west coast; only the north-west and central parts were non-Pama-Nyungan.

Now this in itself is actually rather odd. Human beings had been living in Australia for at least 35000 years, possibly much longer,[17] just as they had on New Guinea, the large island to the north. Yet New Guinea is a patchwork quilt of different language families with no single family showing dominance over others, and this is despite the fact that agriculture in the form of taro farming spread across the island thousands of years ago.[18] So why should Australia be so different? You would naturally imagine there had been some significant development which had enabled Pama-Nyungan speakers to dominate and spread their culture across the land, perhaps a development in stone tool technology or even the appearance of farming. But this was not the case. In fact the most significant developments in stone tool technology took place in north-west Australia, in non-Pama-Nyungan territory, in around 4000BC.[19] So the question remains: what could possibly have led to the spread of Pama-Nyungan language? It's a question to which experts still have no answer. Turning to the language analysis, my own estimate for the date of origin of Pama-Nyungan is 7000BC, with a location in eastern Australia. The date is close enough to 6250BC bearing in mind the uncertainty present, while the location is somewhere in the Great Dividing Range, the highest ground on the continent. Others may express less certainty regarding both date and location but few linguists would dismiss these estimates as unreasonable, and all would admit that there is no clear reason why this language should have been able to expand its territory in this way. Naturally a flood that covered most of the continent and wiped out a large proportion of the population is not normally proposed as the solution to this mystery – but perhaps it should be!

NORTH CAUCASIAN

My final example here is extremely controversial. It concerns the origin of a varied set of languages spoken amongst and just to the north of the Caucasus Mountain range, languages like Chechen, Abkhaz and Circassian. Now, many learned papers have been written and many theories concocted about North Caucasian languages. They are considered by most to be quite different from all other language families on the planet, and it is therefore generally assumed that they have been present in the

Caucasus for a very long time indeed. This, however, is flatly contradicted by the analysis in *The Origin of Tongues* which, so I believe, looks much deeper in time than other techniques in current use. The measurements show distant relationship with Mongolian, which is a branch of what is termed the 'Altaic' family, named after the Altai Mountains on the Russia-Mongolia border. The date at which the measurements show the North Caucasian family to have separated from Mongolian is 7000BC, and analysis of the Altaic family as a whole shows that at that time it would have been spoken in the far east of the modern state of Kazakhstan, almost under the shadow of the Altai Mountains themselves. And there is absolutely nothing remarkable about such a language division. If I am right in my language analysis, Altaic culture had been spreading east from Central Asia into southern Siberia and Mongolia, and as it expanded ever further it would have left a whole series of closely related cultures in its wake; the culture of eastern Kazakhstan would have been one of many, a culture which, it just so happened, sat on the fringe of the great plain of Central Asia in 6250BC.[20]

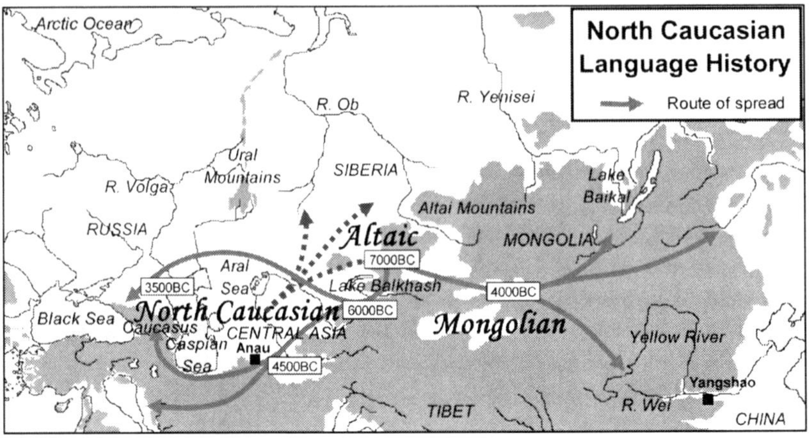

And there is real archaeological support for this proposed spread of North Caucasian language, namely the closeness that several experts have noted between the pottery forms found in Central Asian sites such as Anau and those found in the Wei river valley in China (the previously mentioned Yangshao culture).[21] The only feasible way that this closeness can be explained (other than sheer coincidence) is by suggesting a common ancestor to both, which would be the culture of about 7000BC that divided and became Mongolian and North Caucasian. Mongolian moved east, reaching the Wei river region of China (itself a controversial suggestion to Chinese historians); North Caucasian language and culture were taken west through Central Asia. Archaeology and language speak with a single voice, a controversial voice, but a voice that tells us of yet another spread of language with an origin in the 7th Millennium BC.

If this language analysis is valid, and if this culture really did speak ancestral North Caucasian, it managed to make the 2000-mile journey around the Caspian Sea to the Caucasus. How could that possibly have happened? As I noted earlier, there would have been similarly advanced cultures scattered across Central Asia, all related to that of the Altaic speakers. There seems no way to explain what could have given North Caucasian speakers the required advantage – unless of course there was nothing in the way at all!

SUMMARY

I imagine you are still thoroughly sceptical about the whole idea of a worldwide flood – and I can't say I blame you. Yet it really does look as though something pretty catastrophic must have happened in about 6250BC. There are just too many unexplained spreads of language that originated at this approximate time, and in each case the spread took place across a low-lying plain. Then there is the strange case of Austro-Asiatic and the development of a pidgin – also at just this time. Circumstantial though this evidence is, there is an awful lot of it.

The language evidence also allows some reassessment of flood depth – supposing for a moment that we really are talking about a flood. The completeness with which Pama-Nyungan language took over the continent of Australia suggests only limited survival away from the eastern ranges, which means a depth of 500 metres or more. In Russia and Central Asia around 300 metres would have been sufficient to inundate the steppe completely, leaving just the Ural Mountains sticking up above the flood. Similarly, around 300 metres would have been enough to flood most of the Indus valley and the north Indian plain.

You probably still think that I am off my head even talking in these terms; nevertheless evidence is evidence however crazy it may seem. One thing is for certain; linguistics has failed abjectly to disprove the Great Flood theory, instead providing considerable positive support. But so far I have restricted this investigation to the human evidence. If there ever really was an inundation of vast areas of the globe by seawater then plants, animals and habitats must all have been equally affected. How could experts fail to spot such a catastrophic event? Surely it shouldn't be too difficult for a biologist to scotch the crazy notion of a worldwide flood once and for all? Should it?

5

The Biologist's Report

The first question to ask is: just what sort of evidence should we be looking for? A flood several hundred metres deep lasting several months sounds dramatic, and of course it would have been very dramatic indeed for any plant or creature caught up in it, but just what would its long-term effects have been? I recently watched an excellent television documentary on the subject of what would happen to the earth if human life was suddenly extinguished, and the point was made that actually nature would reclaim our urban worlds in a remarkably short time. The town of Pripyet in the northern Ukraine was abandoned in 1987 following the disastrous explosion at the nearby Chernobyl nuclear power station; much of the local vegetation and wildlife suffered the same fate as many of the human population, radiation poisoning and death. Yet within a couple of decades nature had returned in force and today the region supports a rich and varied wildlife population, thriving in the absence of human activity.

All of this means that if it is difficult to spot the temporary absence of humans from a particular region then it is that much harder to spot the absence of other animals. When dealing with times as remote as 6250BC humans can usually only be detected indirectly, given away by their stone tools, their campfires and, in really advanced societies, by their construction activities. It is actually relatively rare to discover human remains. And since animals created no stone tools, lit no fires and built no structures (beaver dams don't count!), it is much, much harder to find any meaningful clues, let alone to spot any lack of evidence over a period which may only have lasted some hundreds of years. I am not trying to avoid the issue; I am simply being realistic. In the case of birds and insects, re-colonisation after a disaster would be very rapid, giving practically no hope of any useful evidence. You might wonder about such creatures as earthworms, but earthworm eggs can survive long periods under extreme conditions; many would certainly have lived to hatch out even after a long-lasting saltwater flood, once the waters had subsided and the cleansing influence of fresh rainfall had begun to wash the salt out of the soil. After all, remember that Canada and Scandinavia were under miles of ice for thousands of years during the Ice Age, and yet they recovered as fast as the ice retreated.

Turning to plants, the situation is if anything even more hopeless. Seeds are a) extremely resilient and b) easily carried by birds and animals;

it would have taken no more than a few decades before the vegetation had returned to its original state as far as any observer could tell.

So perhaps this chapter should conclude after a single page!

Fortunately I believe there are still places where real evidence can be sought. If a freshwater lake was suddenly inundated by the sea the salt would be there to stay; that should surely have left its mark. If oceans that had previously been separated suddenly found themselves connected, even if it was just for a few months, surely we would find species where they have no right to be; could this have been missed? And if a whole island was submerged then re-colonisation, especially for land mammals, would be much more problematic than on the mainland; that too should show up in the biological record. If there's no evidence in any of these areas then there was no flood; end of argument.

Let's start by investigating the aquatic life contained in some of the planet's lakes and, recognising that most small lakes only have a lifespan of a few thousand years before they silt up, I am going to begin by checking out some of the really large and long-lived lakes of Africa.

LIFE IN THE EAST AFRICAN GREAT LAKES

Lakes are really fascinating ecosystems. For a start there is usually a wide variety of different ecological niches within a small area. For those with a taste for the open water a large lake is really just a small piece of the ocean, with plenty of room for everything from plankton to large fish. On the other hand there is always plenty of shoreline and often a variety of shallow-water habitats, from sandy beaches to marshes to rocky coastline, providing happy homes for molluscs, crustaceans, and numerous exotic fish and reptiles, not to mention birdlife. Lakes provide some of the richest centres for birds anywhere on the planet. Even oceanic mammals such as seals can feel at home in a lake. Add to that the fact that different degrees of salinity are often present, fresh where rivers flow in, more saline out in the open water, sometimes hyper-saline in evaporation lagoons along the shore, and pretty much any variety of water-loving creature can find a home in a lake.

So we could look at the amazing range of creatures living in the 25-million-year-old Lake Baikal in eastern Siberia or the 12-million-year-old Lake Tanganyika in East Africa and we would be in no doubt that these creatures had been living their lives undisturbed in their isolated watery worlds for a very long time indeed. But would we be right to think so? Not necessarily. The clearest warning comes from Lake Victoria, also in East Africa, the second largest freshwater lake in the world in terms of surface area (Lake Superior is the largest). Lake Victoria is home to an amazing variety of brightly coloured fish of the family known as 'cichlids'; there are some 250 species today, filling a wide variety of ecological niches. Each species is different, in looks, size, behaviour, eating habits and chosen habitat. It seems certain that this plethora of species must have taken many hundreds of millennia to develop. But it most certainly hasn't. Hidden unseen in every cell of every cichlid fish is a DNA code, and scientists can read the code (or parts of it anyway) and compare fish with fish. Every fish is an individual, despite the fact that they all look alike to us, and every fish has its own DNA code – although of course all fish within a single species share a great deal in terms of DNA. But in Lake Victoria it is not just the fish within a species that share similar DNA; these similarities cut across numerous species. Two species that occupy quite different habitats, grow to quite different sizes and look quite different from each other often have almost identical DNA. Sometimes the DNA difference between two members of a species is actually greater than the difference between representatives of different species! There can only be one explanation for this unexpected genetic pattern and that is that 'speciation' (division into species) has occurred very recently indeed.[1]

The only possible interpretation is that not too long ago, just a few thousand years ago in fact, there were only a handful of cichlid species in the lake, but that over the course of a few thousand years those few species have diversified as different groups of fish started to colonise different habitats. Their features changed with each new generation as they adapted to their changing environment, but their DNA mutated only slowly, just as it always had. This would be a real puzzle to biologists if geologists hadn't come to the rescue. They have discovered that Lake Victoria, the largest lake in Africa, actually dried out almost completely just 15000 years ago.[2] Those few fish that survived had to

The Great Lakes of Africa

make their homes in the rivers that then terminated in a small saline swamp, all that was left of the giant lake. Then, as rainfall increased and the lake refilled, the cichlids had their chance – and they took it!

So what? Well the point I am trying to make is that just because a lake can boast a large variety of species, that doesn't necessarily indicate eons of undisturbed existence. In the case of Lake Victoria, aquatic life was very severely disturbed indeed just 15000 years ago, almost annihilated in fact, and yet it recovered such that, to most observers today, it stands as a haven of diversity. And there is actually an even more impressive example than this in East Africa, namely Lake Nagubago in Uganda, which has only existed for 4000 years and which now boasts its very own five indigenous cichlid species, all descended from a single group of colonists.[3] Now I am not actually going to suggest that Lake Victoria, at 1194 metres above sea level, was ever inundated by the ocean. The biological evidence is that the whole ecosystem suffered a disaster a few thousand years ago and a saltwater flood would be one logical cause of such a disaster – except in this case we know perfectly well that the cause was actually the complete drying out of the lake. But the reason I wanted you to know about Lake Victoria is that it provides a benchmark, a point of reference with a known history to which we can compare other lakes and inland seas.

Moving south from Lake Victoria, the next giant body of East African water is Lake Tanganyika at 773 metres above sea level, which has an array of cichlid fish to rival Lake Victoria. In fact many of them look very similar to those in Lake Victoria and they occupy similar niches; but they are not the same at all. The ancestor cichlid, whose descendants now fill Lakes Victoria and Tanganyika, lived some 7.5 million years ago, according to the difference seen in various parts of the genetic code.[4] Not only so, but individual species in Lake Tanganyika are genetically quite different from each other, as well as looking different; and there are large numbers of other aquatic life forms, notably crustaceans as well as numerous non-cichlid fish species. And genetically hard-wired into every cell of these creatures is the signal that Lake Tanganyika has not suffered the sort of disaster that afflicted Lake Victoria, at least not for many hundreds of thousands of years.[5] Many geologists believe that the lake level fell dramatically, by up to about 600 metres, during the same period in which Lake Victoria dried out, but there was still enough water in Lake Tanganyika to support the varied life we see today. The only biological signal that this dramatic fall in lake level ever occurred is the fact that the same coastal-dwelling fish species are found on opposite sides of the lake, when there is no way that such fish could make the crossing with water levels as they are today.[6] The biology of Lake Tanganyika effectively proves that no massive influx of seawater has disturbed its peace for hundreds of millennia. In this part of the world therefore, if there ever was a Great Flood it never reached the 773-metre mark.

But what about the most southerly of the African great lakes, Lake Malawi, at only 474 metres above sea level? It too is home to an amazing variety of cichlid fish species, over 500 by most counts. The lake is geologically very much like Lake Tanganyika, a deep gash in the surface of the planet formed by the splitting apart of two of the Earth's crustal plates. As in the case of Lake Tanganyika, there is evidence that levels fell dramatically between about 15000 and 11000 years ago, perhaps by as much as 400 metres; as in the case of Lake Tanganyika however, the lake hasn't dried out completely for well over 50000 years.[7] So you might expect the genetic signal from Lake Malawi to be similar to that from Lake Tanganyika – but you would be quite wrong! The signal from Lake Malawi is actually very similar to that from Lake Victoria. There has been a massive and very recent (in evolutionary terms) 'speciation', i.e. an explosion of new species colonising all the different corners of the lake; and no-one knows why. It is obvious that a disaster of some kind occurred, at least amongst the cichlid fish species. It isn't easy to say much about the other species in the lake because there aren't many – which in itself is rather surprising. As for the date of this disaster, it is not possible to say with any precision because estimating the rate of genetic mutation is an imprecise business, but it was certainly within the last 17000 years or so.[8] This is a serious mystery and, whether saltwater flood was the cause or not, that cause must lie in a real event.

If the evidence of Lake Malawi biology genuinely points to an influx of seawater then we are talking of a very deep flood, over 474 metres, which means that the remaining East African great lake, Lake Turkana in northern Kenya, would also have been in danger. Lake level today is around 375 metres above sea level and falling, since evaporation exceeds river inflow. But this was not always the case. Before about 4000 years ago the lake level stood at around 455 metres above sea level and a river drained the lake to the north-west, eventually reaching the Nile. It is therefore no surprise to find that the majority of Lake Turkana fish species are also found in the Nile. It is however a little bit of a surprise to discover just how low the general level of biodiversity in the lake is. There are only about 50 fish species, compared with hundreds in the other great lakes, and only 7 snail species compared to 30 in Lake Victoria and over 100 in Lake Tanganyika. Admittedly the water is now slightly salty, but only just outside the freshwater salinity range. Some have even proposed that it may have been a recent (but hitherto unexplained) episode of high salinity that caused the relatively low number of species.[9] Seawater inflow could certainly have done the job!

To sum up the biological evidence from the East African great lakes, there are real signs that a disaster of some sort affected Lake Malawi in the recent past, possibly Lake Turkana as well, and a massive increase in salinity would be one logical explanation. And if this was actually caused by a flood then its maximum height must have been at least 474 metres above sea level.

However Africa is not the only continent with large bodies of inland water. You might immediately think of the American great lakes, but these have only been in existence since the end of the last Ice Age and so can tell us little one way or the other. At the time of this possible flood they would only have been a few thousand years old themselves. Asia on the other hand has some very ancient lakes indeed.

THE INLAND SEAS OF ASIA

The oldest, deepest, most biodiverse lake on the planet is Lake Baikal in Siberia, at 456 metres above sea level. If a seawater flood really was the cause of the disaster that befell Lake Malawi's cichlid fish and if the same level occurred in Siberia, then Lake Baikal would have been swamped by the sea. But it certainly hasn't been. The remarkable variety of species is no mirage, as it was in Lake Malawi. There are well over 1000 species of various different forms of lake life that are found nowhere else on earth, like the famous candle fish,[10] and there is no evidence for any recent speciation events,[11] which means no significant disturbance to the ecosystem. We might wonder about the Lake Baikal seal, an animal that is closely related to the Arctic ringed seal, and there has certainly been plenty of speculation as to how it made the 1500-mile journey from the ocean – and when. However, the 'when' question has now been addressed by genetics and, though experts differ in their opinions significantly, they

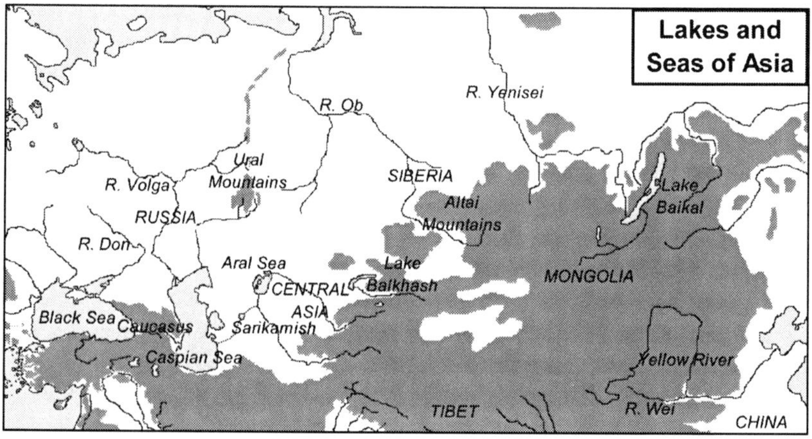

agree that it was a lot longer ago than 6250BC.[12] So, even if it was a massive sea level rise that allowed the seal to access the lake, it wasn't recent enough for this book.

OK; so whatever happened in East Africa, no flood higher than 456 metres occurred in Siberia. But what about the largest inland body of water on earth, the moderately salty Caspian Sea, whose current water level is actually about 28 metres below that of the oceans? It would only require the oceans to rise by about 50 metres to bring the sea flooding in.

The Caspian is inhabited by fish and other life forms from a number of sources.[13] Some can probably be traced back to the time that the Caspian basin first separated from the ocean, about 14 million years ago according to geologists; some are colonists from the Mediterranean, including plenty of very recent arrivals via the Volga-Don ship canal; some have managed the journey from other Central Asian rivers and lakes; and fourteen species have arrived from the Arctic. And it is this last group which is the hardest to explain. The Arctic species all arrived quite recently, most since the last Ice Age; otherwise there would be signs of difference between Caspian and Arctic populations, and there aren't any. They include fish, crustaceans and molluscs. A walrus tusk has even been discovered on the sea bed. So the question is: how on earth did these creatures get there?

There have been several theories over the years, the current favourite being that they became isolated in a large glacial lake that was held back by the ice sheets over Scandinavia and northern Russia, and that this lake eventually overflowed south into the Volga river system and thence to the Caspian.[14] On the other hand there have been dozens of Ice Ages over the course of the last two million years and it seems that it was only during (or after) this last one that most of the Arctic species were able to invade.[15] Unlikely though such a scenario may still seem to you, if the Arctic were to have risen by a little over 100 metres, it would have overflowed south into the Caspian basin, bringing various of the more warmth-tolerant species with it. You may still think this is an utterly absurd suggestion of course – but if so then read on.

There are several other oddities about life in the Caspian Sea. Like Lake Turkana it is relatively poor in terms of overall biodiversity, some five times poorer than the Barents Sea for example[16] (the part of the Arctic Ocean nearest to the Caspian), and there is very little life below about 100 metres depth despite the waters being perfectly adequately oxygenated.[17] The greatest number of species types is found among the crustaceans; in fact crustaceans in the Caspian are rather like cichlids in Lake Malawi in that they have diversified to fill almost every available niche. And, as in Lake Malawi, much of this diversification is very recent indeed, evidenced by similarities in DNA.[18] So, as in Lake Malawi, we are looking at some sort of environmental disaster that wiped out much of the lake's ecosystem, and whatever it was occurred within the last few thousand years. One thing we can be quite sure of; the Caspian Sea never dried up, which means that an episode of greatly increased salinity is just about the only possible explanation. Deep water species would have stood no chance unless they were salt-tolerant; near-surface species would have had the option of life in the river mouths.

But perhaps the greatest mystery of all is the presence of *cardium edule*, the common cockle. It suddenly appears in the sediment record shortly after 6000BC – and it just shouldn't be there! There was no connection between the Caspian and the oceans at that time as far as anyone knows. The standard explanations given are that either a bird or a human was responsible, but it is a little hard to see how this could have been achieved since a journey of some 300 miles would have been required.

I'm going to leave the lake evidence at that. It isn't complete; and I'll be referring to other bodies of water and their aquatic life later in this book. But it has been sufficient to suggest that biology is going to have just as tough a time as archaeology or linguistics in refuting the idea of a Great Flood. In fact the pro-flood biological evidence is starting to stack up quite impressively. Anyway, leaving lakes and inland seas, my next port of call is the subject of oceans temporarily being connected, something which, if true, would surely have left its biological mark.

OCEAN TO OCEAN JOURNEYS

The oceans of the world are of course connected already. If a fish wishes to cross from the Atlantic to the Pacific or *vice versa* then it is just a matter of heading north to the Arctic and then south through the Bering Strait, or else heading south and rounding Cape Horn at the southern tip of South America. To travel between the Indian and Atlantic Oceans is even easier, simply requiring a journey round the southern part of Africa; and the Indian and Pacific Oceans effectively merge via the Indonesian archipelago. However, for tropical species things are a lot more difficult; they could never survive a trip though the cold seas of northern or southern latitudes. And this means that there are large numbers of marine creatures that are restricted to a single ocean.

I guess you realise the point I am making here; if there was any significant rise in sea level then the Isthmus of Panama which today separates the Atlantic and Pacific Oceans would become submerged – as was the case until two million years ago. Similarly, there would be easy passage through from the Red Sea to the Mediterranean. Surely we should see some sign of this?

Not necessarily I'm afraid. The remarkable colonisation of every part of Lakes Malawi and Victoria by cichlid fish has occurred in an evolutionary blink of the eye; but it still took hundreds, probably thousands of years. The connections which would have opened during a Great Flood may only have been available for a few weeks, perhaps months, if the clues in the flood myths are to be taken seriously. Would in-shore dwelling creatures have had reason to make the 50-mile journey across the flooded Isthmus of Panama? A few perhaps. For those living out in the open ocean, would they have changed their usual pattern of migration? Probably not, since they would have been quite unaware of the sea level rise. In the main, the life forms that you might have expected to make the crossing would have been those minute organisms (eggs, larvae) that just drifted on the tide. As it happens some 13% of east Pacific mollusc species and 17% of corals have actually managed the journey to the Atlantic recently enough for them not yet to have become a separate species, and they are now thriving in the Caribbean and the Gulf of Mexico.[19] One explanation offered is that the larval forms drifted on the current through the Bering Strait and the Arctic Ocean before making it down to tropical Atlantic latitudes, a very long journey indeed. Could they possibly have survived it? Besides, if this were really the route taken then someone needs to explain why no west Pacific species made the journey when they would have found it much easier than east Pacific dwellers to find their way up to the Bering Strait because of the way the North Pacific currents circulate.[20] The explanation simply doesn't make sense – and the same argument would apply to the southerly route around Cape Horn. Somehow it looks as though a direct connection must have opened up through Central America – which is of course completely impossible unless there had been a sea level rise of at least 60 metres!

The issue of a connection between the Red Sea and the Mediterranean is rather more complicated, and this is because a large number of Red Sea species have recently been able to move into the Mediterranean through the Suez Canal which, unlike the Panama Canal, has no locks and therefore presents no physical barrier to marine life. This has happened since the canal opened in 1869. Unfortunately, back in 1869 there was limited knowledge of the species present in either the Red Sea or the Mediterranean, which means that it is difficult to be 100% certain that all the Red Sea species found in the Mediterranean today are actually recent arrivals. I notice that at least one of the presumed Suez Canal migrants, a type of Killifish, has now been found to have a significantly longer history in the Mediterranean,[21] which begs the question: how on earth could any fish have made this journey before 1869? There would have been no route available – unless the sea rose by several metres.

By the way, I have only mentioned one-way traffic through both of these canal zones for the excellent reason that all the traffic really does seem to have been one way. The reason given by biologists is that the Pacific is much more species-rich than the Atlantic and the Red Sea more so than the Mediterranean, both of which are true; but are we really to believe that not one Atlantic species fancied its chances in the Pacific? The ocean currents would certainly be easier to negotiate in that direction. Or could it be that the real explanation for these journeys is quite different, somehow involving ocean currents extending across what is normally dry land?

Whatever the real reason for these colonisation movements the standard explanations appear inadequate – whereas sea level rise over a period of weeks or months might explain things better; which means that here too there almost seems more reason to believe in a worldwide flood than not. Never mind; let's see whether this view is contradicted by the evidence of the world's islands.

ISLAND PARADISES

I suggested earlier that land flora and fauna would reappear so quickly after a flood that it would be quite impossible even to spot that they had ever disappeared. Islands however are different. Islands are colonised in two main ways. Either they were once connected to the mainland (like Britain for instance, or Borneo) and so they would naturally have the same range of species as on the adjacent continent, or they have to be colonised remotely. For plant life, remote colonisation is generally no problem, either by seeds floating on the water or carried in the digestive tracts of birds, or even on the wind. Insects can also be carried in egg form in various ways, often via birds. Some reptiles and mammals can arrive by swimming. Those with the greatest problems are land mammals. Take Madagascar for example. Earth scientists believe that it separated from mainland Africa about 80 million years ago, since which time mammals have been almost unable to cross to the island, although the latest theory (based on DNA studies) is that there were actually four occasions during those 80 million years when a breeding pair of mammals managed to make the crossing from Africa somehow. Small mammals can cross stretches of open water if they are very lucky, on rafts of drifting seaweed or debris such as palm logs; similarly small land reptiles. Large land mammals however generally have no route open to them.

This of course means that any massive disruption to the ecosystem on an island will be quickly repaired except in the case of large land mammals or other earth-bound creatures. This can be seen today in the case of Long Island, not the well known Long Island in New York but another Long

Island about 30 miles off the coast of New Guinea. The whole island blew apart in a massive volcanic eruption some time in the 17th Century, totally destroying all living organisms. Since that time plant life has made a more or less full recovery, and there are now 13 species of mammal, 14 species of reptile and two amphibian species that have managed to make the crossing and then to make a living there.[22] So I guess you can see that if this is the sort of recovery seen after 350 years, it might not be too easy to spot anything at all after eight millennia! If an entire island were inundated by the sea, seeds would still survive in the ground ready to germinate as soon as the conditions returned to normal; eggs of many ground-dwelling creatures (worms, centipedes, snails, perhaps even reptiles) might likewise survive. Other species would have to re-colonise from elsewhere.

Our task therefore is to find islands where there is clear evidence of species that either have or have not survived, although lack of survival is never easy to prove. As in the case of lakes, the mere fact that an island possesses indigenous species is not sufficient since 8000 years is ample time for speciation to take place. For example, large iguanas are found across the northern Caribbean, notably on Cuba, the Bahamas and the Cayman Islands, and several different species are assigned based on differences in appearance and behaviour. Yet, genetically, these species are very close indeed and interbreeding is still quite possible.[23] The whole dispersion of species could easily date from a mere 8000 years ago, descended from a population that survived in Cuba for instance.[24] The fact that island habitats can lead to very rapid change is proved by the Faeroe Island mouse, introduced into the Faeroe Islands just 250 years ago and which is now quite distinct from all other mouse species.[25]

So, we are warned; the search for evidence is not going to be straightforward. But where should one look? Well, islands that are large enough to have a rich and varied set of ecological niches would be a good starting point. The problem is that large islands tend to include areas of high ground, which would form adequate refuges for ground-living creatures even if there was a flood – given the flood depth limits deduced from archaeology and linguistics. The truth is that there are so many islands with so many species that the task is a much larger one than this book can hope to undertake. Fortunately however a helping hand is available from a United Nations list[26] of those islands with the largest numbers of endemic species, i.e. species found nowhere else in the world. At the top end, naturally, are large islands like Madagascar, New Guinea and Cuba, all with more than enough high ground for flood survival. Moving down the list, the first island with no land over 1000 metres is Mauritius, in the Indian Ocean.

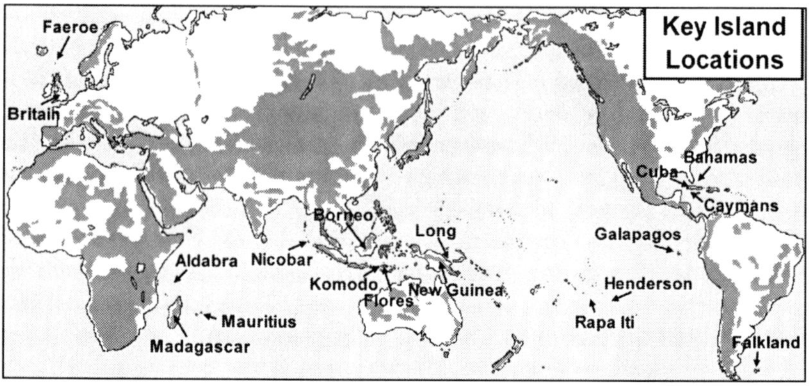

Mauritius is large enough to be home to many endemic species, including nine species of bird and five reptiles. It was also, famously, home to the dodo, the creature whose very name is a byword for species extinction. And the useful thing about the dodo is that it genuinely was unique. There were no dodos, so far as we know, anywhere else in the world. More usefully still for this investigation, the dodo couldn't fly. If a flood had ever covered Mauritius completely the dodo would have met its end long before humans came to the island. Since the highest point on Mauritius is 828 metres above sea level, this gives me another fix on maximum possible flood elevation.

Much less exciting than the dodo but just as useful here are the 14 or so remaining indigenous species of Mauritian ant. What makes these ants so interesting is the fact that every one of these native ant species is only found near the tops of the mountains. Invasive species are found at lower elevations. Why should this be? What sort of event could have wiped out those ant species suited to lower levels, leaving just the mountain-top species? The scientific world has no answer.[27]

Scanning further down the United Nations list, Rapa Iti in French Polynesia, with its 98 species of land snail, might appear to bring the limit down to 650 metres at that point. However the issue of snails brings me back to the rather important question of whether eggs could have survived a long-lasting saltwater flood. After all, an egg laid by an animal is not so different from a seed produced by a plant, and there is every reason to believe that seeds could have survived. Those who are gardeners know that seeds can sometimes germinate years after they were formed. They have encoded into their DNA a trigger mechanism which means they wait until conditions are right – rather annoying for those of us trying to grow vegetables when the weather is less than ideal! In the same way earthworm eggs wait until the soil is just the right warmth before hatching, which again means there is good reason to suppose that some at least could have survived several months of unsuitable conditions (low temperature; raised salinity). As it happens, the same is true of land snails.[28] Even in more complex life forms the same mechanism can apply. Reptile embryos will dramatically slow down their development if the temperature is too low, extending the time until hatching by several weeks in some cases.[29] So, in theory, many such creatures could have survived in egg form so long as the time period involved wasn't excessive. But then there is also the issue of whether the eggs would have been sufficiently protected to prevent them from being carried away on the tide. Burial in soil would probably do the trick; gluing to plant stems (as some insects do) might be satisfactory in some cases although survival rates would surely have been low; anthills and termite mounds might be rather less likely to survive – hence my point about the ants of Mauritius. Bird eggs would seem to stand no chance, quite apart from the fact that warm-blooded creatures do not seem to be able to delay hatching appreciably.[30]

The conclusion from all this is that the survival of the 98 land snail species on Rapa Iti is perhaps not quite as significant as it first appeared. Nor should we be particularly impressed at insect survival in cases where eggs are securely anchored or buried. Even the survival of quite distinct lizard species on various islands in the northern Caribbean, including low-lying islands like Andros in the Bahamas and the Cayman Islands, may indicate nothing more than the remarkably flexible incubation periods displayed by lizards. The species that really count are mammals, flightless birds and some of the larger land reptiles.

Taking the larger reptiles first, Komodo dragons, the world's only known man-eating lizards, could probably have survived on their 735-metre-high island. If not, then the island of Flores, with peaks rising to over 2000 metres, lies just a few miles away – and Komodo dragons are competent swimmers.

Across the other side of the Pacific, the Galapagos Islands are rightly famous for their giant tortoises and numerous other large reptile species, which have clearly been able to develop in isolation for much longer than eight millennia. True; with a maximum elevation of 906 metres the Galapagos Islands could accommodate a pretty large flood without suffering 100% extinction, but most of the islands are much lower-lying and so a much lower limit on sea level rise seems to be implied, probably no more than a couple of hundred metres at most. This is significant. Taken in conjunction with the various clues gleaned from archaeology and language, as well as the evidence of lake ecosystems, this suggests that if we really are talking about a flood then the depth must have differed appreciably in different parts of the world for some reason.

The other centre for large reptiles is the western Indian Ocean, where most of the islands once boasted giant tortoises; now they are only found on Aldabra, a coral atoll rising no more than 10 metres above the ocean. On the other hand DNA studies show that these tortoises originated in Madagascar, from where they spread to the other islands.[31] Although the Aldabra tortoise is designated a 'land' tortoise since the land is its preferred habitat, they have been known to survive long ocean journeys and so could have arrived from Madagascar more or less at any time. The same point applies to the various endemic land bird species of Aldabra, all of which made the journey from Madagascar at some indeterminate time in the past. The differences between the species on Aldabra and their close relatives on Madagascar are all very small, to the degree that there is debate in some cases as to whether they should be accorded separate species status.[32] In fact the message from Aldabra, known as one of the least spoilt island paradises on the planet, is that there are no endemics that definitely date from the distant past.

Aldabra is Number 23 on the United Nations biodiversity list and the first of the really low-lying islands. The next (Number 33) is Henderson Island, far out in the Pacific, somewhere between French Polynesia and Easter Island, with a maximum elevation of 33 metres above sea level. We should probably ignore the four endemic land snail species for reasons already discussed, but the four endemic land birds are a different matter, not to mention the four further bird species known to have existed there in the past. If there was a dodo-like creature on Henderson Island then we would seriously have to question the whole idea of a Great Flood. And there is! The 'Henderson Island crake' is a flightless bird of the class known as 'rails', and similar flightless rails are found on islands right across the Pacific. If the Henderson Island crake can be shown to have been present on Henderson Island 8250 years ago then this represents very serious anti-flood evidence indeed. The question is: was it there?

Genetic studies show that the various flightless rails of the Pacific are most closely related to a bird with full flying skills known as the 'spotless crake'. But the slightly odd thing about the spotless crake is that it only spread across the Pacific during the last 2000 years or so; its original home was Australia. So the question arises: how (and when) did the flightless rails get to Henderson Island and the other islands of the Pacific – bearing in mind that they are flightless? The genetic evidence strongly suggests that all of the current species of flightless rails descend separately from spotless crake parents rather than being directly related to each other,[33] which means that spotless crakes must have been present right across the area – yet there is no evidence for spotless crakes earlier than 2000 years ago. It's a puzzle; and the logical answer to the puzzle is that all the different flightless rail species have come into being during the last 2000 years, displaying an evolution rate comparable to that of the Faeroe Island mouse.[34] What this means of course is that even the presence of a flightless bird on low-lying Henderson Island is actually quite compatible with the island having been totally submerged just 8000 years ago.

As for the three remaining bird species on Henderson Island, as well as the four driven to extinction by human settlers, they are (or were) a) able to fly, and b) very closely related to species on other islands with much higher ground. They could therefore easily have arrived within the last 8000 years. The Henderson Island lorikeet may even have been introduced by Polynesian setters, who are known to have kept lorikeets as pets.

I could go on for ever here – but don't worry; I won't! We should just mention the mammals though. There aren't too many of them. Islands relatively close to continental landmasses can be reached by small mammals such as mice, rats and shrews. Larger mammals such as the Falkland Island wolf (or 'warrah') – now extinct but remarked on by Charles Darwin – or the crab-eating macaques of the Nicobar Islands and Mauritius almost certainly had the assistance of humans in reaching their destinations. In the case of the Mauritius crab-eating macaque this is well documented and occurred in the 16th Century; they were brought as exotic pets by Portuguese sailors.[35] It is a sobering thought that the Mauritius macaque is now classified as a separate species; evolution doesn't hang around in island habitats! In fact I am not aware of a single species of mammal endemic to any low-lying island that could not have reached its home within the last 8000 years either by natural processes or by human intervention. In no such case does it appear that any large genetic difference has developed between related species in island and continental habitats, although there may often be quite striking differences in appearance or lifestyle, caused by the need to adapt to a new environment, new food sources etc.

And this observation does much more than merely fail to disprove the flood; the lack of species on low-lying islands with genuinely large genetic difference from those elsewhere is really very hard to explain, rather like the cichlid fish of Lake Malawi or the crustaceans of the Caspian Sea. Where islands have been in existence for hundreds of thousands or millions of years this really should be evident in the diversity of those species such as mammals that, once they arrive, are effectively trapped there. Only an ecological catastrophe of some sort could prevent this being the case.

SUMMARY

Despite the quite extraordinary ability of life on planet Earth to repair any damage inflicted and to present an appearance of variety and species-richness, there are signs still readable in the biological record that something happened a few thousand years ago that drastically affected several parts of the globe. Lakes in East Africa and Central Asia seem to have suffered significant 'wipe-out' events, allowing subsequent bursts of diversification from the remaining life forms, cichlid fish in East Africa, crustaceans in the Caspian Sea. Something was responsible for bringing Arctic species to the Caspian, and for the introduction of the common cockle. Something allowed a parent iguana species in the Caribbean suddenly to diversify and colonise several islands. Something was responsible for the fact that indigenous Mauritian ants are now only found near the tops of the mountains.

These are nothing more than scattered signs, clues to one or more ancient catastrophes. Yet, when these clues are pieced together, the evidence points straight at a flood. Low-lying islands right around the world are found to have no indigenous land creatures of ancient lineage, whereas some of those with mountains do indeed possess such species. A flood would also explain the colonisation of Atlantic waters by east Pacific corals and molluscs. In most cases the information is much too imprecise to fix a date to this catastrophe, although not in the case of the cockle's arrival in the Caspian. There it is found from 6000BC in well-dated sediment layers, quite compatible with initial arrival of a few parent organisms a few hundred years previously.

In summary therefore, the biological evidence does nothing to dispel the notion of a Great Flood and gives plenty of reason for taking it seriously. Biology too has failed the challenge thrown down by legend and myth.

However biology cannot be divorced from its environment. If, for example, salty seawater actually invaded what had previously been freshwater lakes then this should surely show up in geological records. We may not be talking of an event that would have caused any drastic change to the surface of the planet, but the opinion of a geologist is nevertheless most definitely required.

6

The Geologist's Report

Did anything happen to the Earth in around 6250BC which can still be seen in the geological record? That is the key question here. And what might we expect anyway? A rise and fall in sea level is hardly going to reshape the landscape on its own, certainly not if it is all over in a matter of months. However, if the sea really did rise and fall by several hundred metres then there was a cause – that is self-evident – in which case geology may be able to give some clue as to what that cause might have been. First, though, as I suggested at the end of the last chapter, let's take a look at what geology can tell us about those lakes and inland seas that showed evidence of serious disruption to their aquatic life.

THE STORY OF SALT

There are a number of clever techniques for indirect measurement of salinity in times past and most involve detailed evaluation of cores through lakebed sediment. Microscopic organisms known as 'diatoms' inhabit all the world's waters and they come in many different varieties. Some like it fresh, some medium and some salty; some like it shallow, others deep. So, by inspecting the relative abundance of different diatoms in a sediment sample it is possible to get an estimate of past salinity, as well as water depth. Similar clues can be obtained by checking on the relative quantities of different mollusc species. In theory, therefore, geology provides the means to prove or disprove the whole idea of a Great Flood once and for all.

Unfortunately it isn't as easy as that. Take Lake Turkana in East Africa for example. We know that today it receives a volume of river inflow each year equivalent to about one twelfth of the total lake volume – and that this inflow is matched by evaporation. However, during the period we are concerned with here, the river inflow was considerably greater due to the wetter climate in the region at that time, and a significant proportion of the river inflow would have overspilled and flowed down into the Nile valley (allowing Nile fish to colonise the lake).[1] Even if this outflow volume was only 10% of the inflow, and even if the salinity of the lake had been raised to that of the ocean, it would have returned to freshwater conditions within about 300 years, which means we might well see nothing at all in the sediment record since those 300 years may only be represented by a few centimetres of sediment thickness, and not every centimetre is sampled and tested. Of course what makes the situation rather trickier in this particular case is that we have no sediment cores stretching back further than 5000 years! We are therefore left with the remarks made by certain researchers that the geological evidence implies either a period of high salinity or else a near-total drying out of the lake[2] – but we have no clear way of deciding which is correct. As I noted in the last chapter, raised salinity is the usual explanation given for the rather depleted species count in the lake today; it could also explain why certain Nile fish species are found in the rivers feeding Lake Turkana but not in the lake itself.[3]

In Lake Malawi on the other hand there are excellent sediment cores, giving datable information back well over 20000 years[4] – and the awkward truth is that they reveal absolutely no sign at all of any period of significantly increased salinity. There are indications that the lake level fell in around 6500BC, recovering after a few hundred years; there is also a very strong signal that the lake water temperature took a sudden 2°C nosedive at the same time,[5] taking about a thousand years to recover. But there is no sign of any significant increase in salinity. Whatever caused the explosive speciation of cichlid fish, the sediment core evidence gives reason to doubt the theory of a saltwater flood.

Admittedly experts tend to advise a high degree of caution when interpreting sediment records, warning that the way in which the samples are analysed is critical and that some organisms tend to be better preserved than others, which may lead to false conclusions. Nevertheless, the fact is that no high-salinity signal has been detected – and that cannot simply be dismissed. If the entire lake had actually become as salty as the sea, and if today's inflow and outflow rates are assumed to have applied in the past, it should have taken over 2000 years to return to freshwater status and at least 6000 years to reach today's ultra-fresh state. It's hard to see how this could have been missed in the sediment record. But if it wasn't increased salinity, what on earth could have caused the dramatic speciation of cichlid fish in the lake? For now I think we will just have to admit that the geological evidence does not support the view that a saltwater flood ever reached Lake Malawi. It's a setback for the pro-flood argument – there's no denying it – one that will need addressing if that argument is to prevail. However, before agreeing to any reduction in flood level let's take a look at the rest of the salinity evidence, starting with the other large inland body of water that showed signs of major upset to its ecosystem, namely the Caspian Sea.

THE CASPIAN SEA

In the Caspian Sea approximate estimates of past salinity have been made based on the forms of certain molluscs found at different locations associated with different ancient shorelines,[6] and it is fascinating how conditions have changed over the years.[7] During times when the Caspian has been an enclosed sea with no outlet, salinity has increased as more and more salt has been brought down the rivers. At other times it has overflowed into the neighbouring Black Sea and this has led to a rapid lowering of salt concentration. Unfortunately there is plenty of disagreement as to just when this high-water condition last existed. It seems pretty clear that the Caspian was high enough for outflow to occur around 45000 years ago, but some suggest a reoccurrence about 11000 years ago, and there is even a Carbon 14 date from a high-water shoreline suggesting as little as 8000 years ago, i.e. 6000BC. However, what does seem clear is that the salinity jumped from what may have been as little as 0.4% (almost fresh) to a reading of 1.5-2.0% some time prior to about 5500BC.[8] Could this be a sign that seawater had gained access?

If the Caspian Sea really was at 50 metres above the level of the world's oceans in 6250BC, the approximate level of the outfall to the Black Sea, then this means that the river inflow rate must have more than compensated for evaporation, i.e. it was about twice what it is today. If the whole basin was then filled with seawater (at 3.5% salinity), the salt content would have immediately begun to reduce again (by up to about 0.3% per century[9] by my estimate), assuming that water continued to overflow into the Black Sea for a while. However, as river flow decreased and the water level dropped toward today's level, 28 metres below the level of the oceans, the salinity would have increased again due to the reduced water volume; and this brings me to one of the most interesting features of the Caspian, the 'Kara Bogaz Gol'.

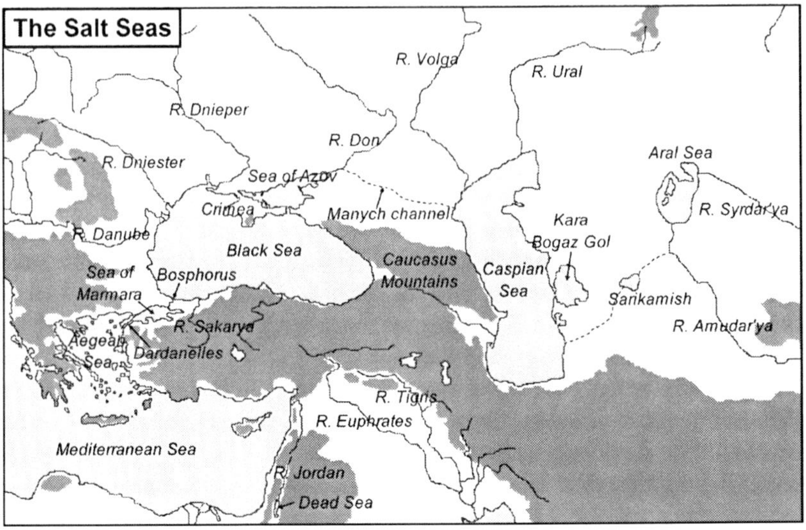

The Kara Bogaz Gol is really a giant evaporation lagoon situated on the eastern side of the Caspian. It is connected by a 10-kilometre-long strait and it acts as an outfall, taking about 10 cubic kilometres of water out of the Caspian Sea every year, together with its salt content. Historically (i.e. 100 years ago) the outflow volume was much greater,[10] but it is quite impossible to say with any certainty what the situation was in earlier times. Nevertheless, at today's outflow rate it is possible to calculate that it would have taken about 8000 years to change the salinity of the Caspian from 3.5%, the salinity of seawater, to today's 1.2%; at the rate of 100 years ago it would have taken only 4000 years. So, even without any outflow to the Black Sea in the centuries following a saltwater flood, the Kara Bogaz Gol provides an alternative way in which the salt content of the Caspian may have been reduced, the way in which it is still being reduced today.

The Kara Bogaz Gol is a key commercial source of salt – and there is plenty of it. There are three (or possibly four[11]) distinct layers of salt present across the area, the last of which is still being added to and probably now contains about 1000 years' worth of deposition.[12] This is logical as historical records tell us that the level of the Caspian Sea was much lower during the 1st Millennium AD,[13] in which case there should have been no connection to the Kara Bogaz Gol at that time. The second and third layers are thicker and both are thought to date from the last 10000 years or so.[14] The total salt volume deposited in the Kara Bogaz Gol represents an apparent loss of about 0.5-1.0% salinity from the Caspian Sea as a whole,[15] although this doesn't take into account the leaching of salt into groundwater and so the true salinity loss would certainly be significantly greater. The Caspian Sea was therefore at a much higher salinity a few thousand years ago than it is today – possibly close to the salinity of the ocean. Yet salinity had been much lower just a few millennia earlier – according to the mollusc shell evidence. Can this increase really be put down to salt from the rivers alone?[16]

In fact, standing back for a moment and considering the Caspian, it is really rather surprising that it holds as much salt as it does. There is of course a steady supply being washed in from the rivers, but whenever there has been an outflow, either to the Kara Bogaz Gol or to the Black Sea, the salinity must have decreased rapidly. There are only two explanations; either the current condition with an outflow to the Kara Bogaz Gol is exceptional when the whole history of the sea is considered, or else there has been a recent influx of salty water.

Looking around the other large inland bodies of water in Asia, all at different levels of saltiness, there don't appear to be many more clues to be gleaned. The Aral Sea, eastern neighbour to the Caspian, has become a small and highly saline lake since the rivers supplying the basin now have much of their water siphoned off for irrigation purposes; however the total salt content is just about what would be expected from the slow build-up of salts brought by these rivers. It is known that the Aral Sea was once much larger and that it used to overspill into the adjacent Sarikamish basin, and then on into the Caspian and, although precise dating of level changes is extremely difficult, the arrival of the common cockle, presumably from the Caspian, suggests that overflow to the Caspian was occurring as recently as 4000BC.[17] This overflow situation would, of course, have led to a marked lowering of salinity, effectively wiping clean any possible signs that the Aral Sea had ever been inundated by seawater. The current level of salt build-up dates from the end of this outflow connection to the Caspian.

Moving 600 miles to the east, Lake Balkhash is a fascinating body of water, being half fresh and half saline, the two halves connected via a narrow strait. It sits in a large basin rimmed by hills 500 metres or more above sea level, and it seems almost certain that the sea never flooded the basin – at least not in recent millennia; it simply doesn't look as though there is enough salt in the system for this to have been the case.

However there is one further Asiatic lake that positively demands our attention. The Dead Sea is a byword for saltiness. Sitting over 400 metres below sea level, with just a 50-metre-high land barrier protecting it from the oceans, it is in a potentially vulnerable location. Furthermore, the nearby city of Jericho has already given us a clear signal that something brought civilisation to a sudden halt in the valley of the river Jordan in about 6250BC. As its name suggests, the Dead Sea is biologically dead, which means there was nothing to investigate from a biologist's standpoint. There should, however, be geological evidence. If this is not the case then I think we might have to conclude that the Great Flood really is nothing more than a myth.

THE DEAD SEA

As you might expect, experts disagree as to the correct interpretation of evidence from ancient shorelines, sediment deposits, signs of erosion etc.; however it is generally agreed that the level of the Dead Sea was much higher than today during the depths of the Ice Age, and this is presumed to be because there was much less evaporation compared to today. There is evidence of an ancient shoreline 250 metres above today's water level, which is still about 150 metres below ocean level. This ancient sea is known to researchers as 'Lake Lisan', and the signs are that it was at a relatively low salinity.[18]

As the Earth warmed up and the evaporation rate increased, so the lake level dropped; but how far? There are those who believe that it had almost dried out completely by 8000BC – and this is based on the finding of steep-sided canyons on the slopes of the lakebed down to an elevation of 700 metres below ocean level, i.e. virtually to the floor of the Dead Sea basin. On the other hand, it has been pointed out that this should have been a physical impossibility because the salinity would have increased too much in the small remaining water volume, preventing such high evaporation from taking place, and a limit of around 500 metres below ocean level has been suggested.[19] Yet pretty obviously something caused the lakebed canyons.

At this stage there occurs what is known as an 'unconformity' in the sediment evidence, which means a sudden change. In some places Lake Lisan sediments are immediately overlain by deposits more recent than 8000BC. There is also a massive salt deposit right around the Dead Sea marking this unconformity,[20] and organic debris immediately overlying this deposit has yielded alternative Carbon 14 dates of 6000BC and 9300BC.[21] The unconformity appears to coincide with a sudden (at least in geological terms) refilling of the basin.[22] This conclusion is supported by evidence from caves in a salt massif known as Mount Sedom, which implies that the Dead Sea was 400 metres below ocean level (slightly higher than the modern Dead Sea) in 4500BC but that it had been 100 metres higher in 5100BC (again dated from organic debris[23]) and, prior to 5100BC, the lack of cave-forming in the Mount Sedom massif strongly suggests that the water level was higher still, submerging the whole formation.[24]

So what does all this mean? It's easy to see why experts are a little confused. The physical evidence of erosion on the lakebed to a depth of 700 metres below sea level does not sit easily with the supposed salt content of the water. But if the water was much fresher than has been supposed then where has all today's salt come from? And what about all the extra salt contained in the several-metre-thick deposit? At face value the evidence implies that the Dead Sea had a lower salt content in former times, allowing the water to drop to 700 metres below ocean level by 8000BC. Yet by about 6000BC the basin had filled to cover

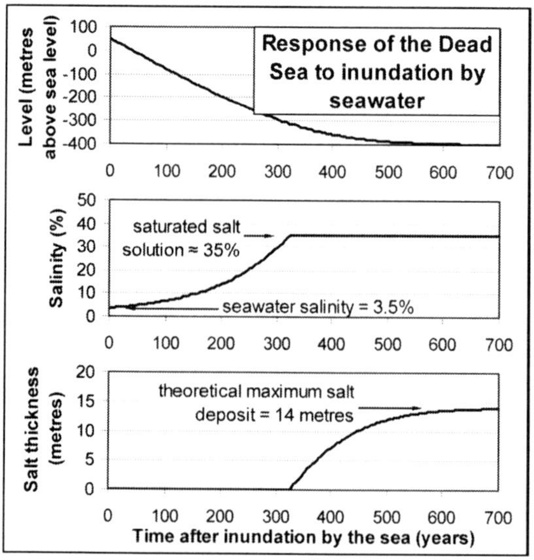

Mount Sedom completely, while at the same time somehow managing to create the massive salt deposit seen today, which means that the salt content of the water must have become very high indeed. However unbelievable, it's hard to see any explanation that matches all these pieces of evidence other than a sudden filling of the whole basin with seawater some time before 6000BC.

If the Mediterranean Sea really did flood the entire Dead Sea-River Jordan valley it would have reset whatever salinity had been there previously to around 3.5%, creating a large salt lake with a surface about 50 metres above ocean level. This level would have dropped off quite rapidly since evaporation would have greatly exceeded rainfall and river inflow and, as it dropped, so the salinity would have increased. The figure shows graphically what would, in theory, have happened over the course of seven centuries.[25] The ruins of Jericho, at 250 metres below sea level, would have emerged after about 250 years. After 330 years, with the lake level at about 300 metres below sea level, the salinity would have reached saturation point, which means that, as the lake fell further, salt would have precipitated out of solution and built up on the lake bed, forming a deposit just like the one which is seen today.[26] If the whole idea wasn't so crazy, this would surely be accepted as the logical explanation for current Dead Sea geology.

By the way, US readers might wonder whether the Salton Sea in southern California might show similar evidence since it has many similarities to the Dead Sea, being below the level of the oceans and requiring only a small sea level rise in order to be inundated. The answer however is a very definite 'no'. The Salton Sea has only existed in its current form since 1905 when an irrigation scheme taking water from the Columbia River went rather drastically wrong! The only clue that the basin might have been inundated by the sea over 8000 years ago is the salt content of the Salton Sea today (4.4%). This is presumed to be a consequence of highly saline run-off from agricultural irrigation, but it may also owe much to the slow dissolving of salt deposits from underlying sediments, deposits that may well date to an earlier drowning of the basin by seawater.

There is however one further and extremely important body of water, which was once an inland sea but which has since suffered inundation by the ocean, an inundation from which it has never recovered. I speak of the Black Sea which, as I said in Chapter 1, has become many people's favoured location for Noah's flood itself.

THE BLACK SEA FLOOD

This is a highly controversial subject, one that has generated heated debate between supporters and sceptics – and my contribution here is hardly likely to lessen the controversy.

The Black Sea is a vast reservoir of salty seawater today, slightly less salty than the rest of the world's oceans because of the large number of rivers that flow into it, but still pretty salty. If you look back two or three pages to the most recent map you will see that the only outlet is the narrow Bosphorus channel, flowing past the city of Istanbul and into the Sea of Marmara. This channel, 15 miles long and no more than about a mile wide in most places, has a depth of around 40 metres at its outlet to the Sea of Marmara. The Sea of Marmara itself is a relatively small body of water lying between the Bosphorus and another narrow channel, the Dardanelles. This second channel is about 50 miles long, two to three miles wide and has a depth of some 75 metres; it connects through to the Aegean Sea, which is part of the Mediterranean.

During the course of their work in oceanography and earth science, two geologists, Bill Ryan and Walter Pitman of Columbia University, began to realise that the history of the Black Sea had been somewhat out of the ordinary. In fact it had already been noted by others that at some time in the not-too-distant past the entire Black Sea must have been a freshwater lake with a much lower surface level than today.[27] Ryan and Pitman put together their own evidence, finding that the shoreline had once been over 100 metres below the current surface but that the water level had risen very quickly indeed since the features of this old shoreline were remarkably well preserved. Another highly significant piece of evidence was that Carbon 14 dates from the lowest layer of saltwater mollusc shells, immediately overlying earlier freshwater mollusc remains at the bottom of the sea, all came out at around the same date, 5600BC. The implication seemed clear and Ryan and Pitman went public in 1997.[28] Their contention was that the level of the Black Sea had fallen during extremely dry conditions at the end of the last Ice Age, conditions that were dry enough to mean that the evaporation rate from the surface of the Black Sea exceeded the inflow from the rivers. At that time the level of the world's oceans, including the Sea of Marmara, would also have been substantially lower than today due to the vast quantities of water still tied up in ice sheets, particularly in North America. This meant that the bed of the Bosphorus channel must have stood high and dry, 50 metres or more above the level of the Black Sea and also well above the level of the Sea of Marmara. Then, as the ice sheets melted and the oceans rose, flooding the Dardanelles Strait and the Sea of Marmara, there came a time when the Sea of Marmara had risen sufficiently to overtop the bed of the Bosphorus and flow through to the Black Sea. However, according to Ryan and Pitman, for some reason, perhaps earthquake, the Bosphorus channel had become blocked, creating a dam. As the oceans rose still further this dam was holding back ever more water until, in 5600BC, the dam broke; billions of gallons of water burst through, washing the debris from the dam far out into the Black Sea.[29] The water level over the entire Black Sea would have risen at a foot or two per day, rapidly submerging the old shoreline features.[30] That at least was Ryan and Pitman's interpretation of the evidence.

Since their initial publication in the scientific press, Ryan and Pitman have been closely involved with the notion that this flood could actually have been the very flood that led to the Noah story.[31] However, their explanation has certainly not gone unchallenged. Let me now put forward some of the evidence which their opponents have gathered.

i) A study of deposits around the mouth of the Sakarya River in northern Turkey has revealed strong indications that the Black Sea was only 18 metres lower than today in 5600BC (i.e. the same level as the rest of the world's oceans at that time), although the study confirmed that it had been around 100 metres lower two or three thousand years previously. This same study also confirmed the transition from freshwater to saltwater at a time that could easily have been around 5600BC.[32]
ii) A sediment outflow delta has been mapped at the southern end of the Bosphorus channel, dating to between 8000BC and 7000BC. This implies continuing outflow from the Black Sea during this period, supporting the evidence in point i) that the level of the Black Sea was at least as high as that of the Sea of Marmara.[33]
iii) A study of micro-organisms present in seabed cores allows the oxygen level in water at the seabed to be assessed. Low seabed oxygen is associated with highly stratified water (usually fresh over salt) which, in the Sea of Marmara, would indicate a strong freshwater outflow from the Black Sea. These conditions have persisted at the Bosphorus end of the Sea of Marmara since 7000BC, implying continuing outflow from the Black Sea ever since.[34]
iv) Indicators of salinity suggest that the water in the north Aegean was of unusually low salinity between 8000BC and 4500BC, again suggesting strong outflow from the Black Sea, the only possible source of fresh water.[35]

Although there is general agreement among opponents of Ryan and Pitman's theory that the Black Sea did indeed become salty at some time during this period, there also seems to be irrefutable evidence that the waters of the Black Sea were already spilling out through the Bosphorus by around 8000BC and that this situation has persisted ever since.[36] The standard explanation for this phase of Black Sea history given by Ryan and Pitman's opponents is that the ever-rising ocean levels led to the Bosphorus channel becoming too deep for its own good. The relatively fresh surface waters of the Black Sea would have continued to pour out through the upper 20 metres or so of the Bosphorus channel, while denser, saltier water would have started to push its way in from the Sea of Marmara at lower depths, setting up one of the strange features of the Bosphorus as it is today, namely a two-way water flow – southward near the surface; northward at depth.

This is excellent logic and good fluid mechanics; unfortunately it does not explain the strange fact that low oxygen conditions appear to have taken hold in the Black Sea all at one time. The material which Ryan and Pitman dated (from mollusc remains) was taken from a layer of so-called 'sapropel', an organic-rich mulch which is only formed under conditions of low oxygen, and their date for the appearance of this layer, 5600BC, is pretty consistent right across the seabed. Admittedly it should have taken a few hundred years for these low-oxygen conditions (due to stratified water) to establish themselves once the Black Sea became salty,[37] but it certainly implies that saltwater status was achieved relatively suddenly at some point in the centuries before 5600BC. In fact Ryan and Pitman also published Carbon 14 dates for freshwater molluscs found immediately beneath the sapropel layer and have a range of results (reflecting the fact that it was a disturbed gravely material), the most recent of which is 6250BC.[38] But the point is that, according to the conventional model, not only should it have taken several hundred years to achieve the layering of the waters, fresh overlying salt, necessary for sapropel production, but that development should have been progressive, starting with the deepest parts of the Black Sea basin and working its way slowly up as the salt-water content increased.[39] Ryan and Pitman's cores on the other hand showed quite clearly that the same start date applied everywhere in the Black Sea and at all depths.

The key pieces of evidence are therefore as follows:

i) The waters became salty all at one time.
ii) The date was a few hundred years before 5600BC but no earlier than 6250BC.
iii) The Black Sea was already flowing out into the Sea of Marmara at that time.

Ryan and Pitman's theory is undone by point iii). If the Black Sea was already just as high as the Sea of Marmara and the rest of the oceans, then there is no reason for any sudden northward rush of water to have occurred. Yet it did occur. The transformation of the Black Sea from freshwater to salt at a single point in time demands it. It is a difficult conundrum and it is easy to see why there has been no resolution of this disagreement. If the concept of the oceans rising well beyond their normal boundaries was not such an outrageous one, it really should be put forward as the only logical explanation of the Black Sea evidence.

Enough said; however unbelievable, the conclusion is clear enough. In this instance at least geology has failed to come up with a credible alternative to the Great Flood. You might also like to know that botanists have no ready explanation for the fact that certain Mediterranean plant species arrived in the Crimea, the peninsula that juts south into the Black Sea, in around 6000BC.[40] A possible cause which has not been considered for obvious reasons is that seeds were transported north by a massive influx of Mediterranean water! Like it or not, the Black Sea evidence goes a long way to proving that the Great Flood was a real event.

RUMBLINGS IN THE EARTH

To be fair, geology has not failed entirely in its task of refuting the flood. It certainly has failed as far as the Black Sea is concerned, although it probably wouldn't have taken more than a few tens of metres rise in sea level to produce the sudden transformation of the Black Sea that Ryan and Pitman found. It has also failed in relation to the Dead Sea, and here a 50-metre rise would be required; and the same sort of sea level rise would also explain Caspian Sea geology – another failure. On the other hand in Lake Malawi geology has done what biology couldn't. There is no arguing with the fact that sediment cores through the lake floor deposits indicate that the waters above never turned particularly salty despite the fact that some sort of disaster must have set off the spectacular explosion of cichlid fish species. We are therefore left with conflicting signals from biology and geology and real doubt as to whether an East African flood could ever have reached the 474-metre mark.

But once we leave the issue of salt behind there is a limit to what we can expect to see in the geological record. A flood of a few months duration would not lead to the formation of any significant depths of sediment; there would have been little noticeable erosion and no movement of rock. On the other hand, if the flood was a real event, as the myths tell us and as other evidence increasingly seems to imply, then I will have to address the cause at some stage, and that cause must have been pretty dramatic whatever it was; and if something dramatic took place that affected the planet as a whole then we might at least expect to see something in the geological record, earthquakes perhaps or volcanic eruptions – if only we knew where to look!

Well, nowadays the first places to look for records from the distant past are Greenland and Antarctica. The great ice sheets hold embedded within them a record of the past, a record that can be fairly accurately dated because of the useful fact that ice sheets develop distinct annual layers, a bit like tree rings. The conditions (temperature, evaporation rate) are different in summer and winter and the result is a series of different-looking layers of snow, which then consolidate into different-looking layers of ice. The ice can then be analysed for a multitude of different things, one of which is its chemistry, and the key point here is that the acidity of the ice has been found to be a reliable indicator of volcanic activity. Now you may have imagined that volcanic activity is essentially random; it certainly seems to have been pretty random in modern times. However, when looking over timescales of millennia the truth is that it has not been random at all, and the greatest concentration in recent millennia took place between 7000BC and 5000BC. Over the course of these two millennia three times as many eruptions took place as in the most recent two millennia, and average eruption magnitude was significantly greater as well.[41] This may just be coincidence of course, but it is certainly worth noting. You might recall from Chapter 2 the tale told by the Purus River tribes of the Amazon that "once upon a time people heard a rumbling above and below the ground"; and "the sun and moon turned red, blue and yellow". These signs are reported to have immediately preceded the Great Flood.

Volcanic activity is a sign of disturbance in the Earth's crust and is often associated with earthquakes; and *vice versa*. The problem however is that it is much harder to date earthquakes than volcanic eruptions. Earthquakes leave no mark on the atmosphere or the sea. We can see their effect on the landscape but dating can only be crude, based on estimates of such things as erosion rates, rock patination patterns etc. Besides, in most fault zones earthquakes are regular occurrences, set off by relative movement between the various tectonic plates of the Earth's crust and, whatever I might eventually dream up as the cause of a Great Flood, it is unlikely to involve any change to the rate of 'continental drift'. No; the places to look are those where earthquakes are relatively unusual – northern Sweden for example. Here, a thousand miles from any active fault, lies brutal evidence for something really impressive that occurred some time between about 7000BC and 5000BC. The Parvie fault runs for 160 kilometres across the landscape, a continuous cliff which, investigations have revealed, represents the top edge of a vertical slip reaching some 40 kilometres down into the Earth. The 50-kilometre-long Landsjarv fault is similar and is also located in northern Sweden. Most geologists would suggest that the high-magnitude earthquakes that produced these faults were caused by the 'rebound' of Scandinavia after its compression under a massive weight of ice during the Ice Age – but could there be an alternative explanation?

SUMMARY

In no way can I pretend that this has been an exhaustive report on geological issues. I have simply concentrated on those areas where I figured that real evidence for or against a flood was most likely to be found. I have not spent time trying to prove or disprove the view that fossils of marine creatures found on mountain tops were actually formed during Noah's flood; that was disproved centuries ago. Those who cling to this view simply refuse to see what they do not wish to see. However, if you approached this book with anything like an open mind then you should be seriously wondering by now whether there might not actually be some truth in the Great Flood story. It seems that wherever I turn there is good reason to believe that something rather unusual happened to the Earth round about the year 6250BC. The volcanic record and ancient earthquake faults may be nothing to do with it, but you would have to admit that none of the branches of human knowledge consulted so far have come remotely close to disproving the theory, based on ancient myth, that the oceans really did once rise to cover the land. In fact in every case they have provided pretty solid support.

However, returning to earthquakes and volcanic eruptions, if such events actually do form part of the overall picture then we are moving into an area where we would also expect an effect on the climate. In fact even without earthquakes or volcanic eruptions, if sea level rose to such an extent that the shapes of the oceans and land masses changed significantly then that might be sufficient to trigger climate change by itself. Or, standing back and looking at the bigger picture, if something happened to the planet that was big enough to cause sea level rises of hundreds of metres then, whatever it was, it was probably also big enough to change the climate. Whichever way you look at it therefore we would be fools not to call in the specialist assistance of a climatologist.

7

The Climatologist's Report

Climate change is a very modern subject – or so most of us seem to assume. Yet that is only because we find it difficult to imagine what we have never experienced. So, while I may bemoan the lack of snowfall these days in England and remember with fondness the icicles that used to hang from the eaves each winter, and I would be right to put this down to climate change, the fact is that climate has changed much more radically in the past, and not only in the dim and distant past. The 'Little Ice Age' is the name given to the centuries between about 1450 and 1850 during which the river Thames in London used to freeze over, something which is unimaginable today. Yet if we go back another few hundred years the climate in the northern hemisphere was significantly warmer than today, allowing cattle farming on the slopes of Greenland's mountains, just a short distance from the great ice sheets of the interior. I have mentioned already the fact that many of the great deserts of the world weren't deserts at all just a few thousand years ago. Rock drawings out in the middle of the Sahara showing boats and the sort of wildlife you would expect on the Serengeti today rather give the game away! Even in Roman times it was possible to drive chariots and horses across the Sahara, where now only camels tread.

The story of past climate is therefore a complicated one. So can we really hope to see anything from 8000 years ago, with no written records?

RECORDS IN THE ICE

Despite the lack of written records our planet actually has many, many climate-related sources of data and, just as was the case for past volcanic activity, the Greenland and Antarctic ice sheets are definitely the best places to start. As I said in the last chapter the ice in these great ice sheets is layered in annual bands and so it is possible to take a core right down through thicknesses measured in kilometres and to know fairly accurately what date each layer of ice was deposited (as snow on the surface). In the last chapter I was interested in the acidity of the ice; here however the key quantity needed is the average molecular weight of water in the ice. This has been found to correlate with how easily the molecules managed to make the transition from liquid to gas and back again, which in turn correlates to the ocean temperature at the time that water evaporated to form the clouds that eventually deposited snow onto the surface of the ice sheet. The chemistry of the ice sheet therefore preserves a record of ocean temperature at the time it formed, a really quite detailed and sensitive record, as shown in the next figure.[1] You could certainly debate the extent to which this record relates to local effects rather than global, but it is undeniable that similar patterns emerge from both Greenland and Antarctica, at least in some of the records.

Looking at the figure you can see that from about 18000BC, the low-point of the last Ice Age, temperatures started to rise but that, in Greenland at least, this trend was checked until about 13000BC when a serious increase in temperature occurred, almost to present levels. However the trend was rapidly reversed again for a reason which is yet to be discovered, leading to the so-called 'Younger Dryas' cold period – from 11000 to 10000BC. This was then followed by the final great warming, in around 9500BC. Since then the most significant fluctuation was a lowering in temperature commencing a little before 6000BC – exactly the period of interest in this book. Compared to the Younger Dryas cold spell, or to the Ice Age itself, what has become known as the '8.2ka BP climatic event' may seem relatively insignificant, not much more severe than the Little Ice Age, the final low point on the graph. It does however seem to have been a bit more significant than it looks in terms of its effect around the planet.

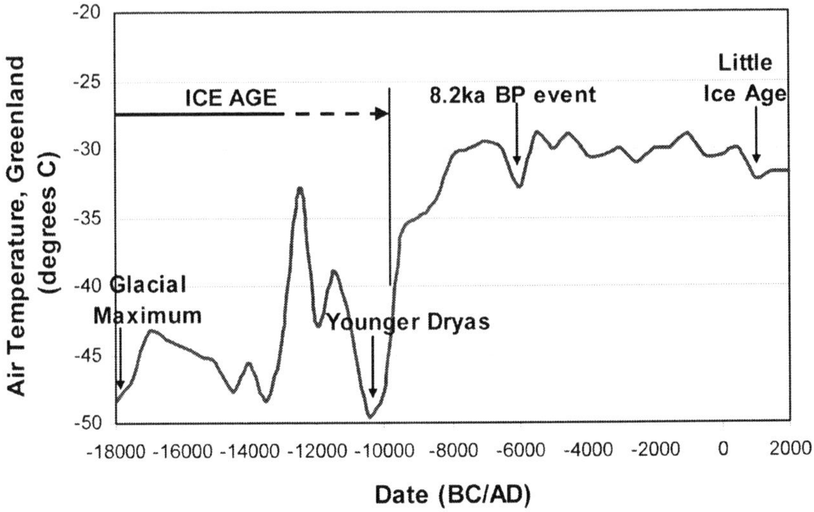

THE 8.2ka BP CLIMATIC EVENT

In case you are confused, *ka* means *thousands of years* and *BP* means *before present* which, odd though it may seem, means before 1950.[2] The net result is that we are talking about something which is dated to around 6250BC.

As the figure illustrates, the first evidence for this event came from a Greenland ice core and was based on interpretation of ice chemistry. And the consistent picture that has now emerged is that the temperature in Greenland fell by a few degrees, up to 7°C according to some core data. This immediately made investigators around the world look for similar signs elsewhere.[3] In Antarctica a clear signal was found in a core from Vostok,[4] right in the middle of the ice sheet, although it is true that other cores from elsewhere in Antarctica failed to show anything similar. However it isn't just in the polar regions that evidence has been found. An ice core through a Tibetan glacier appears to show a surprisingly large temperature drop of around 9°C.[5] There are also large numbers of records that suggest a near worldwide fall in ocean temperature. For example, a core from the North Sea shows a significant increase in a particular cold-water plankton species datable to 8.2ka BP.[6] Another, from the Norwegian Sea, gave an estimated cooling of 1-2°C;[7] one off Portugal showed about 0.5°C.[8] To the west of Ireland there was a marked reduction in the growth of a particular cold-water coral mound.[9] Off the African coast several sediment cores also suggest temperature reductions of up to 2°C.[10] The same is true in the Mediterranean, the South China Sea and the western Pacific.[11] Similar signals have been noted in organic lake deposits from the Ammersee in Germany,[12] from snail remains in south-east England[13] and from cave formations in Ireland[14] and Israel,[15] all implying a temperature reduction of up to 2°C. I could go on and mention the expansion of cold-loving trees in the Swiss Alps and sediment evidence from numerous lakes across the United States and Canada.

There are also several indicators that suggest not only a reduction in temperature but also a shift to a drier climate. This is particularly marked across Africa where low lake levels are seen, notably in Lake Chad in West Africa,[16] and where a core through the ice sheet on the summit of Mount Kilimanjaro reveals a high aerosol level, which implies a drier climate.[17] In Oman there was a significant reduction in monsoon rainfall, deduced from cave deposit evidence,[18] while sediment records also suggest reduced precipitation in India and Pakistan.[19] In Spain there are signs of a concentration of natural forest fires,[20] and this is broadly supported by evidence of fall-out from fires contained in a Greenland ice core.[21]

There are now so many pieces of evidence, many more than I have listed here, that scientists are in absolutely no doubt that something significant must have occurred. All the evidence dates to the same period, a period of approximately 300 years commencing in about 6250BC. Some even concerns the chemistry of the atmosphere itself, notably a fall in the concentration of both methane and carbon dioxide.[22] The question of course is: just what caused it all?

Well, one thing is clear and that is that the effect felt on land was intimately tied in with something that happened in the oceans. In the Mediterranean for example 8.2ka BP represents a disaster of stupendous proportions, a disaster which saw a massive reduction in marine life and the permanent loss of many species. For some reason the circulation which is so necessary for a healthy ocean, bringing oxygen to the depths, suddenly ceased, and for the next several thousand years nothing could live at any significant depth below the surface, especially in the eastern Mediterranean.[23] Across the Atlantic, sediments from the Cariaco Basin off the coast of Venezuela suggest an increase in winter upwelling in that part of the Caribbean, which in turn has been interpreted as a change in the latitude of the trade winds and their associated ocean currents.[24] In the north Atlantic, off the coast of Norway, changes in the properties of the ocean-bed sediment also suggest a change in ocean currents,[25] and the majority of researchers are now of the view that a major alteration of the North Atlantic circulation pattern occurred during this period. But why?

GLACIAL LAKE AGASSIZ

Whatever the detailed mechanisms involved it is clear that the strongest signals are in the northern hemisphere and that they are particularly strong in the North Atlantic and surrounding lands (Europe, Greenland and North America). That, therefore, is the place to concentrate the search for a cause. And there are two particularly telling pieces of evidence. The first is an abrupt increase in the volume of debris found on the ocean floor of the North Atlantic, debris which could only have got where it is now found if it had been transported by icebergs.[26] The second narrows down the hunt further still; it is the finding of a layer of red silt on the bed of the Hudson Strait, the stretch of water leading from Hudson Bay in northern Canada out into the Atlantic Ocean.[27] This has been interpreted as signalling a massive flow of water out from Hudson Bay. Bearing in mind that the Ice Age had recently ended and that ice sheets still lay across many parts of Canada, including the Hudson Bay area, it seems likely that something had suddenly caused large sections of that ice to be carried in the form of bergs out into the Atlantic. And there is only one possible agent that could have been responsible for this event, namely 'glacial lake Agassiz'.

The glacial lakes of North America were a fascinating phenomenon. There has recently been considerable publicity surrounding the stupendous flood that, probably on more than one occasion, roared down the Columbia River when the ice dam holding back glacial lake Missoula collapsed, creating giant ripples in the landscape.[28] Yet this was nothing compared to the biggest ice dam collapse of them all. There are signs from North Dakota through central Canada towards Hudson Bay that much of the area was once under water – and not that long ago either. The glacial lake known as Lake Agassiz after Louis Agassiz, a famous geologist from the 19th Century, first started to form in about 9700BC in the Red River valley of North Dakota and Minnesota, a river which today runs north through Canada and into Lake Winnipeg. At that time however the path north was blocked by ice and the water had to spill out south into the Minnesota River and thence to the Mississippi. As the ice sheet retreated northwards under the impact of global warming, Lake Agassiz managed to drain into Lake Superior and the Great Lakes system, but ice sheets prevented flow down the St Lawrence, so the only route was still south and into the Mississippi.

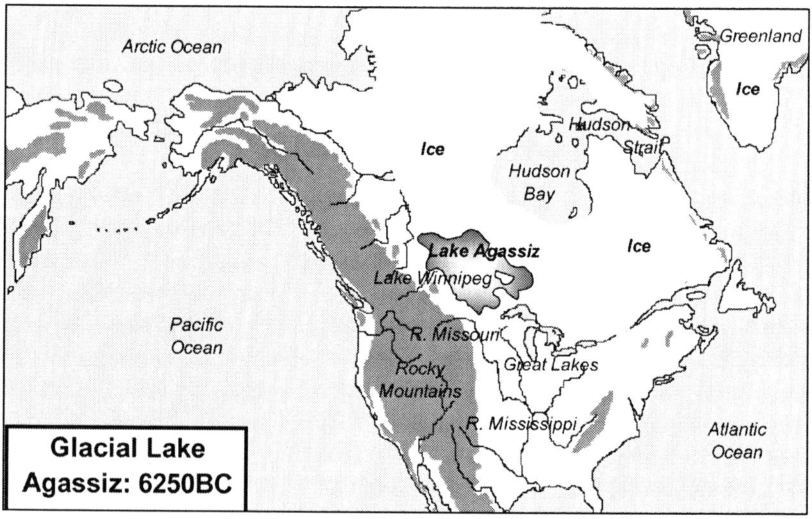

James Teller of the University of Manitoba, Winnipeg, is well known for his extensive investigations into the progress of Lake Agassiz as it grew ever larger northwards, as more and more glacier was replaced by lake.[29] He has traced eighteen separate occasions on which the level of the lake fell abruptly as an ice barrier gave way, but seventeen of them pale into insignificance compared with the last and greatest release of water. Teller's estimate for the volume of the lake at the time that it issued catastrophically into Hudson Bay is 163000 cubic kilometres, just over twice the volume contained in the Caspian Sea today. Estimates for the total volume of fresh water released into the oceans, including the water released by the subsequent rapid melting of the ice sheet, range up to about 400000 cubic kilometres. Global sea level would have risen almost instantly by about half a metre, and by a further half metre or more over the course of the next few decades. This was the event which, climatologists are pretty certain, was responsible for the sudden cooling seen in the Greenland ice core records and in so many other records from around the world. The excess of fresh water in the North Atlantic temporarily diverted the Gulf Stream, allowing less relatively warm water to penetrate to the areas of ocean from which Greenland's precipitation derives. And a change in the Gulf Stream spelt a major climatic change in Europe.[30]

So; climatologists have found their culprit. Many computer simulations have now been run, tracing the global effects of this pulse of fresh water, and they consistently model the reduction in Atlantic sea temperatures, European air temperatures and African rainfall.[31] It is true that many have expressed surprise that this phenomenon should have been responsible for changes on such a global scale as those observed (remember the temperature falls in the Pacific, in India and Tibet), but the scientific consensus seems to be that, whatever the models may or may not predict, this event simply has to have been responsible for all the oddities in climate-related records datable to that time.

The problem is that we have still not found any sign of a Great Flood. A sudden half-metre rise in sea level may have been the talk of coastal dwellers for many a month but, as a flood, it hardly deserves the title 'Great'. Even when half a metre became a metre it is hard to see too many generations getting excited about it. And there is no way that this can have been responsible for the Black Sea flood or any of the other phenomena noted in previous chapters. It's even questionable whether it really explains all the climate data from far-flung parts of the world.

So has consulting a climatologist been a complete waste of time?

SUMMARY

Something big happened in 6250BC (i.e. 8.2ka BP); that much is clear. The draining of Lake Agassiz and the change in climate are acknowledged facts; so is the transformation of the Black Sea from freshwater to salt; and the collapse of Pre-pottery Neolithic B civilisation. Some of the other evidence has been a little less precise, for example the sudden expansion of so many language groups and the equally dramatic explosion in Lake Malawi cichlid fish species, and in Caspian Sea crustacea.

In Chapter 2 the challenge was thrown down as to whether science could 'debunk' the persistent myths from all around the world that one day a very long time ago there had been an unprecedented worldwide flood; and despite the suggestion being patently absurd to most people today, science has quite obviously failed the challenge. Indicator after indicator has pointed straight at a rise in sea level, of several hundred metres judging by some of the evidence. Yet here, just when we should be getting to the root of the mystery, all we have is a paltry half metre. It is one thing to produce evidence that 'something' must have happened. If it is scientifically impossible that any Great Flood ever occurred then it didn't – it's as simple as that! Despite the strength of the evidence, we would just have to turn around and find alternative explanations. Perhaps there really is an inherent propensity in human nature to make up flood stories. There could certainly be other explanations for the end of Pre-pottery Neolithic B culture in lowland locations, and for the patchy progress of agriculture across China, India and the Nile delta. The language evidence seems to imply a disaster of some kind, but it need not have been a flood. And the calculations of past changes of salinity in various inland bodies of water are a long way from being precise; similarly the observations on recent speciation events. I guess the Black Sea evidence looks to be the hardest to get around, but given time someone would probably find a plausible alternative explanation.

So the time has come to face the big question, the question that has so far been avoided. Back in Chapter 1 I spoke of the need to find a) a possible time window, b) clues that something big happened and c) a mechanism by which it might have happened. Points a) and b) have been answered many times over; it is time to rise to the challenge of point c) and to ask whether any conceivable mechanism could have brought the sea high enough to flood into Lake Malawi – or to shipwreck Noah and his family high in the Mountains of Ararat. We need an explanation. Without it the Great Flood remains nothing more than a myth.

In Part 2 therefore I will be seeking an explanation. If the emptying of Lake Agassiz genuinely was the event that triggered the greatest catastrophe that mankind has ever known, rather than the mere half-metre rise in sea level which it would seem to be capable of producing, then I need to understand how this could have happened. And in order to do that I shall have to delve deeply into Earth science and some of the key laws of physics. It will not be a particularly easy journey, but then if it was many would have got there before me! I hope you manage to stick with me as I peel back the layers of complexity to arrive at the truth. If the thought of anything mathematical turns you off then feel free to skip the detail, but you might at least like to dive into the second half of Chapter 11 where the final conclusion from Part 2 is revealed.

PART 2

THE EXPLANATION

8

Newton's Law

Sir Isaac Newton (1643-1727) is best known today for having an apple fall on his head. And rightly so! He may have been one of the greatest scientists the human race has ever produced, but we all need an easy way to understand science and falling apples is something we can all relate to. Science is really just a proper understanding of the blindingly obvious. It's obvious that apples fall to the ground when their stalks break – we don't need a great scientist to tell us that – but we need a great scientist to express this mathematically so that we can go on to calculate things properly and design the various aids to modern life that we take for granted today. Newton simply formulated a mathematical equation to describe gravity, an equation that took into account the mass of the Earth, the mass of the apple (or other falling object) and how far apart they were.

Actually Newton's equation for gravitational attraction was just one of his many achievements. The law that really concerns us here is another expression of the blindingly obvious. He noticed that if you apply a force to a mass then it will accelerate; i.e. if you put your foot on the accelerator it works because the motor in your car produces a force, and the lighter your car the faster it will accelerate. A powerful motor in a light car (as in Formula 1) gives very rapid acceleration. As I say, it's blindingly obvious but it needed someone to come along and write down the equation that engineers use today. This equation (Force = Mass × Acceleration) is, I believe, going to help us to get to the bottom of just what happened to the Earth in 6250BC.

However, before getting too carried away, if we are serious about the possibility of a Great Flood then I think the first thing to worry about is just where all the water could have come from. The evidence from all the various odd events of 6250BC may point straight at a flood, but in order for floodwaters to cover the land there has to be a source of water. What was it?

WHERE DID THE WATER COME FROM?

There are about 1300 million cubic kilometres of water in the oceans today; a 300 metre flood would require another 130 million or so – an extra 10%. That's a lot of water. And don't forget that not only did the water have to appear from somewhere, but it also had to disappear afterwards. Now a perfectly logical explanation would be to say that the Great Flood was an act of God and, that being the case, God could have simply created the extra water and then made it vanish again – and I would have no answer to that. Personally I don't believe that was the case, but it is not something I can disprove. I would be more inclined to believe that the God who created the laws of science would continue to use those laws to achieve what he wanted, but I couldn't prove it. Anyway, for better or worse I shall continue to pursue the path of science and see where it leads.

Some have suggested that the water may have been contained in the atmosphere somehow and that it was released at the time of the flood; hence the references to long-lasting rainstorms in many of the flood myths, including 40 days and nights of rain in the case of the Noah story in the Bible. It is also true that the story of creation in the Bible speaks of the waters above and below the 'firmament', where the firmament means the sky above us. If there was once water high in the atmosphere then couldn't it have been released by some effect yet to be understood and then re-absorbed somewhere afterwards? I'm afraid my answer has to be a resounding 'no'. The atmospheric pressure we feel today is due to the weight of gas (oxygen, nitrogen, carbon dioxide, water vapour etc.) above us, of which only about 1% is water in the form of droplets (clouds) or vapour. If there had ever been 130 million cubic kilometres of additional water then atmospheric pressure would have been some twenty five times what it is now. I am not sure that I could prove what the effect of this would be but I am pretty confident that neither our bodies nor those of the animals and plants around us would be suited to such an environment. Air resistance would be twenty five times greater; every breath we took would fill our lungs with water; and I guess (though cannot prove) that the planet would be as dark as it is on Venus under their 15-mile-thick mass of cloud – and probably nearly as hot.[1] No; I'm afraid all that I can attribute to the atmosphere in relation to a flood is a little rain, enough to raise sea levels by no more than a few centimetres.

Another proposal is that the water could have been present within the Earth somewhere – but I can detect absolutely no evidence for this, and there most certainly should be evidence; the release (and then re-absorption) of such a large volume would have to have caused serious geological upheaval. It is true, as we saw in Chapter 6, that there was an increased level of volcanic activity in that general period, but nothing on the sort of scale which a 130-million-cubic-kilometre discharge would require.[2]

No; from a rational point of view there is only one possible source for flood water on this scale. It must have come from the oceans themselves. Actually, when you think about it, we are lucky to have any land to live on at all. Nearly 70% of the planet is ocean, with an average depth of some 4 kilometres; the other 30%, the land, sticks up by much less than 1 kilometre above sea level on average. The continents are like icebergs floating in water, except that they are made of granite and float in a sea of even denser part-molten rock. Just as 90% of an iceberg is below the water line so 90% of the thickness of the continental plates extends down into the underlying denser rock. If 5 kilometres of a 50-kilometre-thick continental plate sticks up above the level of dense rock (the bed of the oceans) then some 45 kilometres are hidden. Imagine: if the thickness of my idealised continental plate was only 30 kilometres instead of 50 kilometres then the height protruding above the beds of the oceans would be reduced to just 3 kilometres and, since ocean depth averages 4 kilometres, the whole continent would be submerged! Is there any conceivable geological process that could possibly reduce the thickness of the continental plates? Or could they somehow be pushed down into the underlying denser rock? All I can say is that I can't see how. There's not much you can do to sink an iceberg! It has the density it has – a bit less than water – and by the laws of physics it will continue to float. Likewise, I can't see how any mechanism could make the continental masses sink into the rocks beneath. Violent volcanic processes such as magma plumes, upwellings of molten rock from deep inside the mantle of the Earth, might do a fair bit of damage as has happened many times in the Earth's history; but they can't do anything to reduce the difference in density between the continents and the rock below. Damaged or otherwise, the continents will continue to float as they do. I need some other explanation.

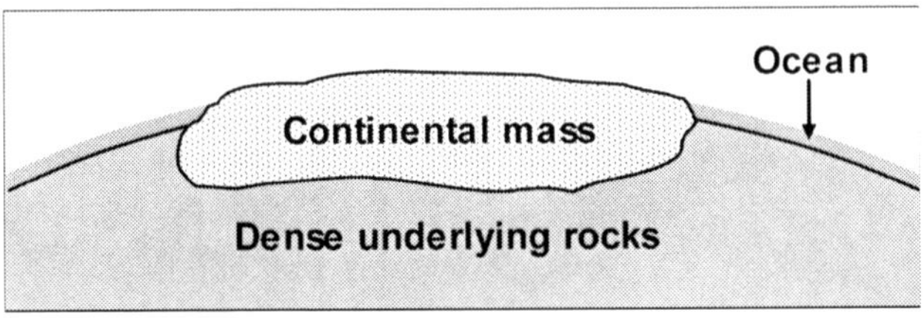

So, if the elevation of the continental plates cannot change dramatically, the only other way to create a major flood is to persuade the oceans to redistribute themselves somehow. This wouldn't strictly be a world flood since extra water in one region would be offset by less elsewhere, but the inhabitants of the flooded regions wouldn't know that! As far as they were concerned the whole world would be under water. But the question remains: how is it possible for the oceans to move in their beds? Can gravity be altered in some way? It's difficult to see how, if the shape and mass of the Earth remain the same, at least not if Newton's Law of gravitational attraction applies. So is there any other force involved?

Now that was the right question! Yes; there is another force involved. It is called centrifugal force; the force due to the spin of the Earth, rotating once on its axis every 24 hours. If you imagine the planet as a giant spinning top and you were perched somewhere on the outside, you would experience the unwelcome sensation of being spun off into space. Fortunately the sheer mass of the Earth means that this tendency to spin off into space is dwarfed by the much more powerful effect of gravity, but you should actually feel slightly lighter at the equator than at the poles because of this spinning-off effect. The difference would be very slight, enough to give you about an extra centimetre if you were attempting a high-jump record. However the point is that all the components of the Earth, continents, oceans and underlying strata, also feel a slight reduction in gravitational pull at the equator because of the planet's spin and, over the course of the millennia, this has led to a slight redistribution of the Earth's mass. The planet actually bulges slightly at the equator because gravity appears marginally weaker there, and the upshot is that the equator sticks out about 21 kilometres further from the centre of the Earth than the poles. The true shape of the Earth is a squashed sphere, flattened at the poles and bulging out at the equator, and it has come about as a natural consequence of the spin of the Earth.

Now imagine what would happen if the solid parts of the planet tilted a bit while the oceans remained as they are. For every 100 kilometres you travel away from the equator, the 21-kilometre 'bulge' reduces by about 230 metres. So, if the planet tilted by 100 kilometres, bringing a point that had been 100 kilometres north of the equator so that it now lay on the equator, it would be 230 metres below where it 'should' be. If it had previously been just above sea level, it would now be below sea level. The result: a Great Flood – at least in some parts of the planet. The problem is: what on earth could induce the solid bits of the planet to tilt while the oceans didn't?

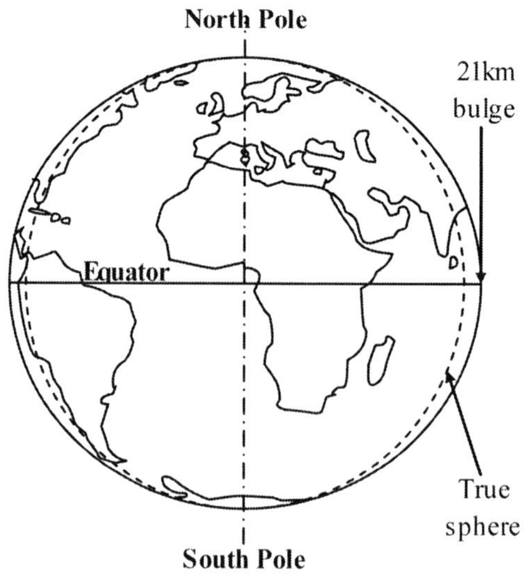

The True Shape of Planet Earth

MAKING THE PLANET TILT

Planet Earth spins on its axis like a top. Everything is pretty much in balance and the motion is nice and regular. It isn't quite perpetual motion. As I write it is New Year's Day and scientists decided to give us all an extra second last night to compensate for a slight slowing in the rate of spin – but then you know that a top eventually loses momentum and comes to a halt. You have probably also seen a top wobble. Maybe it wasn't perfectly made so it had a very slightly uneven weight distribution, or it had been damaged. And actually the Earth wobbles too. It isn't a big wobble. It amounts to about 6.5 metres one way and then the other. It isn't a very quick wobble either; it takes about 14 months to wobble back and forth. This means that if you take the trouble to visit the South Pole and plant a flag exactly on the Earth's axis of spin, the precise pole location, you would find that it had drifted off by a metre or two after a few months. This is the 'Chandler Wobble'[3] and it is exactly the sort of tilting of the solid parts of the Earth that I was referring to just now. There is so much momentum tied up in the spin of the Earth that there is no way that the axis of spin itself is ever going to move; the only movement possible is tilt of the solid Earth relative to the axis. In theory, if a 37-degree tilt occurred then London could move to the North Pole! On the other side of the world, San Francisco would lie on the equator! OK; I am being a little over-melodramatic I admit, but I hope I am getting across what this sort of tilting of the Earth could potentially achieve. By the way, the technical term for it is 'True Polar Shift'.

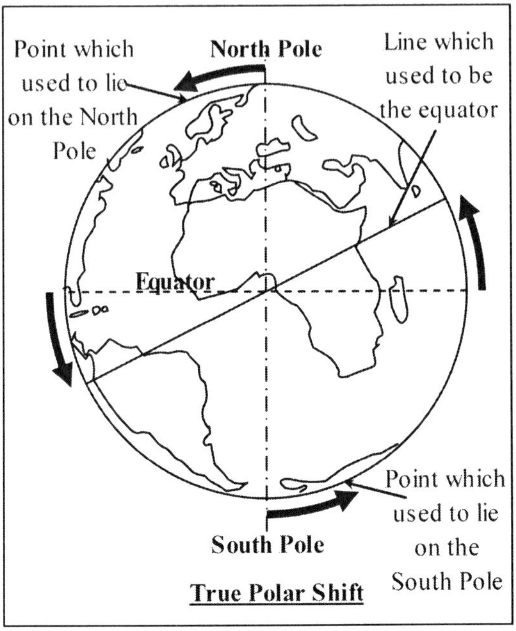

In truth no-one knows what causes the Chandler Wobble, but it definitely represents a slight out-of-balance effect felt by the Earth. Some suggest movement in the deep oceans;[4] others suggest the influence of the atmosphere; personally I favour the effect of snowfall and melt in the different continents. We know for certain that it is caused by the Earth being thrown out of balance because the Indian Ocean earthquake and tsunami of Boxing Day 2004 dramatically affected it, presumably because of significant redistribution of mass within the Earth's crust.[5] And this point brings me straight back to the Great Flood. If the Indian Ocean earthquake upset the balance of the Earth a little, imagine what would have happened in 6250BC when Lake Agassiz, with twice the volume of the Caspian Sea, suddenly drained out into the oceans. This was mass redistribution on an altogether different scale!

Now we're getting somewhere. In the course of just a few days 163000 cubic kilometres of water simply disappeared from one location, Canada, and redistributed itself across the oceans of the world. That's 163 trillion tonnes suddenly not there any more. What would Isaac Newton have had to say about that?

Well, the first thing is to calculate a force, the centrifugal force due to the spin of the Earth which, you won't be surprised to hear, depends on the rate of spin (1 revolution per day), the distance from the axis of spin (about 4000 kilometres in that part of Canada) and the mass (163 trillion tonnes). This centrifugal force is the force that was acting on the water in Lake Agassiz but which suddenly disappeared in 6250BC; this is the force that the Earth suddenly found that it needed for correct balance – but didn't have. One way to look at it is that an equivalent 163 trillion tonne mass on the other side of the world, somewhere in Siberia, suddenly found itself with nothing to counterbalance it.

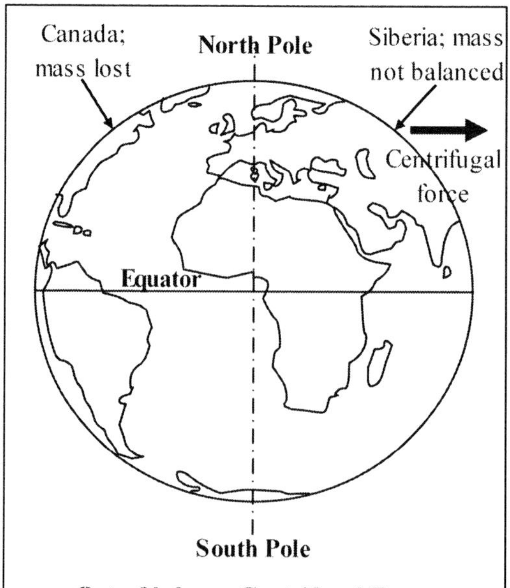

Out-of-balance Centrifugal Force

You can probably imagine what this out-of-balance centrifugal force would do. It would begin to tilt the solid Earth. Following Newton's Law, the force would act on a mass (the Earth) and cause an acceleration. It would be a rotational acceleration – that is to say we are talking about tilt here rather than any actual sideways movement of the planet – and the result would be that Siberia would drift slowly south while Canada headed north. And remember that the shape of the Earth, a squashed sphere, would mean that the further the planet tilted the greater the difference would be between the level of the solid Earth and level of the oceans, which means floods across half the planet while the seas retreated in the other half.

But how far would it go? What would stop it? Well this is where the equatorial bulge really comes in useful. It acts just like the wide central part of a spinning top, giving stability. Any slight tilt of the Earth on its axis would mean that parts of the equatorial bulge would find themselves either north or south of the equator, forming out-of-balance masses which would counteract the one that had just been created when the waters of Lake Agassiz were lost. The result is not too hard to calculate[6] – assuming no change to the overall shape of the planet – and you find that the Earth would tilt by about 120 metres, and that it would take about 5 days to achieve this feat, although it would then wobble back and forth for many months before settling down. The land surface in some parts would rise by 25 centimetres relative to the ocean; elsewhere it would fall by 25 centimetres. No-one would have noticed!

BACK TO THE DRAWING BOARD

C'est la vie. I started with a half-metre global sea level rise due to the waters of Lake Agassiz entering the ocean; I now have just 25 centimetres to add to it due to the tilt of the Earth. It had all looked so promising – and it has all come to nothing. The Earth appears to have built-in stability, courtesy of its equatorial bulge.

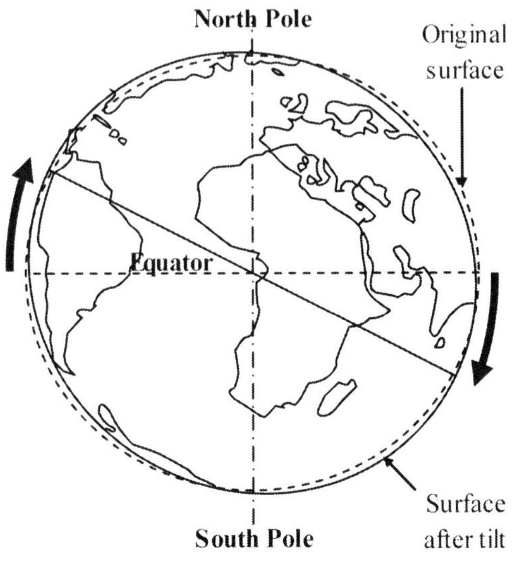

Tilt and the Equatorial Bulge

Yet the evidence in previous chapters has looked compelling; and it can surely be no coincidence that we have identified a potential mechanism for producing a flood as well as a possible trigger, the emptying of Lake Agassiz. Is there anything we have missed?

It is hard to see how the centrifugal force calculation can be wrong, other than the uncertainty in the exact mass of water involved. The inertia of the Earth, the way that its mass resists the rotational acceleration, that too should be pretty reliable. However there was one key assumption that I think we should question, in relation to the effect of the equatorial bulge. Just now I said "assuming no change to the overall shape of the planet", and I am beginning to think that was rather a rash assumption. The Earth may look pretty solid, but just what is down there? And how would it have reacted to the tilting action? These are questions that must be asked. It is time to head off to where no human can ever go – on a journey to the centre of the Earth.

9

Archimedes' Law

Archimedes (287BC-212BC) was famous for running naked into the streets of Syracuse shouting *Eureka!* (Greek for *I've got it!*), and in those days that was probably rather a shocking thing to do. Like Newton, Archimedes was a scientist and during his career he came up with all sorts of handy inventions to improve the world of the ancient Greeks. However on this occasion he was beside himself with joy having just realised one of the fundamental principles of life. He had realised that when he placed a floating object in his bath (rubber duck; model trireme perhaps) it displaced exactly its own weight of water. Well, perhaps you think that should be obvious, as in the case of Newton and his apple, and it probably was obvious to all sea captains as they judged how much cargo to allow aboard their ships, but it takes a scientist to understand the principle properly and write down an equation we can all use.

Archimedes was actually thinking about how to prove the purity of gold in the king of Syracuse's new crown rather than being concerned with continents floating on a mass of dense part-molten rock! But the principle is just the same. A continent will displace its own weight of underlying rock, which means that about 90% of it will sink down into that dense layer. The whole weight of the continent is balanced by just nine tenths (90%) of the volume of denser underlying material.

As it happens I am not really concerned with continents here; I am simply using this as an illustration of how Archimedes' Law can be applied to earth science. And this chapter will most definitely need to apply Archimedes' Law to parts of the Earth. Before that though, we need to take a good look at the internal structure of our planet.

PLANET EARTH

The ground beneath our feet may appear reassuringly solid; the rocks may seem hard and immovable. But we see only the surface of a giant and complex structure and never experience more than a small fraction of what it has to offer. Deep mines may extend several kilometres down into the Earth's crust – but that is as far as any human has ever ventured. Yet a journey to the centre of the Earth would take us nearly six and a half thousand kilometres through varied materials, densities, temperatures and pressures. And despite the fact that none of us can physically make such a journey, the wonders of modern seismic investigation technology mean that we have a pretty good idea of what is down there. The next figure shows the basic structure of our planet.

The layer we live on is the *crust*. It is anything between 5 and 100 kilometres in thickness, thicker under the continents, thinner under the oceans, and it is largely composed of granite and basalt. Current majority opinion is that the continents (largely granite) and ocean floor plates (basalt) have been formed over the millions of years of the Earth's existence as a result of repeated melting and solidifying of materials from the underlying mantle layer. Each time the materials forming the mantle melt, as in volcanoes today, the lighter fractions rise to the surface, just like refining oil – or distilling alcohol. After the first melt these fractions solidify to form 'basalt' and this is the main constituent of the crust beneath the oceans. Next, after further re-melting as basalt plates rub together, the lighter fractions again separate, forming another mineral, which solidifies as 'andesite'. And so the process continues, eventually producing granite, which sits at the light end of the spectrum of so-called 'igneous' rocks, the types of rock that are formed in this way. Of course we get rocks by other means too. Ocean-floor deposits eventually solidify into rock. Vast beds of limestone are found all over the world and these have formed as millions and millions of tiny shell-dwelling creatures have perished and ended up at the bottom of the sea. However the main structural components of the crust are granites, andesites, basalts and the like.

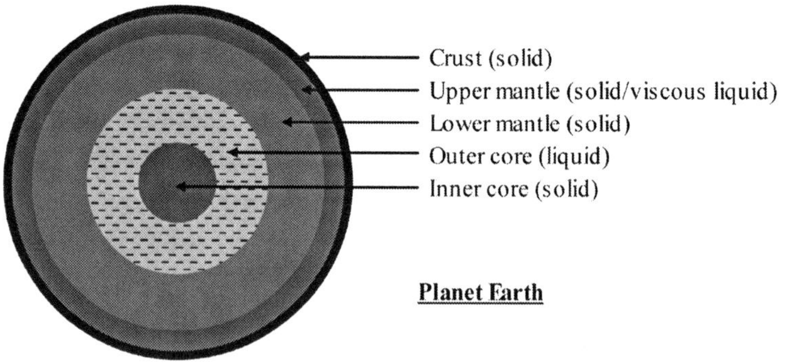

So far so good but we still have over 6300 kilometres to go!

The next layer, the *mantle*, is the source material for the crust. It is composed of a substance known as 'peridotite', which is basically a rock not unlike granite but containing more of certain heavier minerals, so it has a higher density than the crust, which means that the crust is effectively floating on a sea of peridotite mantle. But it would be wrong to think of the mantle as a liquid. It can flow – that's true – but then so do glaciers and ice isn't a liquid either. The Earth's mantle is mainly solid peridotite rock but, being at a much higher temperature than the crust, it is a sort of 'plastic' rock. It can be moulded and deformed. Not only is it more plastic than the rocks we see on the surface, but it also contains a certain amount of genuine molten rock, the magma that fills volcanoes and occasionally spews out across the planet's surface in the form of lava flows.

However I would be lying to you if I claimed to understand the detailed structure of the mantle. We know from seismic investigation that it can be divided into two zones. The upper mantle, down to a depth of about 670 kilometres,[1] is of relatively low stiffness and the combination of semi-plastic rock and lenses of molten magma means that it really does almost behave like a very viscous (i.e. sticky) fluid. The lower mantle, which extends to a depth of about 2900 kilometres from the surface, is still very hot but the high pressures at these depths help to keep it in a mainly solid state. It is therefore stiffer and behaves more like 'normal' rock. To what extent the whole mantle is fractured and fragmented is anyone's guess. We know that fault lines emerge at the surface, lines where crustal plates rub together such as the San Andreas fault complex in California, but it is impossible to know to what extent these crust phenomena are also present lower down, which means it is very difficult to be confident about the properties of the layer as a whole. Nevertheless, while the mantle may be rather less solid than the rocks at the surface, it gives a degree of (possibly misplaced) confidence in the Earth's overall stability.

The next layer however is quite different, and it is the reason why the Earth would rapidly and easily change its shape in the event of any change in the forces acting on it. It is the 2250-kilometre-deep sea of molten iron known as the *outer core*. It is at very high pressure and also at very high temperature, and is subject to internal currents that have an important effect on the magnetic field of the Earth. As a pure liquid, it is weak and unstable. Like all liquids, if you apply pressure then it will simply flow. We are certainly fortunate to have 2900 kilometres of mantle (and a little crust) between us and this unreliable liquid outer core.

Finally, at the point where the pressure becomes sufficient, the liquid iron of the outer core becomes the solid iron of the *inner core*. The final 1200 kilometres or so on this imaginary journey to the centre of the Earth takes us to the middle of an immense ball of iron. It is floating right in the middle of the molten outer core and, being slightly denser than the outer core, it has no desire to be anywhere other than where it is, right at the centre of the planet.

In effect the Earth is not unlike a giant water-bed. The mantle, together with the crust, forms the flexible skin; the liquid iron of the outer core is like the water inside. The whole thing is flexible and will respond to load by changing shape, and the amount of change depends on just how stiff the 'skin' is. So if, for example, I were to dump 3 kilometres of ice onto Scandinavia, as was the case during the last Ice Age, the whole surface of the planet would go down in that region; the mantle would sink into the molten iron outer core until it reached a level at which it felt 'comfortable'. In terms of Archimedes' Law, it would sink down to the level where it displaced its own weight of liquid iron. And the reverse is also true. If the great ice sheet sitting on Greenland melted away we would find that Greenland bobbed up like a ship that had just had its cargo removed as the mantle was pushed up by the pressure in the liquid iron underneath. These examples are not too difficult to visualise once you can picture the Earth as a water-bed, although we need Archimedes in order to calculate things properly.

All of this means of course that my calculation in the last chapter, suggesting that a 120-metre tilt of the Earth would be enough to balance out the loss of Lake Agassiz, was very wrong indeed!

THE REBOUND EFFECT

First things first; as soon as the water drained away from Lake Agassiz, the upward pressure from the liquid iron of the outer core (relieved of the weight of 163000 cubic kilometres of water) would have caused the whole mantle in that part of the planet to rise up until a new state of 'equilibrium' had been reached; according to Archimedes it would have no choice. It's not exactly a straightforward calculation because we have to take account of the way that gravity changes as you go deeper into the Earth. We also have to remember the spherical shape of the Earth, which means that if Lake Agassiz had a surface area of about a million square kilometres, the surface of the liquid iron outer core 2900 kilometres beneath would have an area of only about a third of a million square kilometres. Anyway, the net result once the calculation is done (see Appendix) is that the loss of water mass would be more than compensated for by the extra liquid iron pushing up from beneath, and the supposed loss of centrifugal force that I came up with in the last chapter is utter nonsense; there would actually be an increase in centrifugal force! Canada wouldn't have drifted north at all; it would actually have headed south.

I'm sorry this is all so complicated. It is what happens when you live on an unstable bed of partially molten rock floating on a sea of liquid iron. Nothing is quite what it seems. If the Greenland ice sheet disappeared tomorrow, representing the loss of a very real and extremely large mass, the subsequent rising of the mantle means that we would actually end up with more mass in that part of the world than we started with. In fact you might wonder why we should get so excited about a trifling 163000 cubic kilometres of water when the great ice sheet of North America, with a volume of several million cubic kilometres, has formed itself and then completely disappeared many times over the millennia. The key however is time. Given time the Earth can accommodate these changes quite happily; given time the plastic rock and molten magma within the mantle will deform and flow, increasing or decreasing the overall thickness of the layer, and balance will be restored with a minimum of fuss. The problem comes when the planet gets caught off guard, with no time to react. And thankfully that doesn't happen too often!

So what would really have happened in 6250BC?

THE BIG TILT

Well, if the Earth really had been able to respond like a water bed then we can forget the effect of the equatorial bulge. I suggested in the last chapter that a point 100 kilometres north of the equator was about 230 metres closer to the centre of the Earth than a point on the equator. That's still true; the bulge is a real phenomenon. However, I went on to suggest that if the planet tilted by 100 kilometres, bringing the point that had been north of the equator so that it lay right on the equator, this would mean that it was 230 metres too low – equivalent to a rise in sea level of 230 metres. That was nonsense! If the land thinks it is 230 metres too low then it will simply rise, pushed up by the liquid iron of the Earth's core until it is 'comfortable' once more, i.e. in equilibrium. This is Archimedes' Law again. The whole mantle layer is floating on the liquid iron outer core and it would therefore just bend and flex to maintain the same overall shape as before, like a pontoon bridge floating on a river. There would be no reason for the land surface to be either higher or lower than it 'should' be at any point. And there would be no flood.

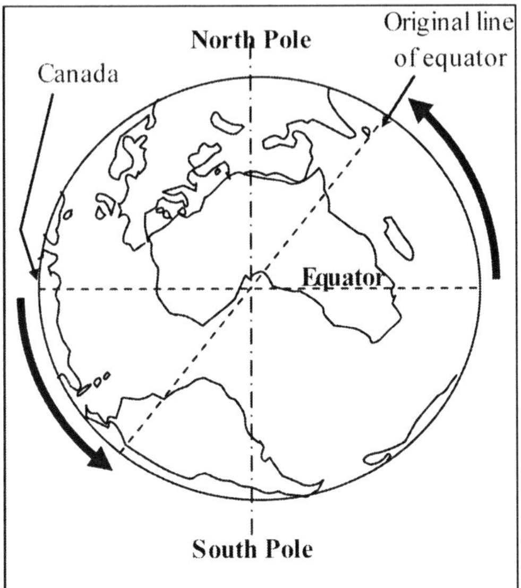

Tilting with nothing to stop it

There would also be no stopping the tilting motion! With no out-of-balance equatorial bulge to counteract the out-of-balance centrifugal force created when Lake Agassiz drained, the tilting would simply continue until the energy of motion had dissipated or until the patch of Canada where Lake Agassiz had been arrived at the equator – and let's face it; this hasn't happened. Clearly I have got something wrong again!

A CLOSER LOOK AT THE MANTLE

I have made one rather dodgy assumption in all this. I have assumed that the mantle is the same thickness everywhere – and it isn't; it varies depending on distance north or south of the equator. Just as the equator sticks out 21 kilometres further from the centre of the Earth than the poles, so the mantle is 15 kilometres thicker at the equator than at the poles[2] – and for the same reason, the centrifugal forces generated by the Earth's spin. This means that, if a particular point on the surface moves north or south, the mantle at that point will end up either thicker or thinner than it ideally should be. This is not easy to show diagrammatically because of the curved shape of the Earth, so on the next diagram I have 'unwrapped' the Earth's mantle, unbending it to lie on a straight line. Hopefully you can see that a tilt of the Earth can be represented by a horizontal shift in the diagram. If, for example, the Earth shifted by 100 kilometres on the surface this would mean that the mantle ended up about 155 metres thicker (or thinner in the other hemisphere) than it should be. Would that have any effect?

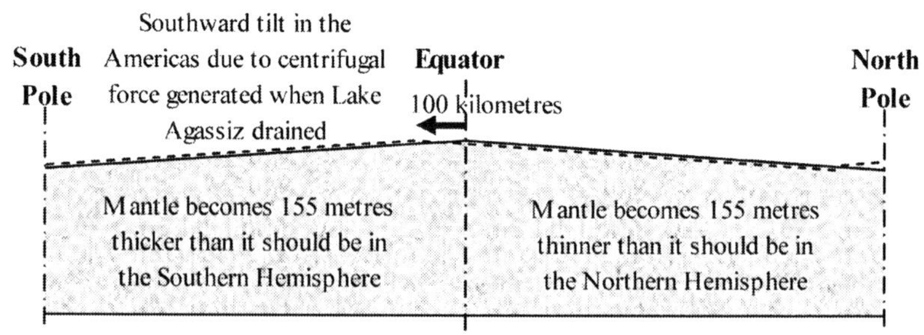

The effect of a southward tilt on mantle thickness

It's time to make use of Archimedes' Law again. Where the mantle is thicker than it should be (in the southern hemisphere in the diagram), i.e. heavier than it had previously been, it will settle down into the liquid iron outer core until it has displaced its own weight of iron – or more accurately the weight of the extra thickness – or more accurately still, a slightly different weight because of the way that gravity varies through the thickness of the mantle. Once again, this is not a straightforward calculation and it is critically dependent on the way that density varies throughout the mantle thickness.[3] However, if I have done my sums correctly (see Appendix) then about 88.5% of the extra thickness will settle back into the liquid iron, leaving just 11.5% sticking up. For a 100-kilometre movement on the surface, leading to the mantle being 155 metres thicker than it should be, this means that it will sink about 137 metres down into the liquid iron core while only 18 metres sticks up, which means there would be an 18-metre rise in ground level relative to the ocean. In the other hemisphere the ground would sink 18 metres – which translates into an 18-metre-deep flood.

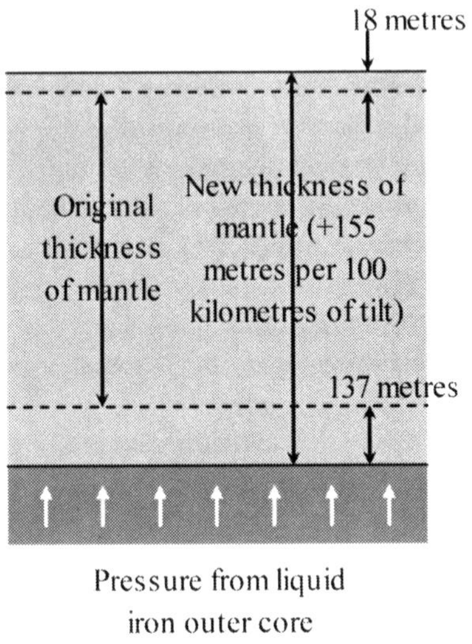

The effect of increased mantle thickness

As soon as Lake Agassiz drained, tilting would have started. This would mean that the mantle ended up either thicker or thinner than it should have been at any given latitude; this in turn would mean that half the planet experienced a rise in land level while the other half experienced a fall. Half the planet would have seen the sea retreat; half would have experienced flooding. Problem solved!

Well, 'partially solved' is as far as I could go. The next thing to think about is how this 'incorrect' thickness of mantle would affect the balance of the Earth. How would it affect the centrifugal forces? Would it perhaps act to resist the tilting motion and so bring it all to a halt before it went too far – just as the helpful equatorial bulge did before we realised how flexible the Earth really was? After all, for every 100 kilometres of tilt, instead of the equatorial bulge we now have an 18-metre increase in the overall size of the planet in the southern hemisphere (in the Americas, where Lake Agassiz was) while the northern hemisphere becomes 18 metres smaller; wouldn't this help?

Quite the reverse I'm afraid. The calculation is not complex although it is once again sensitive to the density assumed at each level within the mantle. And the inescapable and rather disturbing finding from this calculation is that the more the planet tilts the more it wants to tilt! The further it goes, the greater is the imbalance in overall centrifugal force. The 18-metre rise at the surface in the southern hemisphere is a good thing; unfortunately it is more than offset by the loss of 137 metres of liquid iron, replaced by much-less-dense mantle.

This is a very surprising result. It means that once tilting starts there is a serious risk that it will just keep on going. This is not a finding you will read in any existing textbook on earth science that I know of, nor yet in any technical publication. And it obviously hasn't happened! What went wrong?

BACK TO THE DRAWING BOARD AGAIN

Let's recap. I have correctly used Newton's Law to identify the fact that a redistribution of mass on the Earth, giving an out-of-balance centrifugal force, will cause the planet to tilt. I have then correctly used Archimedes' Law to show that the mantle of the Earth will find its own level since it floats on the liquid iron of the outer core. And yet, when I check it out I am left with an impossible and obviously wrong conclusion. If the planet is as unstable as it seems to be according to these latest calculations then the slightest little imbalance and it would just topple – like an iceberg when it becomes unstable due to too much melting low down and simply flips by 90 degrees or so.

But there is something else that I have forgotten. Let's go back to my 'unwrapped' picture of the Earth's mantle, with the southern hemisphere being 155 metres too thick (for a 100 kilometre tilt) and the northern hemisphere being 155 metres too thin. As I then calculated, 137 metres of the southern hemisphere would sink into the core leaving just 18 metres of land level rise; on average, this works out that the mantle would be 59.5 metres (i.e. [137-18]÷ 2) lower than it had been. In the northern hemisphere it would, on average, be 59.5 metres higher. But then what happens at the equator? Looking back at the 'unwrapped' diagram there is a 100 kilometre zone just south of the equator where the transition from 59.5 metres higher to 59.5 metres lower has to take place. Is that reasonable? Can you imagine how hard it is to bend 2900 kilometres of mantle? Archimedes' Law still holds, but the situation here is like tying two ships together and then transferring all the cargo from one ship into the other. One ship wants to ride deeper in the water; the other wants to float higher. The ropes used to tie the ships together will stretch to breaking point and structural damage to the two vessels is not unlikely. And a similar stretching, bending and breaking must have taken place in the transition zone between the northern and southern hemispheres of the Earth as soon as it started to tilt. What does that do to our predictions I wonder?

10

Hooke's Law

The name of Robert Hooke (1635-1703) is, regrettably, rather less well known than those of Isaac Newton and Archimedes; but not to engineers. Engineering is the application of science and for that it is necessary to know how materials behave. And, as in the case of Newton's and Archimedes' Laws, Hooke's Law might be described as nothing more than a statement of the blindingly obvious. He noticed, as probably thousands had noticed before him but not set down in writing, that the amount by which a material stretched was usually proportional to the force applied. So, if a rubber band stretches by 1 centimetre when I hang a kilogram on it, it should stretch about 2 centimetres when I hang 2 kilograms. It's not exactly rocket science but it's pretty helpful to us engineers!

Now admittedly Hooke's Law is not really a universal law applying to all materials; it's more or less correct for metals as well as rubber and it isn't too far wrong for concrete, brick and, importantly here, rock. And it means that we can define the stiffness of a material as the ratio of applied force (well; *stress* actually, force over a certain area) to elongation (well; *strain* actually, elongation divided by original length) and, to sound scientific, we call this stiffness the 'modulus of elasticity'. I'm just going to call it 'stiffness'.

That's enough technical stuff. The point is that in order to calculate how a material bends we need to know its stiffness which, if we were dealing with a standard material like steel or concrete, would be no real problem. It wouldn't be too bad if we were dealing with solid granite. Unfortunately the material of interest here is peridotite, the mineral making up the Earth's mantle, and it is under a rather different set of conditions down in the mantle than it would be if it was in the laboratory, which means it is not going to be easy to deduce the right stiffness value.

I must admit here that the next two or three pages will be a touch technical as they concern quite a detailed aspect of this calculation, although I hope the illustrations will help to explain what is going on. Feel free to speed-read through if numbers aren't your thing.

HOW STIFF IS THE MANTLE?

This is the key question that this chapter is trying to answer. We know that if a solid sample of peridotite is tested in the laboratory we would find it had a stiffness similar to granite[1] – which is about half as stiff as steel. The problem is that it just isn't like that down in the mantle. As I said before, we have no clear idea of the structure of the mantle; we don't even have that good an idea of the structure of the crust. We can guess that the mantle contains faults and joints; we know there must be lenses of molten rock because it appears from time to time at the surface. We also know that there is a fair degree of 'plasticity', at least in the upper part of the mantle, because of the slow way that the Earth continues to recover even today following the removal of the great Ice Age ice sheets,[2] and plasticity suggests a rather lower stiffness (due to high temperatures) than we would measure in the laboratory.

The truth is that it is absolutely impossible to make any direct measurement of the real stiffness, taking account of all these unknown factors. One indirect technique is to measure the way the surface level changes as load is applied, and scientists in Chile have used the fluctuating water level in a large lake to do this. And, sure enough, their finding was that the stiffness was only about a fifth of the normal laboratory value.[3] But this figure only relates to one small part of the crust-mantle layer, with most of the effect coming from the crust. I simply have to find a better way of estimating overall average stiffness – and fortunately I believe such a way exists.

MODELLING THE WAY THE EARTH TILTS

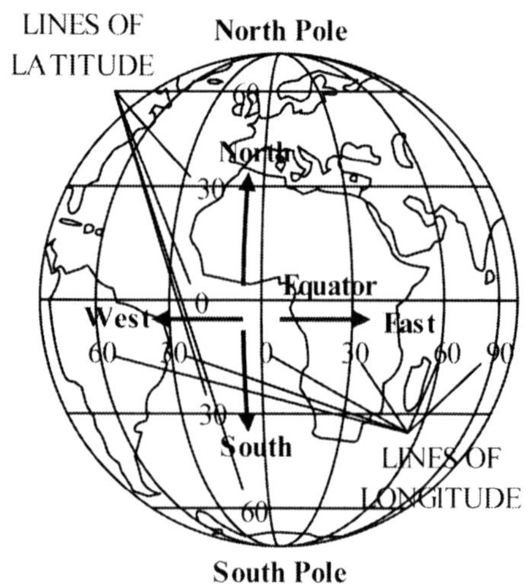

Definition of Latitude and Longitude

Before deciding on the right value for the stiffness of the mantle, let's just review why we need it. It was because, as the planet tilts, so one part of the mantle will become thicker and heavier and will try to sink back down into the liquid iron outer core while another becomes thinner and lighter and wants to rise up a bit. We need to calculate how easily the whole mantle layer bends at the transition between the two. In fact, looking at the planet as a whole, we can divide it up according to which parts are trying to rise and which are trying to sink. If the tilting is set in motion by the emptying of Lake Agassiz then that is where the out-of-balance centrifugal force is, and the tilting will take place on a line running from pole to pole through Canada. This is a line of 'longitude', and if you look at an atlas you will see that it would be about longitude 95 degrees west, just off the left hand edge of the figure.

We can then map out onto a globe just which parts want to rise or sink the most, as shown in the next figure, and it becomes obvious where the problem areas are. Looking for example at the northern hemisphere you can see that there is a gradual change from maximum rising on the left of the figure to maximum sinking on the right, and a gradual change is no problem; the southern hemisphere shows the same thing in reverse. The problem comes at the equator, particularly those bits of the equator on the left and right of the figure where the greatest rising and sinking occur. It is here that we need to be able to calculate the detailed way that the mantle bends.

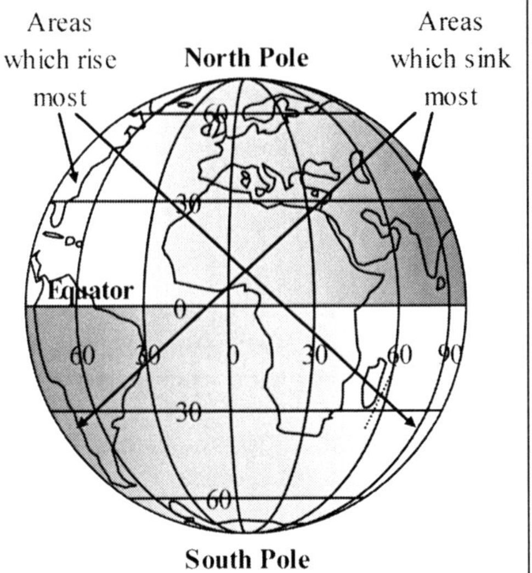

Mantle rising and sinking during tilt

The actual calculation is described in more detail in the Appendix. It isn't by any means a precise calculation. Bearing in mind the uncertainties, particularly in the stiffness of the mantle, there isn't really anything to be gained from increased precision. What this calculation does is to compute the shape taken up by some imaginary line characterising the average level somewhere in the middle of the mantle, and it will include a 'wiggle' just next to the equator, as you can see on the next figure.

Obviously the stiffer the mantle the more gradual the 'wiggle' will be, which means it will be increasingly different from the idealised shape. To calculate what effect this has on the way the Earth tilts, we first need to predict the real shape of the mantle, i.e. the shape of the 'wiggle' at the equator, and then to add up all the components of centrifugal force. And the answer will be different now from the rather dramatic picture painted at the end of the last chapter because of this improved analysis of the exact level of every bit of the mantle. Once the centrifugal forces have been calculated, this lets us know whether the planet wants to go on tilting further or whether resistance is building up and slowing the movement down. After each little increase in tilt the calculation must be repeated, and so on until the motion stops.

So much for how to do the calculation, but we still don't know what stiffness to take for the mantle layer, so how do we know if we have the right answer? Well, the key to answering this question lies in the Chandler Wobble, the real tilting motion that I mentioned back in Chapter 8, a motion that happens today and that has been accurately measured. As I said, it is a relatively small wobble – a maximum of just 13 metres in all, 6.5 metres either way – and we know exactly how long the main oscillation takes, 14 months. In theory therefore all I have to do is to model the Chandler Wobble accurately and that should mean that my assumptions are correct, including that all-important mantle stiffness value. Of course since no-one really knows what causes the Chandler Wobble, I don't really know how to set it going correctly, so I shall just use an out-of-balance centrifugal force like the one created by Lake Agassiz's disappearance but a great deal smaller.

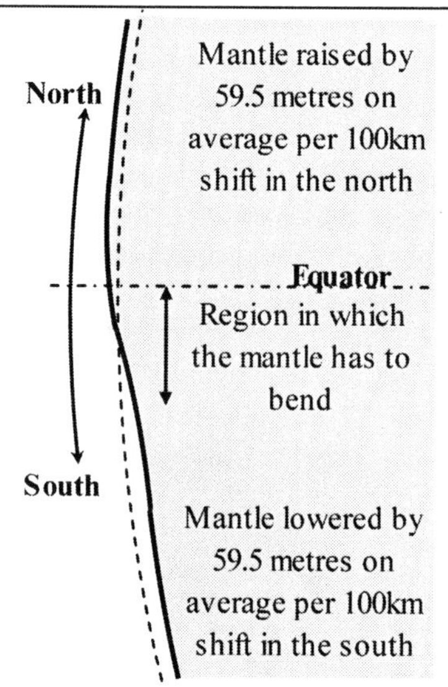

Bending of the Mantle near the Equator

And the result? If I assume a mantle stiffness equivalent to solid peridotite rock at normal Earth-surface temperatures, which would be about 100 'GigaPascals', I find that the Chandler Wobble should, in theory, oscillate back and forth every 5 months – which is wrong. In fact I have to reduce the stiffness to 64 GigaPascals in order to match the actual cycle time of 14 months more or less exactly. It's a rather lower value than we would find in the laboratory, but it's a lot higher than the value deduced by scientists studying the effect of lake level changes in Chile (18 GigaPascals).[4] By the way, I needed an out-of-balance force of just 0.05%

of the force created by Lake Agassiz's demise, which is probably about the sort of impulse that differences in snowfall and melt between America and Siberia would generate – not that this is relevant here.[5]

Please don't worry about all these 'GigaPascals'. Most engineers wouldn't really know what to make of them either! I needed to give you some numbers so that you had a feel for how the stiffness of the mantle (taken as a whole) compares with laboratory values. Anyway, the key point is that I now have a stiffness value, which means I can now do the 6250BC calculation for real. The excitement is almost too much to bear.

Unfortunately your excitement will have to be contained for a while longer. I'm afraid the result of the prediction is not nearly as exciting as you might have hoped. With a full Lake-Agassiz-scale impulse I predict that the tilt would be just 25 kilometres and that it would take 7 months to develop, which I have to say is a slightly disappointing finding. I guess it's a bit closer to matching the evidence of the flood myths in that we have a duration of several months; but 25 kilometres simply isn't enough. It gives me a maximum flood in middle latitudes of just 5 metres, an absolutely stupendous event – don't get me wrong – but quite inadequate to explain any of the evidence from archaeology, biology etc. It certainly isn't enough to flood the Jordan valley and the Dead Sea, nor to bring Pre-pottery Neolithic B civilisation crashing down or to wipe out all life on the Indus plain; neither could 5 metres inundate Lake Malawi or Lake Turkana. And remember that 5 metres is a maximum at middle latitudes; it would be less the further away you were from the danger areas, the two edges of the shaded globe in the figure before last. The only significantly deeper floods are predicted to occur near the equator and the poles because of the difference between the calculated 'wiggle' in the mantle and the idealised shape; in fact I predict a 20-metre-deep flood near the equator, quite a sight in coastal Ecuador I would imagine but still nowhere near enough to match the evidence.

YET ANOTHER TRIP BACK TO THE DRAWING BOARD

Well, let's look on the bright side. I am getting ever closer to the sort of event that the evidence demands. A couple of chapters ago I had a majestic 25-centimetre flood lasting a few days; in the last chapter I had an unstoppable overturning of the planet and complete extinction of all life on Earth; at least this time I have something a little more reasonable. But the question is: just what else could I possibly have forgotten? Is there anything wrong with any of my assumptions? Newton's Laws are pretty much absolute – unless you start approaching the speed of light and I don't think we are in that sort of ball park. Archimedes' Law is similarly absolute as long as I have taken proper account of the geometry of the Earth and the way that gravity varies as you go down through the mantle. But what about Hooke's Law? I said that it was an excellent law for metals and that it was 'about right' for rocks, but does it really apply to the mantle with its lenses of molten magma, its faults and fractures?

We could just give up at this stage and claim, quite rightly, that no-one knows exactly what the properties of the mantle layer are. Or we could give it our best shot and make a few estimates. Let's give it one more go.

11

Murphy's Law

Einstein may have his law of relativity, Keppler his laws of planetary motion, but of all the great laws governing human endeavour, Murphy's Law must surely be the most universally accepted. Put simply it says: "if something can go wrong then it will"! It is a law that is ever-present in scientific research, with obvious application to military strategy, economics and, probably, human relationships. OK; I admit it. My tongue is in my cheek. It's not really that anything particular has gone wrong with the calculations I have been trying to do over the course of the last three chapters but there always seems to be another layer of complexity just when I think I should be arriving at the answer to the riddle of what happened in 6250BC.

Anyway, there is no escaping it. I simply have to revisit Hooke's Law. It's true that a simple application of Hooke's Law with a stiffness of 64 GigaPascals for the Earth's mantle enabled me to model the Chandler Wobble pretty well, but it is equally true that the material comprising the Earth's mantle is far from being the nice uniform material that this implies. We need to think about it in a little more detail I'm afraid.

THE NATURE OF THE MANTLE

As I said before, a sample of peridotite, the principal component of the mantle, would have a stiffness of about 100 GigaPascals in the laboratory; yet I find that when I look at the very slight degree of bending induced in the 2900-kilometre-thick layer as a whole by the Chandler Wobble its stiffness appears to be just 64 GigaPascals. Why should this be?

Well; I can think of three excellent reasons. The first is that the very high temperatures in the mantle layer mean that the rock is a bit less 'rock-like'. I used the word 'plastic' earlier because, given time, we know that it will deform. And we would not expect the stiffness of a 'plastic' rock to be quite as high as a really hard and relatively cold rock.

The second reason is that the structure of the mantle probably includes faults and joints, such that it resembles a giant three-dimensional jigsaw of interlocking pieces. The pieces may be massive, many hundreds of miles across perhaps and with a similar depth, but that wouldn't alter the fact that it was a 'discontinuous' material. Each giant segment of intact peridotite may be slipping against its neighbour. As an engineer, I am used to effects like this in fractured concrete, and I know that it wouldn't take that many faults or joints to drastically reduce the stiffness of the layer as a whole.

The third and final reason for reduced stiffness is the presence of liquid rock, i.e. magma. Overall there isn't very much, not enough to interrupt shear waves from progressing through the layer according to seismic investigations. Nevertheless, liquids are quite different in their properties from solids, even a solid that's a little 'plastic'. Liquid has no stiffness at all – all it has is the property known as 'viscosity', a measure of how sticky it is. And molten rock is quite fluid. You may not personally have witnessed a lava flow, but you will surely have seen television pictures of fast-flowing streams of red-hot lava pouring down the sides of a volcano. As I write Mount Kilauea in Hawaii is in full flow. This is the type of 'lubricant' which probably fills some of the faults between solid peridotite blocks. All liquids have a viscosity, and molten rock is no exception. It's a lot stickier than water, but on the other hand it's not nearly as sticky as asphalt, and you may have noticed the tendency for asphalt on a road surface to go out of shape in hot weather. Given time, it will flow; given time, so will the mantle of the Earth.

So, I have three reasons for reduced stiffness. The first, that you would expect a plastic rock to have a lower stiffness, in no way invalidates Hooke's Law; the stiffness may be lower but it is still just a stiffness. The second, however, is a bit of a headache. You see; if the mantle is actually faulted, like a fractured concrete slab, then its behaviour will be different and it won't obey Hooke's Law. Its stiffness will tend to reduce the more it deforms. So, if 64 GigaPascals is a realistic stiffness value when the deformation of the mantle is very small (as in the Chandler Wobble), then you would expect it to be a little less if it underwent a much larger deformation (for example tilt due to the draining of Lake Agassiz). It probably wouldn't reduce much – after all, the mantle is still mainly solid rock – but I wouldn't be at all surprised if it reduced by several percent, and that will make a difference to the calculation.

The third reason for low stiffness, the presence of liquid magma, also makes life a bit complicated. Liquid flows, and the longer it has to flow the further it will flow. So, if the deformation of the mantle happens quickly then the whole layer might appear to have a certain stiffness; if it takes longer then it might appear to be less stiff – because the liquid within it would have had more time to flow. This means that if 64 GigaPascals is the right stiffness for a 14-month-long wobble, it should reduce a bit if the movement takes significantly longer. On the other hand, when I look at estimates that scientists have made for the overall 'viscosity' of the Earth's mantle[1] then I have to say that I can't see this adjustment being too significant.

I am sorry for having to be so thorough but, mindful of Murphy's Law, I don't want to be caught out again. Anyway, the conclusion from all that was that, while the first reason (hot, plastic rock) may be responsible for much of the stiffness reduction, it is the second reason (faults and fractures) that gives me most cause to doubt the applicability of Hooke's Law. And it is a serious doubt, one that I can't ignore. I need to include some sort of a rule which says that the stiffness reduces slightly the more the mantle deforms. You can see the way I have chosen to do this in the Appendix if you wish.

THE DAY THE EARTH TURNED

I fully admit that I have no direct means of knowing how much stiffness reduction to build into my prediction. As I said, it probably wouldn't be much. But let's take a look anyway at what would have happened to the planet following the sudden death of Lake Agassiz if the mantle stiffness had actually been a little lower than 64 GigaPascals. How much difference does a small change in stiffness make? The answer is that it makes a great deal of difference. A modest reduction to 60 GigaPascals merely trebles the tilt from 25 to 75 kilometres. But if we go a little further, to 56 GigaPascals, the movement becomes almost unstoppable, increasing the tilt to a massive 1000 kilometres; the resulting flood would be measured in hundreds of metres over much of the planet! In fact, when I link the reduction in stiffness to the amount of deformation then I find there is something of a 'tipping point'. The prediction suddenly jumps from a moderate 1-degree tilt (just over 100 kilometres on the surface) to a mind-boggling 20 degrees (over 2000 kilometres on the surface) when the rate of stiffness reduction reaches a certain level. If this calculation approach is right then the flood of 6250BC would either have been quite modest, no more than about 20 metres deep, or it would have been of stupendous proportions, many hundreds of metres deep. There is no middle ground. Once the planet had passed a 'point of no return' it would have just kept on going.

Even with all the evidence from Part 1 of this book, it is still a shock to see that there really is excellent physical reason for this flood. From what I know of the behaviour of fractured materials, it would be no surprise at all if the Earth's mantle lost 10-20% of its stiffness as it deformed,[2] although I have no way of estimating the true figure with confidence based on the materials alone. On the other hand we have a large body of indirect evidence from all around the world. I am seeking an explanation for a flood deep enough to inundate much of Australia as well as the steppe land of Russia and Central Asia, the Indus and Ganges valleys, Egypt, Iraq and northern China. It may even have reached Lake Malawi. By way of an upper limit I am quite sure that it didn't enter Lake Baikal. And, remarkably enough, it seems that all this indirect evidence is compatible with a 20-25 degree tilt of the planet, the Lake Baikal limit steering me down toward the lower end of the range. I am therefore almost forced to conclude that the true tilt was indeed approximately 20 degrees.

But now the question arises: what happened next? The prediction as it stands would be for a continuing oscillation back and forth, between zero and 20 degrees. Of course the motion would not go on for ever. Energy would be lost within the mantle as it deformed, converted into heat, melting rocks and creating magma, possibly explaining the increased level of volcanic activity for the next thousand years and more. Energy loss inevitably occurs when you have a faulted material with slip taking place between solid blocks; it is equally inevitable when you have molten rock flowing back and forth along the faults. And in the end, after many centuries of ever-decreasing cycles of oscillation (and repeated floods), the planet would have come to rest at some intermediate position, around 10 degrees different from its starting point. But I see no evidence at all that this is what really happened.

In fact I have neglected one last thing. The overturning force generated when Lake Agassiz vanished would immediately have started to diminish as the plastic rock of the mantle slowly 'flowed'. It would have been a little bit like pushing back the pendulum of a clock and then half letting go. With an ever-reducing 'push' from the Lake Agassiz mass imbalance, the Earth would not have been slowed down on its return journey quite as much as it had been 'speeded up' initially – which means that when it returned it would have overshot the mark, passing right through its original orientation and tilting the other way. It wouldn't have gone quite so far this time since the Lake Agassiz effect was now acting against it, not to mention the continuing loss of energy caused by all that deformation.

But what then? Would it have swung back for a third time?

Well; three possibilities present themselves. Either the loss of energy was enough to prevent the planet from ever regaining its original orientation after its second tilt, or the remaining push from Lake Agassiz was just enough to get there but no more; or else, possibly, it may have been enough to carry right on through for a third trip. It is not too difficult to predict the first 20-degree tilt, nor the second, at just under 20 degrees, but I certainly could not claim to be able to calculate which of the next three options was correct. However I think we have enough indirect evidence to be pretty sure which one it was. It is reasonable to believe that the Earth tilted first one way and then the other since there seem to be flood myths from all parts of the world, but there is little in the myths to suggest more than one flood anywhere,[3] nor that the end point was anything other than a return to the original orientation. In the next illustration I am therefore assuming that the Earth made a full recovery from its second tilt, but that it never managed a third.

You can see in the next figure that, if the assumptions made are correct, then this most remarkable of dramas was played out over a period of 6 years. Depending on the land elevation at a given location, the resulting flood would have lasted anywhere from a few months to well over a year. For 2 years following Lake Agassiz's demise not much happened. The Earth was tilting steadily but the combination of forces was only just enough to keep the motion going. You could think of it as a roller-coaster trundling slowly down the first gentle part of its run. But then things began to accelerate – as if the roller-coaster took a sudden dive down a really steep dip in the track. Resistance built up as the polar regions found themselves ever further out of position, and this led to a rapid slowing down and reversal of motion – like the roller-coaster reaching the bottom of a dip and then shooting up the next slope. If you really were in a roller-coaster you would know exactly what was coming next however; you would have a 'breather' for about a second at the top of the rise before you plunged headlong once more into another stomach-churning valley. The Earth behaved in a similar fashion. It slowed as it regained its original orientation – but it had too much momentum; it kept going and then speeded up again as it tilted the other way. The same slowing down process happened again, at a slightly reduced maximum tilt angle this time, and the planet returned once more to its original orientation, slowing as it approached. However, sufficient energy had now been lost from the system and there wasn't enough momentum to take it on a third excursion.

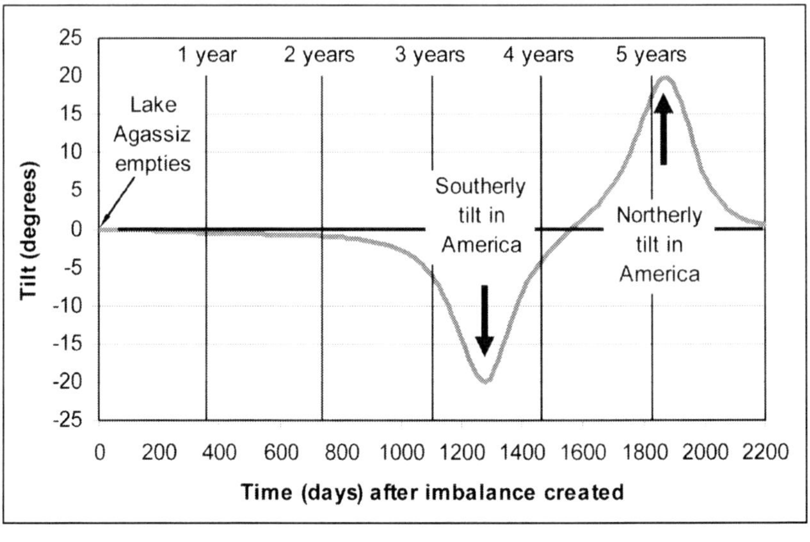

So, out of all this theory a very clear picture emerges; the Earth really could have flipped by at least 20 degrees in response to the sudden emptying of Lake Agassiz, enough to cause severe flooding in many parts of the world. There really is a mechanism that could have caused it. Now if we were discussing some far away planet in the vastness of space this would be perfectly acceptable. But here? On planet Earth? Can I be serious? Yes; absolutely. The combination of indirect evidence (language, myth, archaeology, nature) with direct modelling of the planet's response to Lake Agassiz's disappearance is, in my view, practically conclusive.

By the way, you might be wondering if there is any danger of this happening again – perhaps even soon. Well, if the calculation is right you would need to shift over 90% of the volume of water in Lake Agassiz to get the Earth to tilt in this dramatic way; anything less and the mantle would be stiff enough to return the planet to its rightful position with minimal fuss. And as I look around the planet today I simply cannot see any possibility that this sort of thing could happen. There doesn't appear to be any such water volume waiting to be released,[4] and it is hard to envisage any other mechanism that could possibly redistribute mass on this scale over such a short time period. I wouldn't want to give you the impression you were safe, but I would seriously doubt that mankind is in danger of another 'Great Flood'.

THE GREAT FLOOD, 6250BC

A 20-degree tilt would be truly devastating. The sea level rise (or fall) on the longitude of tilt, the line from the North Pole through the spot where Lake Agassiz was, down to the South Pole and back up on the other side of the world, would be 400-500 metres in middle latitudes. The further you were from this line the lower the flood would be, and if you were exactly 90 degrees from it there would be very little flood at all. New Zealand for example lies on this most fortunate of longitudes.

However, as the next figure shows, the bending of the mantle near the equator and the poles would give much greater flood depth locally, over a kilometre for those unfortunate enough to live on the 20-degree line of latitude and just the wrong longitude (in India or Mexico). Conversely, no-one living on the equator (parts of South America, central Africa, Singapore) would have seen any flooding at all.

This flood was therefore quite different in its depth at different locations. It also varied considerably in duration. The maximum rate of rise in middle latitudes was just over two metres per day, giving some hope of escape depending on the local lie of the land. At latitude 20 degrees you would have had to flee from an ocean that rose a full metre every four

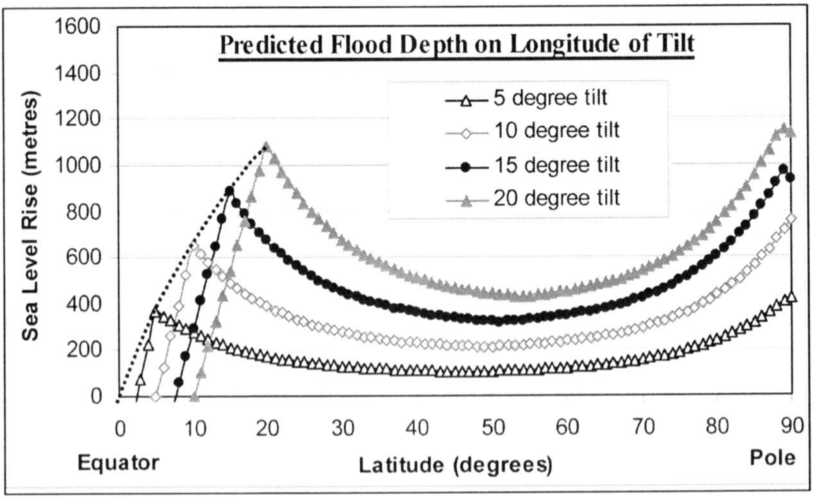

hours. Closer still to the equator, although the overall rise was less the rate would actually have been even more rapid than this. This was a flood to be taken seriously!

SUMMARY

The conclusion from the calculations described in Part 2 is that, in all probability, the Earth had no choice but to tilt dramatically in response to the release of water from glacial Lake Agassiz and so to cause massive floods. If the laws of physics applied and if realistic estimates are made for density and stiffness (and stiffness variation), then the prediction is that the planet underwent around 20 degrees of tilt, on a line of longitude through the location of Lake Agassiz. The absolute magnitude cannot be predicted with full confidence simply from the physical properties of the Earth but, based on the indirect evidence of myth, archaeology, language, biology and geology, 20 degrees is likely to be approximately correct. Furthermore, the loss of energy due to the bending and flexing of the Earth's mantle means that the movement could not have gone on for ever; it is quite reasonable to suggest that it shifted first to the south (on the longitude of Lake Agassiz) and then by a slightly smaller angle to the north, before eventually returning to its original orientation.

So the pieces of the jigsaw have fitted together in the end; the mystery has been solved. Part 1 supplied a time window (around 6250BC) and plenty of evidence that something seriously destructive occurred at this time. We now have a mechanism. In my view, we can say without reasonable doubt that we now know the true cause of all those flood myths. We now know without reasonable doubt that the 'Great Flood' was a very real and very dreadful occurrence.

If you still doubt me then I respect your view, but I hope that you will nevertheless be prepared to join me as I try to paint a picture of what I believe happened during those fateful 6 years. In Part 3 I am going to take you on a world tour. I want you to see this event through the eyes of those who were there. I want to show you the true magnitude of this disaster and the effects that it had on life on earth, both human and animal, as well as those many mysteries – not spoken of in Part 1 – that have puzzled experts in various fields for years but which find their logical solution in this quite remarkable event.

PART 3

THE EXPERIENCE

12

The Native American's Tale

It's official; it really happened. A myth is just a myth – but in this case all the many hundreds of flood myths have a real foundation in truth. And it all began in North America. The Ice Age was in its death throes; Lake Agassiz and the ice dam that retained it were the last reminders of millennia of freezing temperatures and mile-thick ice sheets. The average temperature across the planet was actually very similar in 6250BC to today, but the sheer volume of ice that had covered North America meant that it took thousands of years to melt. And as it melted back to the north, so it acted as a dam behind which Lake Agassiz was contained. When the dam broke, presumably in late summer or early autumn when the season's ice melt had reached its maximum, the immediate effect would have been the sudden exposure of thousands of square miles of lakebed. It would be three years before the truly earth-shaking consequences of this event became apparent.

THE NORTH AMERICAN FLOOD

The next map shows the zone which would have been flooded with a 20-degree tilt of the planet. It includes the whole of the Mississippi-Missouri basin, in fact the whole of the great plain between the Rocky Mountains in the west and the Appalachian Mountains in the east. Only the high ground known as the Ozark Plateau would have stuck up above the high water mark. The speed of advance of the waters would not have been particularly dramatic in North America; it would have been like the tide coming in and just not stopping. In fact, that is exactly how the Haida people of the Queen Charlotte Islands described it.

> …… *As the tide rose and touched her feet, she moved up a little and sat down again. The tide kept rising, following the woman. The villagers soon became alarmed at its unprecedented height and, having no canoes, they prepared rafts and provisioned them with fish and water. At last the tide covered the whole island. The people saved themselves on rafts.*[1]

The maximum rate of sea level rise would have been around 2 metres per day. So, for those who had high ground available nearby it would not have been difficult to escape. Of course, without knowing when or if the sea would stop its advance many will have chosen their high ground unwisely and found it to be insufficiently high. The vast majority of the population across the central United States would certainly have perished.

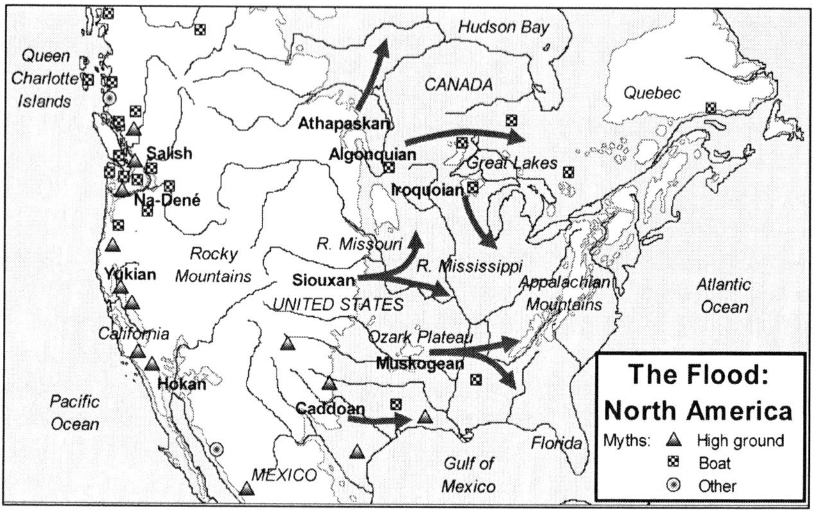

EAST OF THE ROCKIES

The map shows my estimates for the locations of the various language families of North America in 6250BC, together with subsequent directions of spread, based on the sort of language analysis presented in Chapter 4, and they undeniably fit well with the extent of flooding predicted.[2] There would of course have been survivors in the east also, speaking languages with no descendants today. The cultures of the west would eventually prevail right across the continent.

By way of support for this language analysis, the geographical closeness shown on the map between two of the language families, Athapaskan and Algonquian, actually ties in very nicely with the distribution of one of the more widespread flood myths from North America. Back in Chapter 2 I introduced the story told by the Chippewa people. They speak an Algonquian language and today their territory lies close to where the word 'Algonquian' is written on the map. The story was of an old man who had foreseen the flood, built a canoe and survived – not in any way unique so far. However the distinctive features were that the man took on board a beaver, an otter, a muskrat and a duck, which he sent in turn to find land. The duck returned with mud in its bill and the old man somehow changed the mud into solid ground by blowing on it. Here are the versions told by two other Algonquian tribes, the Cree people who live a little to the east of the Chippewa and the Montagnais from Quebec.

Wissaketchak was an old magician. A certain sea monster hated him and, when the old man was paddling his canoe, the monster lashed the sea with his tail, causing waves that flooded the land. Wissaketchak, though, built a great raft and gathered on it pairs of all animals and birds. The sea monster continued its exertions and the water continued to rise until even the highest mountain was covered. Wissaketchak sent a duck to dive for earth, but the duck couldn't reach the bottom and drowned. He then sent a muskrat which, after a long time, returned with its throat full of slime. Wissaketchak moulded this slime into a disk and floated it on the water; it resembled a nest such as muskrats make on ice. The disk swelled and Wissaketchak made it grow more by blowing on it. As it grew and hardened he sent the animals into it. It became the land we now inhabit.[3]

God commanded a man to build a large canoe. The man did so and when he embarked the water rose until no land was visible anywhere. Weary of seeing nothing but water the man threw an otter into it. The otter dived and brought up a little mud, which the man breathed on and caused to expand. ....[4]

The animals may vary but the stories are essentially one and the same. In the Montagnais version by the way the mud also eventually grows to become dry land. Now take a look at three further versions, this time told by Athapaskan peoples (the Sahtu, the Tinneh and the Sarcee) from different parts of the far north of Canada.

The wise man, foreseeing the possibility of a flood, built a great raft, joining the logs with ropes made from roots. .... *Then came a great flood, with water gushing from all sides, rising higher than the trees and drowning all people but the wise man on his raft. As he floated he gathered pairs of all animals and birds he met with. The earth disappeared under the waters and for a long time no-one thought to look for it. Then the muskrat dived into the water looking for the bottom, but he couldn't find it. He dived a second time and smelled the earth but didn't reach it. Next beaver dived; he reappeared unconscious but holding a little mud. The wise man placed the mud on the water and breathed on it making it grow.* ....[5]

The deluge was caused by a heavy snowfall one September. One man foresaw the flood and warned his fellows, but in vain; the flood covered their intended mountain escape. The one man survived in a canoe he had built and he rescued animals from the waters as he sailed about. In time, he set the beaver, the otter, muskrat and arctic duck to dive into the water in search of earth, but only the duck succeeded, bringing some slime in its claws. The man spread the slime on the water and breathed on it to make it grow. ....[6]

The world was flooded and one man and one woman survived on a raft on which they collected all kinds of animals and birds. The man sent a beaver (or some say a muskrat) diving to the bottom and it brought up a little mud. The man shaped this to form a new world. It was at first so small that a little bird could walk around it, but it grew and grew.[7]

There can be little doubt that all these stories have a common origin, yet they are told from one end of Canada to the other. Language analysis however places the ancestors of the Athapaskan and Algonquian language families in adjacent territories in 6250BC[8] (on the shores of Lake Agassiz as it happens), and it has to be supposed that the story originated then and there, not far from modern Chippewa territory. Notice some of the details. The flood is reported to have come on the land in September which, according to the prediction in the last chapter, is compatible with the emptying of Lake Agassiz some 3 years earlier, at the end of the summer. After 3 years the waters should have risen to about 180 metres above sea level, more or less the level at which Lake Agassiz had previously stood; 6 months later and the flood would have peaked at about 450 metres above sea level.

Basically the essential elements of this story make good sense: the inexorable rising of the water; mass drowning of those with no escape route; survival on a home-made craft; and the fact that the flood lasted a long time (6 months to a year would have been typical in that region).

Far to the south, if my map is correct, the Muskogean-speaking people managed to survive in the hills in and around the Ozark Plateau. Here is the story told by one of their descendant tribes, the Choctaw, who would later make the journey east to Alabama.

> *A prophet was sent by the high god to warn of a coming flood, but nobody took notice. When the flood came, the prophet took a raft. After several months he saw a black bird. He signalled it but it just cawed and flew away. Later he sighted and signalled a bluish bird. The bird flapped, moaned sadly, and guided the raft towards where the sun was breaking through. Next morning he landed on an island with all kinds of animals.*[9]

The duration (several months) is right; the island filled with animals is just what would be expected as all living creatures tried their best to escape the rising tide. Actually this story and that of the muskrat and his friends are two of relatively few to have originated to the east of the Rocky Mountains, and there is good reason for this. For a start there has been considerable population movement east of the Rockies and stories are now told in locations distant from their place of origin, something that might logically contribute to memories being lost as they lost their geographical meaning. However I believe a more important reason concerns the lie of the land. While in the west many would have seen the full development of the flood, simply retreating as necessary up the hillside, in the flatter east few would have seen the waters and lived to tell the tale. Basically, if the flood reached your village or encampment you would probably drown. In the gently-sloping landscape to the east of the Rockies there would have been nowhere to go to avoid the waters. And if the flood never reached you, then you would probably never realise that it had even occurred! There would only have been a narrow strip of territory near the high water mark where survivors would have had tales to tell and retell; hence the relative paucity of flood myths from the eastern lands. As for those in the far east, in the Appalachians, they would certainly have had stories to tell – but unfortunately, though their genes may have survived, their languages and cultures have not.

Returning to the languages, there is actually something a little odd about what happened in North America. Modern Native American cultures can be traced back to a parent culture known to archaeologists as 'Clovis', with an origin in around 13000BC somewhere in the western United States.[10] So the question arises: why did the language of the Clovis people apparently travel less than 1000 miles over the course of the next six and a half millennia – at a rate of only about 3 miles per generation? A more typical rate seen in other language spreads from around the world would be 6-10 miles per generation,[11] which means that Clovis languages should really have reached the Mississippi by 6250BC. The Great Flood of course provides a reasonable explanation. The progress of language and culture probably had indeed reached the Mississippi by 6250BC – only to be wiped out right across the flood-plain.

ARCHAEOLOGICAL CLUES

In 7th Millennium BC America there were no cities like Jericho and there was no agriculture. The evidence for human occupation comes in the form scattered finds of stone tools, spear heads and the like, 'middens' – i.e. heaps of debris such as shells or nut husks serving as evidence of food consumption, fire hearths etc. It isn't much to go on and most of what there is cannot be accurately dated, but it's a lot better than nothing! The problem for many archaeologists however is that 'nothing' is exactly what we seem to have in the years around 6000BC, at least in certain parts of North America. There is widespread reference in the archaeological literature to a so-called 'cultural hiatus' lasting one or two thousand years from about 6000BC, which in practice means a lack of evidence, and this situation applies across the plains of the mid-west, the Great Lakes region, and the southern and eastern coastlands.[12] Now a lack of evidence does not necessarily mean a lack of human beings and there are plenty of researchers who reject the idea of any widespread reduction in population. Along the coasts, so it is often argued, the evidence now lies beneath the sea since ocean levels have risen by tens of metres since those times; on the other hand where underwater archaeology has been carried out, off the coast of Florida, there is clear evidence for a major change in settlement pattern and, probably, an actual gap in occupation at exactly this time.[13]

Archaeologists in states either side of the Mississippi river draw comfort from the fact that some archaeological sites can still be found from the 6th Millennium BC, but on closer inspection these sites are almost all in areas of high ground (the Ozark Plateau or the Appalachian Mountains).[14]

It is also noticeable that clear archaeological 'horizons', i.e. levels where particular types of artefact are found over large areas, dry up from about 6000BC. In the 7th Millennium BC the so-called 'Kirk' horizon can be seen over much of the eastern United States dating down to about 6500BC. This is followed by a relatively short-lasting 'bifurcate' horizon covering much the same territory. And then that's it – until the 'Morrow Mount' horizon, which can be dated to about 5200-4500BC.[15] Those who seek what they would term as a rational explanation for the missing years commonly claim that the 6th Millennium BC was a period when each part of the United States did its own thing and artefacts were not traded or copied widely for some reason, or that the evidence has been there all along in the form of various odd unclassified finds in styles not widely represented elsewhere. On the other hand, if this is correct then one might ask: what prompted this change in human lifestyle? The usual answer is a highly plausible one, namely the climatic change seen all over the United States (to a much drier climate, particularly in the west) and this in turn is tied into the 8.2ka BP event discussed in Chapter 7. The same reason is given for a marked decrease in the number of bison that roamed the plains in the 6th Millennium BC.[16]

Clearly these archaeological conundrums would prove nothing on their own. Some archaeologists are happy to admit that the 6th Millennium BC is virtually devoid of human evidence in several parts of the United States; others are not. However I can't help noticing that wherever one looks in the archaeology of the United States there are signs of continuity of occupation in the high ground east and west of the Mississippi basin, while there are disputes over the interpretation of lack of finds from all the lowland areas. Given the cautious nature of archaeologists this is about as ringing an endorsement of the Great Flood as we could hope for!

Anyway, so much for those living and dying east of the Rockies; let me now give you a taste of what those in the west experienced.

THE WEST COAST

The greatest concentration of American flood myths comes from British Colombia and Washington State, where steep-sided mountains rise abruptly from the sea. Many are the tales of escape by canoe or by climbing the mountainside; many too are the tales of drowning and loss. Here is a selection from various West Coast peoples.

When the Squamish saw the great flood coming they held a council and decided to make a giant canoe. The men worked day and night to make this canoe, the biggest ever, and the women made a long rope of oiled cedar fibres with which they tied the canoe to a giant rock. They put every baby into the canoe with food and water. They selected the bravest young man and the mother of the youngest baby to go as their guardians. No-one cried as the waters rose and drowned everyone else. After several days the man saw a speck far to the south. By the next day he could see that it was a mountain top, Mount Baker. He cut the rope and paddled to it, and made a new home there.[17]

One of the good men heard from heaven that a flood was coming. He told the other good people and they decided they would make a dug-out boat from the largest cedar they could find. Soon after the canoe was finished the flood came, filling the valleys and covering the mountains. The bad people were drowned; the good people were saved in the boat.[18]

A great rain came, making rivers and lakes overflow the country. A man named Ntcinemkin took refuge with his family in a very large canoe. The others fled to the mountains but the flood rose to cover them too. The people begged Ntcinemkin to save at least their children. He didn't have room enough to hold all of them, so he took one child from each family, alternating males and females. The flood covered all land except the peak of Split Mountain on the west side of Lower Lillooet Lake. When the waters dropped, the canoe grounded on Smimelc Mountain.[19]

A great rain came which lasted a long time and waters covered the land. The people retreated to high land, but they were all swept away and drowned except for one pair who found safety on the highest peak. They lived on fish, which they cooked by placing them under their arms. They had no fire and, as everything was wet, they couldn't get any. The waters sank and all present Native Americans are descended from that couple.[20]

Water covered the world except for the top of the highest mountain. People escaped to there, but they were starving. The water went down, leaving the ground a soft mud.[21]

A great flood once forced the Zunis out of their valley to take refuge on a nearby tableland. But the flood rose nearly to the top of the tableland and the people, fearing it would drown them all, decided to offer a human sacrifice to appease the angry waters. A youth and maiden, children of two priests of the rain, were dressed in finery and thrown into the flood. The waters began subsiding immediately.[22]

As you can see on the previous map, there are many, many more tales from the western seaboard than these six, each throwing its own individual light on an event which none who saw it could possibly comprehend and which caused untold human misery and loss. For example, the story told by the Maidu people that only one couple escaped when the whole Sacramento valley of central California became like an ocean is fully understandable in the light of the flood predictions.

CENTRAL AMERICA

As we move south of the 30-degree line of latitude, crossing the border into Mexico, so the waters deepen. The inhabitants of Central America were therefore fortunate that they lived in a mountainous land with near-continuous chains of peaks stretching from northern Mexico to Panama. Speakers of the four Central American language families shown on the next map would certainly have been inconvenienced and those living on the Yucatan peninsula would have drowned, but most others would have survived. Many would have seen it all. They would have watched as the coastal plain was inundated, and they would then have had to retreat ever higher up the mountainside. Stories of escape by boat would be entirely unsurprising.

Because the zone of devastation was comparatively narrow, there would have been no subsequent large-scale population or cultural movement. Yucatan was the only sizeable area which would have been left depopulated, and Mayan speakers would rapidly have filled it once more.

Central America has many folk memories of the year the Great Flood struck. Here is a tale told by the Nahua people, the Aztecs of old.

> *The deluge overwhelmed mankind. Only a man named Coxcox and a woman named Xochiquetzal survived in a small bark. They landed on a mountain called Colhuacan and had many children. These children were all born dumb until a dove from a lofty tree gave them languages, but different languages so that they couldn't understand each other.*[23]

Many of the tales from Central America show unmistakable signs of influence from the Noah story, so it isn't always easy to isolate original elements; but here is another which seems to have survived uncorrupted, this time from the Huichol people of north-west Mexico, like the Nahua, speakers of an Uto-Aztecan tongue. It is a bit flowery in language and I have omitted the highly mythical ending, but it certainly paints a picture of a pretty impressive flood.

> *Grandmother Nakawe told a man that a flood was coming in five days. Following her instructions he built a box from the fig tree and entered it with five grains of corn and beans of each colour, fire with five squash stems to feed it and a black bitch. She closed him in and caulked the cracks and he floated in the flood for five years, first floating south, then north, then west, then east, then rising upward as the whole world flooded. Finally the box came to rest on a mountain near Santa Caterina.*[24]

I won't make you plough through further Central American flood myths with their various gods and mythical creatures. Suffice it to say that the one uniting theme is that the sea once flooded the land in a very major way. However I do want to draw your attention to a serious mystery that, in my

view, lies hidden amongst the languages of Central America. One of today's language families is not shown on my map at all since I suspect that it was not yet present in Central America in 6250BC. It is a language family that may well owe more to this flood than any other on earth.

THE ORIGIN OF OTOMANGUEAN LANGUAGE

'Otomanguean' is the name given to one of the largest linguistic groupings in Central America before the Spanish conquest, stretching right across central Mexico from coast to coast. The great 1st Millennium AD city of Teotihuacan and the civilisation it governed was almost certainly Otomanguean speaking. And in most language references you will read that Otomanguean, like almost all the other language families of America, is to be placed in a single massive grouping known as 'Amerind', although it is true that many linguists doubt the validity of this Amerind 'super-family'. My own measurements, reported in *The Origin of Tongues*, support the linking of the four Central American language families shown on the map, Uto-Aztecan, Mixe-Zoque, Mayan and Chibchan, together with all the languages of South America; but these measurements definitely do not support the inclusion of Otomanguean. In fact Otomanguean languages are so different in grammar and form from those of neighbouring families that it is as if they simply emerged from thin air! This, of course, is impossible. Everything has an explanation somewhere – and in this case the Great Flood may well be the key to that explanation. For a start, the time depth of the Otomanguean family is, in my estimation, about 8000 years; the ancestor language was therefore spoken around the time of the flood. And, remarkably, the only other languages which I find to bear a significant resemblance to Otomanguean are to be found some 7000 miles away on the other side of the Atlantic Ocean in southern Nigeria, languages such as Igbo and Efik. There are strong grammatical similarities; word form is also similar; and my evaluation of the language family that includes Igbo and Efik (known as 'Niger-Congo') suggests that Otomanguean separated some time between about 10000BC and 6000BC.

I need hardly tell you that this explanation for the origin of Otomanguean is not yet 'mainstream'! But then neither (at the time of writing) is the Great Flood. However, once the Great Flood is accepted with its countless stories of escape by boat, the matter becomes distinctly plausible. As we shall see in a few pages' time, the whole floodplain of the river Niger and its tributaries, the region where Igbo and Efik are spoken today, would have been flooded, forcing people to seek higher ground. With no significant high ground for 100 miles, many would have taken to boats and tried to reach safety that way. For most there could be no safety; the journey was too far and the currents impossible to fight. Hundreds of boatloads of suffering humanity may have been swept out to sea.

But what then? The currents of the Atlantic sweep across from Africa, along the north-east coast of South America and into the Caribbean and the Gulf of Mexico. These were the currents which Thor Heyerdahl utilised when he 'navigated' his reed boat *Ra* across the Atlantic. For any of the Nigerian boat people who managed to keep themselves alive long enough, a new life awaited on a new continent, a continent inhabited by cultures at a lower technological level. For any who made it, long-term survival was not only possible but likely. Their descendants would have overwhelmed the native Central American population just as European settlers would nearly eight millennia later.

I might also suggest that the giant stone heads carved by the Olmec civilisation in around 1000BC, some of which have features that look distinctly African, are further evidence for this trans-Atlantic colonisation. Unfortunately, although Mexican genes tend to be around 10% African in origin, the recent influx of slaves from Africa means that it is quite impossible to use this as meaningful evidence.

Both Mixtecs and Zapotecs, two of the main Otomanguean-speaking peoples today, have flood stories to tell, although in neither case is it possible to infer a specifically African setting. Here is an unfortunately rather brief and uninformative account given by the Mixtec people.

> *The earth was once well populated, when mankind committed a magical fault for which they were punished by a great deluge. The Mixtec people descended from the few survivors.*[25]

There is no way I can prove that the cultural ancestors of the Mixtecs arrived from Africa. Nevertheless, the fact that a language-based deduction finds such a neat solution in the Great Flood, an event which I now consider virtually proven, raises this proposal far above the level of 'utter madness' where anthropologists and linguists would otherwise place it!

TALES FROM THE AMAZON

Although Africa was once known as the 'dark continent', that title today belongs more properly to South America. Even this year (2008) a hitherto unknown tribe was discovered deep in the jungle of the western Amazon. And this of course means that there is every chance of tales surviving uncorrupted by the influence of other civilisations. If you look back at the flood map you can see that vast swathes of South America would have been under water, although notice the 200-mile-wide strip along the equator, and notice too that three of South America's language families may well have survived courtesy of tribes inhabiting this central belt.[26] Admittedly the time depth of these families is much greater than the 8250 years since the flood, but the land area was large enough to accommodate a variety of tongues from each group. The rather patchy distribution of Arawakan languages today, with pockets of speech from the Andes to the north coast, is almost certainly a consequence of the flood, which left speakers both in the Andes foothills and in the equatorial strip while wiping out all traces in between. And in case you are reluctant to rely on what you might consider dubious linguistic evidence there is now real archaeological data confirming that vast areas of central Brazil were apparently devoid of all human life for a millennium or so at exactly this time[27] – something which would defy all logic without an event such as this extraordinary flood.

Notice the precarious survival of Tupian and Waikuruan languages. Most Tupian languages can be traced to an ancestor dating to about the time of the flood, an ancestor which presumably survived in the Andes foothills. Those Tupian languages that had separated earlier may have already reached the safety of the Mato Grosso. Waikuruan found refuge in the sierras to the south. As for the Cariban and Panoan families, they can both be traced to ancestor languages spoken in approximately 6250BC and, as you can see on the map, both families stem from areas of high ground.[28]

In Chapter 2 I illustrated the rich variety of flood stories from South America, tales of escape to mountain caves in the slopes of the Andes, of people placing their children on rafts and, in several cases, of escape in the tops of trees. In a jungle environment it would have been natural for people to seek sanctuary in the forest canopy. Most would have died as the water rose high above the trees but those around the edges of the flood, where the depth was less, would have experienced a survivable few weeks before the waters receded. Those just north or south of the equatorial strip would have had the rather depressing experience of a second flood about a year after surviving the first, as the land they lived on crossed and then re-crossed the line of the equator. The water level would have risen and fallen very sharply each time.

The next few tales allow us to catch a glimpse of what it must have been like for those Amazon peoples who lived through it – and those who did not.

> *Omauwä and Yoawä dug a hole for water, but they dug so deep that water gushed forth and covered the jungle. Many drowned. Some of the first beings survived by cutting down trees and floating on them. This was such a strange thing to do that they became foreigners and floated away, and their language gradually became unintelligible. The Yanomami survived by climbing mountains, namely Maiyo, Howashiwä and Homahewä.*[29]

> *In the time of the great flood, the age of water, the sea broke against the Encamarada mountain chain and people were forced into canoes. One man and one woman were saved on the high mountain called Tamanacu, on the banks of the Asiveru.*[30]

> *The pious and wise chief Marerewana was informed of the coming of the flood and saved himself and his family in a large canoe. He tied the canoe to a tree with a long cable of bushrope to prevent it drifting too far from his old home.*[31]

> *In a former time when there were a great many people, the earth sank. Then water began to seep out. It kept rising until it became a flood. Some boys were saved, plucked from the water by a white bird; all other people drowned.*[32]

Naturally, with the passage of time these stories have grown in the telling; hence the various clearly mythical ingredients such as the actions of the bird in the last tale. But the essential elements are still clear enough, and they tell the story of a terrible human catastrophe, an event so traumatic that its memory is alive to this day, transmitted orally though over 300 generations.

LANDS OF THE SOUTH

The vast sea that Amazonia had become during the Great Flood extended south through the plains of Bolivia, Paraguay and northern Argentina. Apart from the tops of a few inland sierras, where Waikuruan-speaking tribes survived, the waters extended uninterrupted until they merged with those of the South Atlantic. It is therefore unsurprising that archaeologists find little evidence of human activity in lowland Argentina during the 6th Millennium BC.[33] Only in the coastal ranges of the east and the Andes to the west would life have been possible. The next two stories reflect experiences on either side of the continent.

A flood once covered the whole earth except for the top of the coastal range, Sierra do Mar. Members of the three tribes Coroados, Cayurucres and Cames swam for the mountains holding lighted torches between their teeth. The Cayurucres and Cames wearied and drowned, and their souls went to dwell in the heart of the mountain. The Coroados made it and stayed there, some on the ground and some in the branches of trees. Several days passed without food and without the water lowering. Then some saracuras, a species of waterfowl, flew to them with baskets of earth. The birds began throwing earth into the water, and the water sank.[34]

The flood came after a strong earthquake and volcanic eruption. The people took refuge on a mountain called Thegtheg which floated close to the sun. Afterwards, when the Mapuche felt an earthquake they would flee to the hills carrying bowls to protect their heads from the sun's heat.[35]

This second story, from the Mapuche people of southern Chile, is particularly interesting. If you remember, I had made the point that there is evidence for increased volcanic activity around the time of the flood from ice core data, which is logical since the titanic flexural stresses induced in the Earth's crust and mantle as the planet deformed would intuitively be expected to produce earthquakes. Here perhaps is further evidence that this did indeed occur. Notice also the rather strange-sounding details about being close to the sun and the need to protect one's head from the sun's heat. The flood in South America occurred as the planet tilted north on the longitude of the Americas, which would have brought the Mapuche from their temperate climate to the latitude of the Atacama Desert!

On a similar subject let me remind you of the tale from Tierra del Fuego that I quoted in Chapter 2.

Léxuwakipa, the rusty brown speckled ibis, felt offended by the people, so she let it snow so much that ice came to cover the entire earth. This happened at the time of Yáiaasága, when men seized power from the women. When the ice melted, it rapidly flooded all the earth. People hurried to their canoes but many didn't make it, and more perished when they couldn't find sheltered places. Some people reached the five mountain tops which stayed above the flood. These mountains were Usláka, Wémarwaia, Auwáratuléra, Welalánux and Piatuléra. The water stayed at its high mark for two days and then rapidly lowered.[36]

The first part of this story is most revealing. The initial movement of the planet following the emptying of Lake Agassiz would have been experienced in America as a southward drift. Tierra del Fuego would have found itself within 1000 miles of the South Pole! Admittedly, if Lake Agassiz emptied at the end of the Northern Hemisphere's summer, in September, then this trip into the Antarctic would have occurred some three and a half years later, which would be late summer-early autumn in the Southern Hemisphere, but it would still have been a serious shock to the system for any who experienced it, particularly since the land would have been raised to an altitude some 400 metres above its normal level. Snow and ice in serious quantities would be expected. As the planet then began to tilt the other way, bringing Tierra del Fuego north into latitudes of unaccustomed warmth, the snow would undoubtedly have melted fast while the ocean level rose; it would be quite logical for the people to make a connection between the two phenomena. As for men taking over from women – that remains a mystery that I cannot explain!

SUMMARY

I have concentrated on the human story of the flood in the Americas since there are few scientific issues to look into other than a clutch of archaeological puzzles. There are no great lowland lakes of significant age, and most of the Caribbean islands are mountainous enough for the survival of most species. The survival of lizard species on low-lying islands and the post-flood dispersion of iguanas were covered in Chapter 5. On the other side of the Americas, off the coast of California, the Channel Islands are known as wildlife havens, but Santa Cruz Island, the island with by far the greatest abundance of indigenous species rises to a height of over 700 metres, compared to a predicted flood depth of a little over 500 metres at that point. There would have been plenty of land for species survival. The same is true of the Falkland Islands and South Georgia, in the South Atlantic, while the famous Galapagos Islands, source of so much inspiration for Charles Darwin, lie almost exactly on the equator and would have seen virtually no flood at all; the many species of Darwin's finches were safe enough.

The American story is a fascinating one and we are fortunate to have so many high-quality descriptions of the event still in circulation. These give us a strong feel for what the Great Flood was really like. But at the same time as the oceans were filling the plain of the Mississippi and Missouri rivers, so, on the other side of the world, they were also beginning to inundate the relatively low-lying continent of Australia, inhabited in 6250BC by peoples who were living as their ancestors had for tens of millennia, deep in the Palaeolithic era (the Old Stone Age).

13

The Australian Aborigine's Tale

Despite the decimation of Aborigine tribes over the course of the last 250 years or so, the memory of an earlier catastrophe is still strong, as I have illustrated already in Chapter 2. And if you look at the next flood map you can see why. Right across the northern and southern parts of the continent and through swathes of the central belt, Australia would have disappeared beneath the waves. Northern Australia sits just at the most unfortunate latitude and would have experienced a sea level rise of up to 750 metres. It is easy to see why this event set in motion major changes in the distribution of human cultures. Once the waters had receded, two thirds of Australia would have been devoid of life, animal or human.

ABORIGINAL MYTHOLOGY

However, every cloud has a silver lining, and the deaths of the many spelt new opportunities for the few. The rules of the survival game had changed; those with the requisite skills now had over half a continent at their disposal, and they and their descendants steadily reclaimed the land. A similar jostling for position must have gone on in the animal kingdom too.

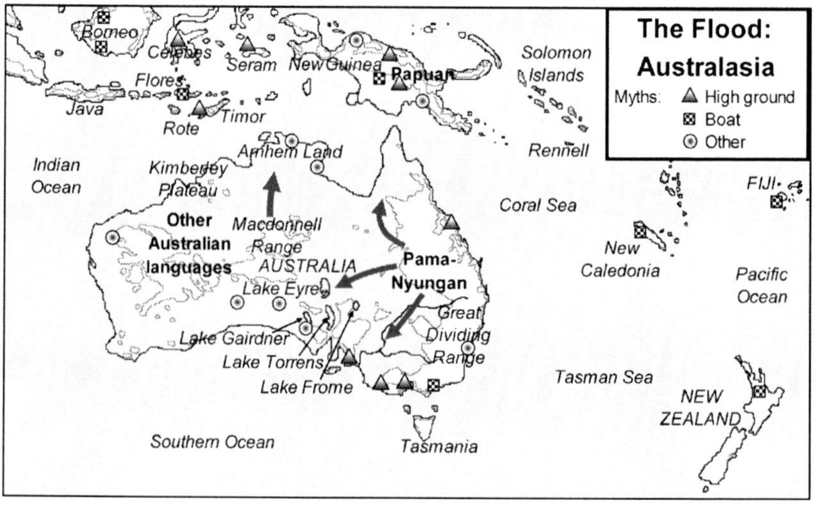

As it happens it was a people from eastern Australia, who survived the flood in the hills of the Great Dividing Range, who were best placed of all. They found themselves with the means and the opportunity to spread and multiply across the deserted lowlands, and the culture and language they brought would, over the course of the next eight millennia, come to cover about 80% of the continent. These were the ancestral Pama-Nyungan speakers.[1] Non-Pama-Nyungan cultures are only found today in central and north-western regions, notably in Arnhem Land which, as you can see on the map, would have been totally immersed. The ancestors of these northern survivors must have ridden out the flood among the peaks of the Kimberley and Macdonnell Ranges. There would also have been other survivors in the south of course, but their culture has since been swamped by that of the Pama-Nyungans.

In Chapter 2 I presented Australian tales of rising waters and escape to the hills, the same types of story as we've just heard from America. I will admit however that there is a very high mythical content in many Australian tales, which makes it more difficult to take them seriously. This one, from Victoria State in the south-east, is a typical example.

> *A man fishing in a lake caught a young bunyip, a fearsome water monster. His companions begged him to let it go lest he anger the water monsters by killing it, but he refused to listen and began carrying it away. The bunyip's mother, in a rage, caused the waters of the lake to follow the man who had taken her young. The waters rose higher and higher, covering all the country. The people fled to a high hill, but the flood rose and when it touched their feet they turned into black swans.*[2]

I'm not too sure what a bunyip is, although it sounds to me like a crocodile, but I am quite sure that it wasn't actually the cause of the flood. But that's not the point; nor is the matter of people turning into swans. The point is that this tale, like all those from America, contains a description of water rising to cover the land. As far as the narrator was concerned it was the waters of a lake that were rising; there was no way he could know that the lake was actually being filled by the ocean. He possibly didn't even know there was such a thing as the ocean.

Let's take a look at another tale from south-east Australia, this time concerning the animal kingdom.

> *The animals, birds and reptiles became overpopulated and held a conference to determine what to do. .... They decided to destroy the over-numerous platypus family. They did their ceremonies repeatedly and a great storm came, flooding the land. The frilled lizards had made shelters on the mountain, and some animals managed to make their way there, but nearly all life was destroyed in the great flood. When the flood ended and the sun shone again the kangaroo called the animals together to discover how the platypus family had fared. But they could not find a single living platypus. ....*[3]

In the real flood of course the platypus would have been safe enough in the upper reaches of the rivers of south-east Australia where they live today. Reassuringly, platypus survivors were eventually found in the flood myth also! And as far as the rest of the animal kingdom goes, the rich and varied wildlife endemic to Australia would have had no trouble surviving in the upland regions in the west, centre and east of the continent. Though their populations would have been greatly reduced they soon recovered to fill the land. Both Tasmanian aborigines and the Tasmanian tiger would likewise have happily survived in the hilly island of Tasmania, both to be rendered extinct eight millennia later by European settlers.

Archaeology is of limited help in Australia unfortunately. The finds are too few and too scattered to give any real indication of population dynamics in these far off times. Geology however has a tale to tell and, like the geological tales told in Chapter 6, it is a tale of salt.

THE SALT FLATS OF THE INTERIOR

As I write, Lake Eyre in southern Australia is once more a sixty-mile-wide stretch of open water – but this is unusual; its normal state is a seemingly endless expanse of white salt. The same is true of Lakes Torres, Frome and Gairdner, each only slightly smaller than Lake Eyre itself. And one subject which geologists have not yet resolved is how to explain the quantity of salt. It's not that there is too much; the puzzle is why there is so little. It is usually assumed that the salt we see today has been washed in by water, either via rivers or groundwater, but if this is the case then the current 400-million-tonne deposit covering Lake Eyre's bed simply isn't enough; it only represents about 5500 years' accumulation based on analysis of inflow water quantity and quality.[4] A similar mismatch can be seen in the other lakes,[5] and this contrasts with the very considerable thicknesses of other sediments found beneath the salt crust, speaking of ages measured at least in tens of thousands of years. Undoubtedly salt loss to underlying saline clays is part of the explanation but, even accepting this, there still doesn't seem to be as much salt as there should be! Compare the situation in Australia with the Lake Bonneville salt flats of Utah (perched well above flood level), the site of numerous land-speed record attempts. The quantity of salt on the Lake Bonneville site is just about what it should be, representing about 11000 years of run-off accumulation since the last time the lake drained out into the Columbia river system. The salt thickness at Lake Bonneville is up to 2 metres;[6] in contrast the thickness in Australia is generally no more than a few centimetres. It just doesn't quite add up.

Logically there are two possible explanations. The first is that there never has been much salt, presumably because rainfall in ancient times was even less than today and so episodes of lake flooding were very rare – but this doesn't sit well with the significant thicknesses of alluvium present. The second explanation is that something has removed the salt, and the only way of achieving that on a large scale is by dissolving it in water. The current salt layer in Lake Eyre (and the other lakes) dissolves whenever the lake fills – only to crystallise out again as it evaporates. But if seawater were to have filled the whole south Australian basin it would have dissolved the salt that had accumulated in earlier millennia,[7] leaving behind a series of large lakes, each with a salinity of 3.5%, that of the ocean,[8] and a total salt load that may well have been about what today's lakebed and salty groundwater deposits contain.[9] Without the Great Flood there is no obvious solution to this geological conundrum.

THE ISLANDS TO THE NORTH

When the aboriginal population of Australia first arrived, whenever that may have been, we can be quite sure that humans had also colonised the island archipelago lying just to the north. The island of New Guinea has its own aboriginal peoples with their own long history; it even has its own population of kangaroos. And here too memories of the day the flood came are still very real.

Over large parts of Indonesia and New Guinea the flood would have been very deep indeed, so it was just as well for the inhabitants that most of the islands are mountainous. The unique wildlife of New Guinea was safe enough. The 735-metre-high island of Komodo, home to the Komodo dragon, would have just about seen off the predicted 600-metre rise in sea level. Besides, Komodo dragons are good swimmers, regularly crossing between islands, and their range in 6250BC, at a time when human disturbance of their habitat was minimal, was almost certainly much wider than today and may have extended to the adjacent island of Flores.

Mention of Flores leads to thoughts of *Homo Floresiensis*, the species of dwarf hominid (known colloquially as the 'hobbit') found on the island, with associated remains dated to as recently as about 11000BC.[10] *Homo Sapiens* remains are only found on Flores from around 9000BC, and there are folktales of 'little people' among the inhabitants of Flores to this day, rather like the folktales of the flood which we have found to contain so much truth – which suggests that 'hobbits' may well have survived to 9000BC and beyond. The Great Flood may even have been the 'last straw', the event that finally saw them give way in the face of competition from their much larger relatives, us!

I am aware of one short flood story from Flores, telling of an ancestor who was saved from a great flood in a ship.[11] But Flores is far from alone in this respect. There are flood myths from the island of Rote to the south, from Celebes to the north, Seram and New Guinea to the east and Borneo to the west. By way of example, here are two of the tales from New Guinea, one from Borneo and one from Rote.

> *Lohero and his brother were angry with their neighbours, so they put a human bone into a small stream. Soon a great flood came forth and the people had to retreat to the highest peaks until the sea had receded. Some people descended, and others made their homes on the ridges.*[12]

> *A flood covered the whole world except for the summit of Mount Tauga. When the wave threatened to cover even that, the rock face cracked and the diamond-studded head of Radaulo, king of snakes, emerged. His fiery tongue licked out to taste the waves, and the water, hissing, retreated. Radaulo slowly uncoiled and pursued the water all the way back to the ocean bed.*[13]

> *A great deluge once drowned many people. A few people survived by escaping in boats to the one mountain peak remaining above water. They dwelt there for three months until the flood subsided.*[14]

> *In former times the sea flooded the earth and destroyed all plants and animals; only the peak of Lakimola remained above water. A man, with his wife and children, took refuge there, but the tide kept slowly rising for some months. They prayed to the sea to return to its old bed. The sea answered: "I will do so if you give me an animal whose hairs I cannot count." A pig, goat, dog and hen failed this test, but when the man threw in a cat the sea sank abashedly.*[15]

Although the mythologies revealed by these tales are all quite different I am sure you will observe that the central theme, a flood that rose to cover the land and that endured for several months, is the same in each case. However, let me draw your attention to one particular detail, from the second of the New Guinea stories, where it is said that the water was pursued "back to the ocean bed". The flood that hit New Guinea occurred during the first tilting of the Earth, and it would have been followed by the sea retreating to several hundred metres below its usual level as the Earth tilted the other way, exposing many miles of seabed. The reference is therefore absolutely logical.

There are certainly questions as to whether all these tales actually originated where they are now told. As far as New Guinea is concerned there is no reason to think otherwise. New Guinea has plenty of mountains to flee to and the population of 6250BC were the direct ancestors, both biologically and culturally, of the Papuan peoples of today.[16] On Borneo however the situation is more ambiguous. The current population speak Austronesian languages, which only arrived in Borneo in about 2000BC.[17]

On the other hand a large part of the population of Borneo are not exactly 'biological' Austronesians; they have merely adopted Austronesian language under the dominant influence of later immigrants. Their culture is a composite, and it's quite possible that the flood tales were inherited from their biological (and doubtless Papuan-speaking[18]) ancestors.

As for Rote, it should actually have disappeared entirely beneath the waves! However the story may well have derived from elsewhere, most likely from the neighbouring and much larger island of Timor.

Overall, the Indonesian islands have a healthy number of flood myths, particularly the Papuan-speaking island of New Guinea. The ingredients of mountains rising steeply from the sea and a very ancient population with a long and largely undisturbed history are exactly those that would logically be expected to give us plenty of surviving folktales of the flood. Elsewhere many memories were doubtless lost when the Austronesian-speaking peoples moved in, although they would of course have brought their own folklore with them. And Austronesian folklore has left its mark much further afield than the islands of Indonesia. If they were indeed carrying their own tales of the flood, these are the tales that are now heard right across the Pacific Ocean.

THE OUTER ISLES

If the stories told on the islands of the Pacific, from places like New Caledonia, Fiji, New Zealand and Hawaii, genuinely relate to events in 6250BC then we definitely have to discount any geographical references; there would be no humans in any of these lands for thousands of years! Colonisation of the Pacific commenced in about 1000BC; Hawaii wasn't reached until about 500AD and New Zealand not until about 1000AD.[19] And in the case of New Zealand there wouldn't even have been much flooding. The country lies almost exactly 90 degrees from the longitude of Lake Agassiz and so would have experienced nothing worse that a few metres worth of coastal flood here and there; yet here is the Maori flood story shown on the map, and it tells of something much more impressive than this.

> *Long ago there were a great many different tribes, and they quarrelled and made war on each other. The worship of Tane, the creator, was being neglected and his doctrines denied. Two prophets, Parawhenuamea and Tupunuiauta, taught the true doctrine about the separation of heaven and earth, but others just mocked them, and they became angry. So they built a large raft at the source of the Tohinga river, built a house on it and provisioned it with fern root, sweet potatoes and dogs. Then they prayed for abundant rain to convince men of the power of Tane. Two men named Tiu and Reti, a woman named Waipunahau and other women, also boarded the*

raft. Tiu was the priest on the raft and he recited the prayers and incantations for rain. It rained hard for four or five days, until Tiu prayed for the rain to stop. But though the rain stopped the waters still rose and bore the raft down the Tohinga river and into the sea. In the eighth month the waters began to thin; Tiu knew this by the signs of his staff. At last they landed at Hawaiki. The earth had been much changed by the flood, and the people on the raft were the only survivors.[20]

Despite the mention of New Zealand geographical features there is no way that this story, if real, stems from New Zealand. Similarly references to various landmarks in stories from Fiji, the Cook Islands, Tahiti, and Hawaii, all have to be treated with a healthy degree of disbelief. The sole thing these stories have in common is the claim that the ocean rose to cover the land, but the stories have clearly been given local meaning in each place where they are now told. Here for example is a Hawaiian tale.

Lalohona, a woman from the depths of the sea, was enticed ashore by Konikonia with a series of images. She warned him that her parents, Kahinalii and Hinakaalualumoana, would cause the ocean to flood the land so that her brothers, the pao'o fish, may search for her. At her suggestion they fled to the mountains and built their home in the tops of the tallest trees. After ten days Kahinalii sent the ocean; it rose and overwhelmed the land. The people fled to the mountains, and the flood covered all the mountains; they climbed the trees, and the flood rose above the trees and drowned them all. But the waters began to subside just as they reached the door of Konikonia's house. When the waters retreated, he and his people returned to their land.[21]

The Polynesians who colonised the islands of the Pacific were all Austronesian speakers. Their forebears set out from the Spice Islands, off the coast of New Guinea, in about 1500BC, and Austronesian history can be traced back archaeologically, genetically and linguistically to the island of Taiwan. That is where the cultural ancestors of modern Austronesian speakers lived in 6250BC and Taiwan is therefore the likely original setting for all the stories now told in all the islands of the Pacific. And Taiwan is a mountainous land, ideal for experiencing the flood in all its power – and yet surviving to tell the tale.

PACIFIC LAKES

But just because there were no human inhabitants of the islands of the Pacific in 6250BC, that doesn't mean that the flood had no impact there. The issue of land-based life in the Pacific has been covered in Chapter 5 already, notably the point that flightless rails found on several islands including low-lying Henderson Island most probably arrived within the last 2000 years or so. But in fact the greatest visible effect of the flood would not be expected on dry land but in some of the enclosed areas of water found on some of the islands, chief of which is Lake Tegano on Rennell Island, which was once a lagoon of the sea surrounded by a coral atoll.

Rennell Island in the Solomon group is now what is known as a 'raised atoll', pushed up over the course of the millennia by some 150 metres, and it is also Number 37 on the United Nations endemic species list. According to the predictions here the flood should just about have covered it completely. Lake Tegano, a large lake of slightly salty water inhabited by several endemic species, should certainly have been inundated. As far as land species go, I see no reason to doubt that the current fauna of Rennell Island have arrived within the last 8000 years, including the Rennell Island flying fox (really a large bat) – cyclones are known to have blown flying foxes across tens of miles of ocean. But in Lake Tegano there is an endemic species known as Crocker's sea snake, and it is quite different from all other sea snakes. How is this possible if the sea invaded Lake Tegano as recently as 6250BC?

Crocker's sea snake is much smaller than other species and if it wasn't for modern genetics we would assume that it had been a distinct species for many tens of thousands of years. Fortunately we now know different. DNA studies prove that it is genetically surprisingly close to another much more widely distributed sea snake, and that separation was actually very recent indeed.[22] This in turn implies either a recent connection between the lake and the ocean or that the ocean has recently invaded the lake. But since Rennell Island is one of the highest raised atolls in the world and has been in existence for many tens of thousands of years, it's hard to see how there could possibly have been any recent connection between lake and ocean – which leaves ocean 'invasion' as the only logical source of Crocker's sea snake and other lake species. Without a flood of sufficient height to overtop the 100-metre coral cliffs surrounding Lake Tegano it is very hard to explain how Crocker's sea snake could ever have arrived; it's also a little puzzling why there are no species in Lake Tegano that show greater than 8000 years worth of separation from oceanic species.

And Lake Tegano is not alone. Palau attracts tourists from all over the world to experience its famous jellyfish lakes. These are lakes with some connection to the surrounding ocean, proved by their tidal nature, but which have now developed their own unique species of jellyfish, which swarm in vast numbers. The time depth of this speciation is just a few thousand years,[23] which is reasonable even without any Great Flood since sea levels were not high enough to create these lakes until long after the Ice Age, but questions remain: a) how did the jellyfish arrive in the first place, and b) why don't they (and other species) continue to arrive today? The assumption is that the connection between lake and ocean was much more direct in times past, but it's not obvious how this could have been the case, particularly in times when ocean levels were significantly lower than today. An alternative explanation of course, not yet considered by scientists, is that the sea actually rose and overflowed into the lakes at some date in the past.

SUMMARY

Neither the Palau jellyfish nor Crocker's sea snake could be said to in any way prove that this flood took place; they simply constitute further pieces of evidence to add to the pile. The same is true of the surprisingly thin salt deposits found in Australia's dry lakes. The art of modelling the way salt is dissolved and transported by groundwater, thus spreading itself widely and deeply through soil strata, is no more than an art, and so the fact that certain scientists have expressed surprise at the lack of salt hardly constitutes solid evidence. But it is nevertheless one more reason to add to the many already found in favour of belief in the flood.

However, as in America, the really impressive weight of evidence is found in the folk myths of the people, both in Australia itself and in the island chain to the north. They are numerous; and, as in America, they are consistent in their portrayal of a flood that rose hundreds of metres and lasted several months. And this makes my next port of call, Africa, particularly interesting since, as I remarked in Chapter 2, Africa is notable for its almost complete lack of flood stories. If the Great Flood is nothing more than a subconscious nightmare hard-wired into the human psyche then this is very odd indeed. On the other hand, even if it was a real event we need an explanation as to why so few in Africa seem to remember it.

14

The African's Tale

Fortunately for Africans of 6250BC, their continent was just about as well placed as it could have been when Lake Agassiz met its sudden end. For a start, Africa is a long way from the longitude of Lake Agassiz; and, for extra protection, much of the continent stands well over 500 metres above sea level. It is therefore predicted to have suffered much less than America or Australia – which means that the lack African folk myths speaking of a Great Flood is not entirely surprising. There are exceptions as we shall see, but in the main this chapter on the African experience will have to be written without the help of orally-transmitted memories.

THE TRIBES OF THE SOUTH

Although, as I say, the flood was much less extensive in Africa than in America or Australia, much of the east coast, including virtually the whole of modern Mozambique, would nevertheless have been under hundreds of metres of water; and the island of Madagascar must have suffered appallingly. Yet the only east-coast tales of which I am aware are adaptations of the Noah story, presumably derived from Muslim or Christian sources; and nothing at all has been recorded from Madagascar. Why should this be?

In the case of Madagascar the answer is simple; the island was uninhabited by humans until about 200AD. If there was a Madagascan flood myth then, like those of the Pacific islands, it would find its true origin in Taiwan, the homeland of the Austronesian people who crossed the Indian Ocean to colonise Madagascar.

The east coast of Africa on the other hand was most certainly inhabited, but the problem is that those who inhabit it today are (culturally at least) not the descendants of those who lived there in 6250BC. Almost the whole of southern Africa, including the east coast all the way from Kenya to South Africa, is home to speakers of Bantu languages, all of which descend from an ancestor that, in 6250BC, would have been spoken somewhere in the northern Congo basin, a basin that saw nothing of the flood. It just so happened that the descendants of these early Bantu speakers would go on to be the lucky recipients of technology from further north (the Nile valley) some time during the 1st Millennium BC. They then proceeded to explode across the map of southern Africa,[1] obliterating most of the cultures (and a large proportion of the people) that had lived there previously, and bringing with them a total and completely understandable ignorance of the flood. Whatever tales of rising oceans and miraculous survival there may have been among the former inhabitants were lost for ever.

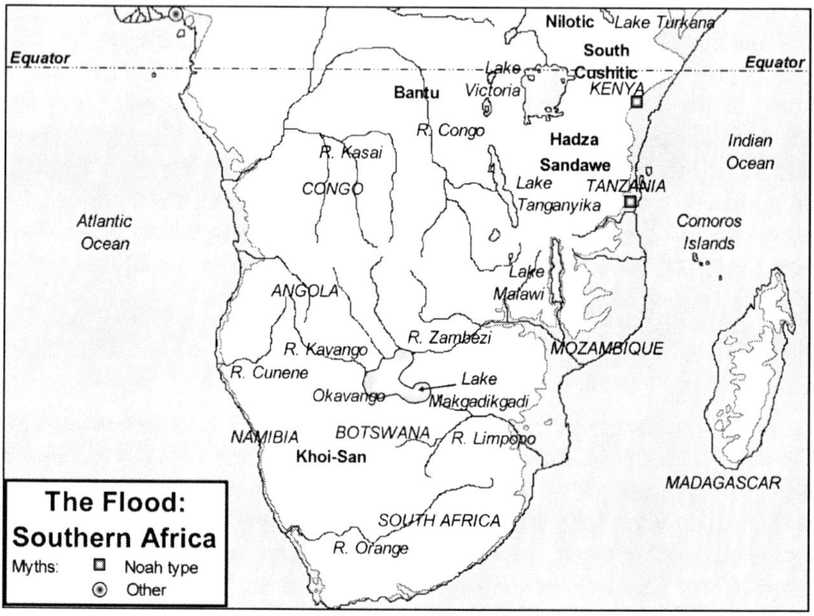

Most of those few non-Bantu people who still survive in southern Africa today are speakers of Khoi-San languages. They live in Angola, Namibia and Botswana as, almost certainly, did their ancestors of 6250BC and, while there would have been a respectable 200-metre flood along the Namibian coast, virtually no-one would have seen it. The coastal region is arid desert today and would not have been particularly hospitable 8000 years ago. The people lived where they could find food – and that meant inland, far from any sight of the flood. The result: no memory of the event survives. Of the other language groups shown on the map, the Hadza and Sandawe tribes are also pre-Bantu remnants, but their territories are some 200 miles from the flooded coast. South Cushitic speakers were on their way south-east in 6250BC, but were not yet in reach of areas subject to flooding.[2] In fact they lived in the safest place on the planet, on the equator. Perhaps some of the Nilotic-speaking tribes living around Lake Turkana might have been expected to remember something, and it is true that the Masai, who are Nilotic speakers and whose ancestors may well have inhabited the Lake Turkana region in 6250BC, do indeed have a flood story.[3] The trouble is that it sounds awfully like the Noah story with different names and a lot of mythical additions. It may possibly contain a highly corrupted indigenous African root – but it is hard to be sure. So, as you can see, there is every reason to expect very little as far as southern African mythology is concerned, and that expectation is amply fulfilled. In fact the lack of stories from Africa would be completely inexplicable if the world's flood myths were really nothing more than the product of human imagination. There would be no reason why these tales should not have blossomed in Africa just as vigorously as in America or Australia.

The bottom line is that the Great Flood, the most appalling catastrophe that has ever befallen mankind, has left no trace at all among the peoples that live in southern Africa today – but it has certainly left plenty of trace in the history of its aquatic life.

A FISHY TALE

Let me return first to Lake Malawi, every aquarium keeper's favourite source of exotic tropical fish. On the flood map you can see that the ocean should have entered the southern end of Lake Malawi. At the height of the flood the water level at that point would have stood at nearly 700 metres above normal sea level, about 220 metres above normal lake level. At the northern end of the lake this would have decreased to around 170 metres above normal lake level since the whole of that part of the continent had been tilted relative to its usual state as the mantle of the Earth reacted to the titanic forces placed upon it. But how much would the inflowing saltwater and the existing freshwater have mixed? Lake Malawi is about 300 miles long, just 40 miles wide and typically around a quarter of a mile (400 metres) deep; seawater would have gained access only via the southern end. A great deal of seawater would have flowed in – that's true – enough to push over half-way along the lake but, in the 3-4 months during which this flood lasted, I can't see that the northern end of the lake would ever have become particularly salty. There is no obvious mechanism that would have brought about thorough mixing. This is important because the only cores ever extracted from Lake Malawi sediments were taken from the far northern end of the lake[4] and, as I noted in Chapter 6, they provide no sign of the significant increase in salinity that the coring team had half expected before they actually got their results. Their expectation was not based on any knowledge of the flood of course but on the need to explain the incredibly rapid speciation of Lake Malawi's cichlid fish. Now we know the actual extent of this flood we can see that they were coring in the wrong place!

However, everywhere except the far northern end of the lake the water would have become too salty for freshwater fish; they could only have survived in the river mouths. When the flood receded, much of the saltwater would have drained out again, leaving behind only mildly saline conditions – but it was too late for most of the fish; the damage had been done. Those species that survived, either in the river mouths or at the northern end of the lake, would have had to re-colonise the numerous desirable habitats once more, diversifying into today's 'species flock' as they did so.

And Lake Malawi isn't the end of the cichlid fish story. The rivers also have a tale to tell. In most of the rivers of Africa there are relatively few cichlid species, and this is presumed, quite reasonably, to be because there are many fewer ecological niches in rivers compared to large lakes. This being the case, it is very surprising how many and varied are the cichlid fish in the Zambezi, Limpopo, Kavango, Cunene and upper Congo river systems. It is also very surprising that these cichlid fish, which are of a different branch of the family from those in Lake Malawi, bear the unmistakable genetic signs of a recent and large-scale 'speciation' event. Fish from opposite extremes of this whole range are sometimes genetically very similar indeed.

Speciation on this scale demands a lake; there is no other habitat in which it could possibly have taken place. And the location proposed for this speciation is a vast ancient lake, Lake Makgadikgadi, which once covered much of northern Botswana, although all that remains today is the famous wildlife haven known as the Okavango.[5] This all seems to make sense. Lake Makgadikgadi is thought to have dried out during the depth of the last Ice Age, just as Lake Victoria did, which means you would expect the same sort of explosion of species when it refilled as Lake Victoria experienced. It then dried up again in about 2000BC which, on the face of it, accounts for the dispersal of these different fish species into the rivers. They were faced with a stark choice: river life or extinction?

Fair enough; except that it doesn't explain things at all! It is true that Lake Makgadikgadi once connected with the Zambezi river system – but not while it was drying out. And how on earth could Makgadikgadi fish have reached the Limpopo, the Cunene or the upper Congo? They are even found in other smaller rivers flowing into the Indian Ocean, between the Zambezi and the Limpopo! By all rights the only river these fish should be found in is the Kavango, the river that still feeds the Okavango swamp today.

At first glance the Great Flood doesn't seem to help solve the puzzle since it never even reached Lake Makgadikgadi. Nevertheless, the answer to this mystery is, I believe, to be found in the events surrounding the flood. Remember that the flood was no more than a side-effect, caused by an unprecedented change in the orientation of the entire planet, and that another side-effect was that the whole 2900-kilometre-thick mantle-crust layer underwent some very substantial deformation. The surface of the land would have sloped first one way and then the other, and the effect would have been particularly pronounced in the tropics.[6] The Lake Makgadikgadi region, lying 20 degrees south of the equator, would have initially tilted northwards and eastwards, imposing a slope of about 25 metres in 100 kilometres or 1:4000, a slope which is greater than that of many of the rivers of the region. The result: the Kavango, the upper Zambezi and all their northern tributaries would have started to flow north, taking the waters of Lake Makgadikgadi with them – and with those waters some of the fish of the lake – and the further north they flowed, the greater the slope of the land became. By the time the Earth reached its maximum tilt angle of 20 degrees, water from Lake Makgadikgadi would have been collecting at about latitude 10 degrees south, among the headwaters of the Congo and its tributaries. There is no mountain range in the way, just thousands of square miles of near-flat land. In the case of the Cunene, the connection is more likely to have been achieved when the planet tilted the other way, giving a south-westward slope to the region. As you can see, the headwaters of the Cunene lie very slightly to the west of those of the Kavango.

The route to the Limpopo and other Indian Ocean rivers is less clear. However, there are several southern tributaries of the Zambezi that rise close to both the northern tributaries of the Limpopo and the headwaters of the Runde (another Indian Ocean river), and the south-westward inclination of the land during the second tilt may have been sufficient to bring Zambezi river water (and fish) right across the watershed. One thing is quite clear however; without this flood and the tilting of the landscape associated with it, today's distribution of cichlid fish is utterly inexplicable.[7]

THE CENTRAL AFRICAN PLAINS

Africa may have got off relatively lightly compared to America and Australia, but the Nile valley was badly affected; so was a narrow strip of land between 5 and 15 degrees north of the equator stretching across to Lake Chad and the Niger river system in Nigeria. The whole basin of the Nile, including territory stretching far out into the Sahara, was under water. When the waters receded the landscape would have been dotted with salt lakes where today's Saharan oases lie. As the lakes dried up under the onslaught of the subtropical sun they would each have left their salt load behind – and there are vast areas of saline deposits throughout the oases, deposits that are presumed to have accrued from the salt content of the aquifers feeding them, but which could equally have been left by the sea.[8] Similarly the Danakil depression of Ethiopia and Eritrea, close to the Red Sea coast, the lowest point in Africa at about 120 metres below sea level and one of the hottest places on earth, would also have been filled with seawater, explaining the extremely young age of the uppermost salt deposits there.[9]

As for the human population, speakers of ancestral Egyptian, then living in the Tibesti Mountain region of the central Sahara, would have found themselves looking out eastwards over an uninhabited land; we can now see exactly why it was that they were able to move east and occupy the Nile valley.

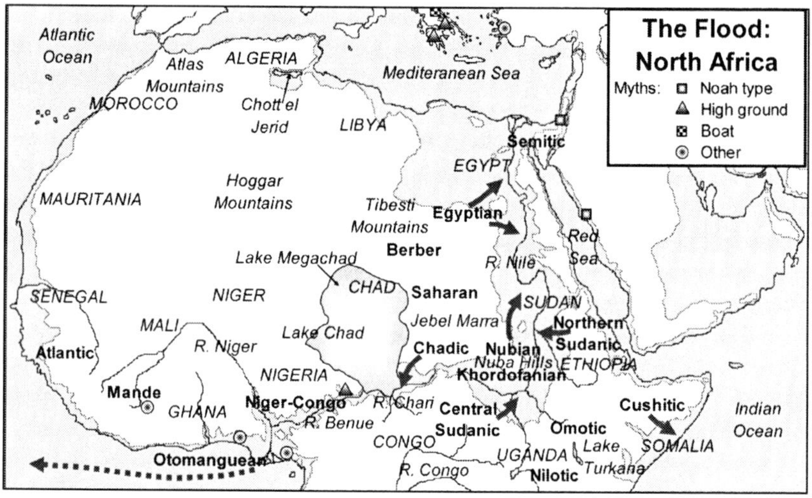

Further north, Semitic-speaking survivors successfully reclaimed the Nile delta, as suggested earlier based on the archaeological similarities between Palestine and northern Egypt. But they had lost the initiative and it would be the Egyptian speakers who would eventually take over. Unfortunately no ancient Egyptian flood story is known other than the tale of the death of Osiris,[10] and that doesn't really resemble the flood described in this book. Never mind; the ancient Egyptians wouldn't be the only people who failed to retain that particular folk memory.

In central Africa some of the rather complex movements of people that took place in succeeding millennia become a little easier to understand once this flood is accepted. Khordofanian speakers today form an isolated pocket, living in the Nuba Hills of southern Sudan, presumably the location they had to retreat to in order to escape the rising tide.[11] All around them the lands were reclaimed by speakers of various branches of the language family known as Nilo-Saharan, namely northern and central Sudanic, Saharan and Nubian. These people today mainly inhabit grassland regions, and it has to be supposed that they were better able to make use of the changed landscape and drier climate following the flood.[12] Nubian speakers had been forced to share the Nuba Hills with the Khordofanians when the floodwaters rose, and they then spread north down the Nile.[13] Further west, Chadic speakers moved into the Chari river basin, and then on into northern Nigeria,[14] while Cushitic (ancestral Somali) speakers reclaimed the low-lying parts of the Horn of Africa.

I couldn't possibly claim that any of these language movements in any way prove the flood, nor indeed can they be known with any great precision, but the flood does appear to provide a degree of logic for them. Perhaps Egyptian speakers would have gone on to dominate the Nile valley even without a flood to clear the way for them – but the fact remains that the death of everyone who stood in their path for several hundred miles must have made things decidedly easier!

At first sight it is slightly surprising how few flood myths there are from this part of the world. After all, many of the tribes who were living around the flooded plains in 6250BC have descendants in the same region today – and of course it may be that many African tales remain unrecorded. On the other hand over much of the affected area the land slopes only gently. Very few who survived would actually have seen anything even if they had lived just a few tens of metres above the high water mark. It's rather similar to the situation east of the Rocky Mountains in America, another region where relatively few tales have survived. In Africa the exceptions are in the Niger delta region and the Benue valley, probably stemming from locations where high ground directly overlooked the flooded plain. Here are two very brief flood descriptions, extracted from the Niger-Benue stories.

> .... *They escaped with a few belongings and looked back to see water covering their village.* ....[15]

> .... *Waters came, covered his farm, and threatened to cover the whole earth.* ....[16]

The stories may be few in number and the flood descriptions brief but they paint the same picture as in America and Australia, a picture of a quite inexplicable and steadily rising tide that threatened to engulf the whole land. By the way you can see for yourself on the map the location that I am suggesting for the origin of the Otomanguean people of Central America, whose language was at that date, according to my language analysis, closely related to those of peoples who live in the lower Niger region today. It is not a connection that mainstream linguists have accepted as yet, but as you can see it is a perfectly logical suggestion – once the Great Flood is accepted of course!

THE LAKE CHAD CONUNDRUM

You might notice that this flood is not predicted to have reached as far south as Lake Turkana – it lies too close to the safety of the equator – and so, despite the fact that some sort of natural disaster appears to have reduced the number of species in the lake today, the flood cannot be held to blame.[17]

However there is another African lake that the flood most certainly reached. Today Lake Chad is nothing more than a rather small and very shallow freshwater terminus for the Chari River. Yet until 6000 years ago Lake Chad was over twice the size of Lake Victoria. The disappearance of Lake Agassiz left Lake Chad as the largest area of fresh water on the planet,[18] offering all manner of tempting ecological niches for enterprising fish species, which makes it slightly puzzling that today it contains no endemic fish species at all. How is it possible that either such 'speciation' failed to take place or else, if it did take place, none of the species that developed has continued to specialise in the lake environment? Admittedly the fact that the vast inland sea known to geologists as Lake Megachad has now shrunk back to the rather modest body of water that some now know as Lake Microchad means that many species would have been lost; but all of them?

A glance back at the flood map and the mystery is solved. Not only would the warping of the land surface as the Earth tilted have tipped much of the contents of Lake Megachad out to the south, but this would have been closely followed by the saltwater flood shown on the map. All endemic freshwater lake species would have perished. Only those suited to river life could have survived in the upper reaches of the Chari and other rivers. Today, 84 of the 179 species found in the Chari river system have found their way back into Lake Chad but none is endemic to the lake alone.[19] It is exactly what you would expect if this flood was real; it is exactly the opposite of what you would expect if there had never been a flood.

And the mystery of the Chari-Chad fish stock doesn't end there. As well as sharing numerous species with the Benue-Niger system – expected since Lake Megachad used to flow out into the river Benue – it includes 89 that are also found in the Nile and 47 which it shares with the Congo.[20] How can this possibly be? Admittedly the map shows a flooded connection between the Nile river system and the Chad basin, but this was a saltwater connection and the fish are freshwater species. The answer, in all probability, is the same as we have just seen in southern Africa; it was due to the warping of the land. In the first phase of the planet's tilting Lake Megachad would have been inclined to the north, but this would then have become a south-eastward slope when the Earth tilted the other way and it would have been a 'close call' as to whether the lake's contents washed into the Benue, its usual outfall, or east down the seasonal river known as the Bahr el Arab and into the Nile. Judging by the shared fish species I am pretty confident that much of it reached the Nile, taking Megachad species with it. This phase was closely followed by the flood itself, wiping out the remaining freshwater fish stock of the lake. At the same time the relatively flat land which lies on the watershed between the Chari and Congo systems would have tilted steeply north, bringing water (and fish) from the northern tributaries of the Congo into the Chari catchment. The fish had little choice; they were simply moving with water that was following the laws of gravity![21]

So, as you can see, many and varied were the consequences of this unique event. Puzzles that seem to be completely unconnected, in biology, geology and the affairs of men and women, many find their answer in this flood.

SUMMARY

I have to say it is particularly pleasing to find that not only does the flood itself explain many things, but the same is true of the warping of the land. This provides real evidence not only that the flood was a genuine event but that the mechanism which caused it really was that described in Part 2. In fact without the clues presented by the distribution of today's fish stocks we would have little supporting evidence in Africa at all. It is true that there are a lot of dormant volcanoes in equatorial Africa that are known to have erupted in this approximate period, and I suggest they were almost certainly activated by the deformation induced in the Earth's mantle during the tilting process, but I would hesitate to put this forward as strong supporting evidence.

But the really striking thing about Africa has been the lack of flood stories in comparison to America, Australia and the islands of Indonesia and the Pacific. Yet once the extent of the flood is mapped out against subsequent movements of peoples and cultures, as well as the topography of the land, then it all makes sense. The truth is that Africa was much less greatly affected. At least 65% of the land surface of Australia would have been submerged; in South America it was over 70%; whereas in Africa it was only 10%. To be sure, it would have been dramatic in the extreme for some survivors. If the inhabitants of the Indian Ocean coast and the Zambezi valley of 6250BC had cultural descendants today we would surely have a crop of stories to match those in America and Australia – but they don't. The Bantu speakers who now dominate more than a third of the continent can be traced back, archaeologically and linguistically, to a tribe who would have seen nothing at all. As I say, it all makes sense; and in my experience this usually means that it is all true!

However, Africa is not the only continent where recent rapid cultural expansion has banished folk memories. The same is true of Europe, a continent perhaps even more favourably located than Africa when the flood struck. If the Great Flood was a real event – and I suggest there has been enough evidence to prove the case many times over – then Europe should be 'the exception that proves the rule'.

15

The Northerner's Tale

This chapter will deal with latitudes far from the tropics. There will be no kilometre-deep floods here and little warping of the land surface. On the other hand a flood of just 100 metres would change most people's world for ever – and there is an awful lot of northern land less than 100 metres above sea level, particularly on the north European plain and in northern Russia. So, though Europe was certainly advantaged by its longitude, its terrain was rather less favourable than Africa's, which means that by no means all would have escaped a watery surprise.

The inhabitants of Europe and northern Asia must have experienced a very strange few years even before the flood struck. The more observant of those villagers who lived next to the sea would first have noticed a sudden sea level rise of about half a metre over the course of just a few days one autumn; though they didn't know it, the ice dam holding back Lake Agassiz thousands of miles away on the other side of the Atlantic had just given way and an unstoppable train of events had been set in motion. Over the course of the next few months those living around the North Sea, the Baltic and the Mediterranean would have realised that the sudden half metre rise was beginning to disappear and by the next summer the level of the Baltic and Eastern Mediterranean had actually fallen by several metres. People must have been very worried indeed. No-one likes an unexpected change and this change was so unexpected it was quite beyond anyone's comprehension.

During the next two years the eastern Mediterranean continued to retreat until it was far out of sight of those who had previously lived along the shoreline, while the Baltic had almost dried up completely. More disturbing still, the winter sun now barely rose above the horizon. Yet by the fourth summer things had improved. The sun was more or less in its right place in the sky; and the waters of the Baltic and the Mediterranean had come into view once more. All eyes would have watched nervously as the sea rose increasingly slowly back towards its original level. But would it stop? We know the answer of course – and the many flood stories I have already shown you give us an insight into the terror that must have ensued when people realised their full predicament.

THE EUROPEAN STORY

In truth, the terror of the inexorably rising tide was experienced by relatively few in Europe. Not only does Western Europe lie more or less at 90 degrees to the longitude of Lake Agassiz, but around most of the Mediterranean the land rises steeply from the sea; survival would not have been a problem. The only Europeans in any real difficulty would have been those who lived out on the north European plain (Netherlands, northern Germany, northern Poland, the Baltic states) or in the Danube and Dnieper basins (Hungary, Ukraine), and I am only aware of a single flood myth from these low-lying plains. It is a Lithuanian tale[1] that speaks of the earth being destroyed by a pair of giants and of people sheltering on the highest mountain. As you can see on the next map, Lithuania is not exactly blessed with mountains, although it does contain one area of highish ground that would narrowly have escaped the flood, and it is just possible therefore that this tale genuinely represents a folk memory from that location. However I use the words 'just possible' because the present language and culture of Lithuania arrived much more recently, in fact only about 2000 years ago. Lithuanian is an Indo-European language and, as we saw in Chapter 4, Indo-European culture has swept through almost all of Europe from the east over the last 7500 years or so. The only non-Indo-European speakers present today are the Basques of north-east Spain and south-west France and the Finno-Ugric-speaking Hungarian, Estonian and Finnish peoples – and we know from Chapter 4 that the Finno-Ugrics are just as new to the continent as the Indo-Europeans. There is therefore

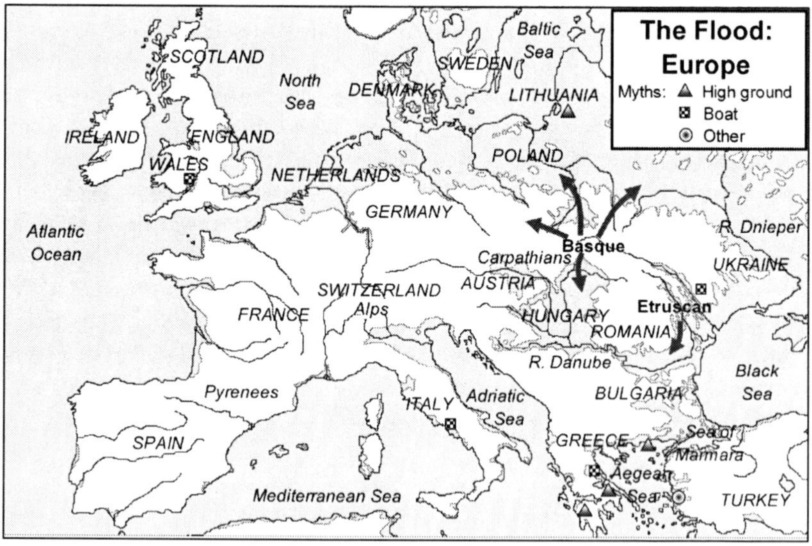

every reason to expect virtually no folk memory at all, at least not from those who actually lived in Europe in 6250BC.

Yet folk memories there are. Some, like the Lithuanian story, may stem from the original Indo-European people, who, according to Chapter 4, escaped the flood in the Caucasus Mountains east of the Black Sea. Certainly the tale told in Wales[2] of a lake bursting its banks and escape in a ship could hardly have originated in Wales, a country that would have seen little more than a series of unusually high tides!

However, the five stories shown in the Aegean region (Greece and Turkey) are much more likely to represent genuine European memories, since Greek culture is really a blend of Indo-European and a pre-existing culture related to that of ancient Crete; it includes much that it inherited from the earlier peoples of the Aegean. Have a look at one version of what is undoubtedly the most famous Greek flood myth, the story of Deucalion.

> *Zeus sent a flood to destroy the men of the Bronze Age. Prometheus advised his son Deucalion to build a chest. All other men perished except for a few who escaped to high mountains. The mountains in Thessaly were parted, and all the world beyond the isthmus and the Peloponnese was overwhelmed. Deucalion and his wife Pyrrha, after floating in the chest for nine days and nights, landed on Parnassus. When the rains ceased he sacrificed to Zeus, the god of escape.*[3]

There are various versions of the story (including the Roman version, shown in Italy) with slightly differing geographical settings, but the essential elements are the same. By the way, the reference to the Bronze Age should not be taken seriously; it simply refers to an earlier age than the one in which the tale was told.

There is also the story of Dardanus, who was driven from his land (Arcadia in southern Greece) by a great flood.[4] And from the Turkish side of the Aegean comes a story of a great flood gushing out from the Black Sea and covering the land around Smyrna (in western Turkey),[5] a story which finds support in the following tale from the Greek island of Samothrace, not far from the Dardanelles Strait, the gateway to the Black Sea.

> *The sea rose when the barriers dividing the Black Sea from the Mediterranean burst, releasing waters from the Black Sea in a great torrent that washed over part of the coast of Asia* [i.e. Turkey] *and the lowlands of Samothrace. The survivors on Samothrace retreated to the mountains and prayed for deliverance. On being saved, they set up monuments to the event and built altars on which to continue sacrifices through the ages.*[6]

At first glance this doesn't make sense. The evidence presented in Chapter 6 implied that the flood had flowed northwards through the Sea of

Marmara and into the Black Sea, not out of it. Yet this flood story has the flow direction reversed, with water forcing its way south from the Black Sea. Why? Are memories at fault?

I suppose that after 8000 years there would be some excuse for memories being at fault! But actually in this case I don't think they are. It is true that the Black Sea flood would have started with a flow north from the Mediterranean; that's the only direct access to the Black Sea. However, when you look at an atlas you realise that the Mediterranean itself was not a particularly easy body of water for the flood to enter. The only inlet point today is the narrow bottleneck of the Strait of Gibraltar, which lies exactly at 90 degrees to the longitude of Lake Agassiz and was therefore not itself subject to any appreciable change in sea level. As the flood rose an alternative inflow point was created, across the Sinai where the Suez Canal is today, between the Red Sea and the Mediterranean; but then the mouth of the Red Sea is another narrow bottleneck. The result of all this would be that the flood level in the Mediterranean must have lagged behind that in the rest of the oceans by a foot or so. However, if you look ahead a few pages to the next map, you can see that once the oceans had risen by about 100 metres a much easier route to the Mediterranean would have opened up. Arctic water would have poured south over the flooded valley of the Volga river, into the Caspian basin and thence to the Black Sea; it would have cascaded across the Gallipoli peninsula from the Sea of Marmara and into the Aegean – in plain view of the terrified inhabitants of Samothrace. The story may be 8250 years old but it still makes excellent sense.

THE EARLIEST FARMERS OF EUROPE

Those who survived the flood on Samothrace were actually some of the first farmers in Europe. The earliest farming settlements appeared in Greece in around 7000BC, and by 6250BC a culture known as 'Starčevo-Körös-Criş' was spreading up the valley of the Danube and across the flat plain of Hungary, doubtless for the excellent reason that it was prime crop-growing land. Knowing what we now know and looking at the previous flood map, you won't be surprised to learn that researchers have noted an unexplained 'hiatus' in the progress of this culture. It seems to have stuttered to a halt in southern Hungary at the end of the 7th Millennium BC.[7] In the 6th Millennium BC it was succeeded by the so-called Linear Band Pottery culture, centred further north, in the Carpathian Mountains, but the connection between Starčevo-Körös-Criş and Linear Band has always been a little unclear to archaeologists. The Linear Band people practised the same sort of agriculture, making use of the same crops and animals, and they therefore must have learnt their skills from the Starčevo-Körös-Criş farmers, yet their material culture was noticeably different.[8] Furthermore the direction of spread in Hungary was now north to south, taking over former Starčevo-Körös-Criş lands. Without this flood it is a mystery why the baton of progress should have been passed from one group to another; seeing the devastation caused across the Hungarian plain on the other hand, it becomes perfectly understandable.

This cultural change also brings me to the language evidence, such as it is. You would expect an advanced agricultural society to spread itself rapidly and widely across the land even without a flood to clear the way for it, and Linear Band culture soon covered all of central Europe, including the recently-flooded north European plain, the Carpathian Mountains and the northern half of Hungary. By the end of the 6th Millennium BC it had arrived in the Netherlands and was mutating into the 5th Millennium BC Rössen culture of western Germany, the Netherlands and eastern France, which then spawned the 4th Millennium BC Chasseen culture of France. A similar spread occurred to the east (Funnel Beaker and Corded Ware cultures) as well.[9] The earlier hunter-gatherer peoples of Europe had a stark choice; join in or die out? And on the back of this cultural supremacy you would expect the language spoken by these farmers to be equally dominant. Logically, therefore, any European language not yet squeezed into oblivion by the later arrival of the Indo-Europeans and Finno-Ugrics is likely to descend from the language spoken by the original Linear Band people. Now, as I indicated a page or two back, only one of today's European languages can trace its lineage back within Europe to pre-Indo-European times, namely Basque, and it should therefore be no surprise that, if my language analysis is correct, the ancestor of Basque was spoken in the northern Carpathian Mountain area in 6250BC.[10] These ancestral Basque speakers just happened to be in the right place at the right time to take advantage of the opportunities created by the flood, having inherited the agricultural know-how of the Starčevo-Körös-Criş farmers.

You might notice that the map also shows ancestral Etruscan somewhere in eastern Romania. This is the one other known language that rivals Basque in terms of its European pedigree – although 'known' is a bit of an exaggeration.[11] Nevertheless I show it where my analysis puts it, somewhere in the southern Carpathians,[12] and, if this is correct, Etruscan speakers too were well placed to take advantage of the flood and spread across the lower Danube valley. I suggest that the 5th Millennium BC Vinča culture of Romania and Serbia spoke an early form of Etruscan and, bearing in mind the extraordinarily advanced state of Vinča society (metallurgy, letter-like signs), it should be no surprise that their language endured and thrived – finally to be extinguished by the Romans.

In fact, if the analysis in *The Origin of Tongues* is to be believed, ancestral Basque and Etruscan formed the vanguard of a great movement of relatively advanced culture that had spread westward from the lands to the north of the Caspian Sea during the millennia from about 9000BC, a movement that was dealt a very serious blow by the flood of 6250BC. The ancestors of the Basques and Etruscans had reached the sanctuary of the Carpathians – but those who remained in the rich lands of the Dnieper, Don and Volga river valleys were obliterated, creating a massive vacuum and new opportunities for those all around the disaster zone to exploit. Cultural top spot was up for grabs once more!

FROM THE VOLGA TO THE YENISEI

As you can see on the next map, we are talking about a very big vacuum indeed. When the waters retreated survivors would have been found in the west (the Carpathians), in the south (the Caucasus), in the centre (Russian uplands and Ural Mountains) and the south-east (the mountain ranges of Central Asia), and I am sure that each population would have expanded vigorously into the empty lands left by the flood. We know from archaeology that those in the Carpathians spread east, the previously mentioned Funnel Beaker and Corded Ware cultures, but their languages have long since vanished from the map. The same is true of survivors from those few hills in western Russia that kept their heads above water. In fact the language evidence is clear; it was the Indo-Europeans spreading north from the Caucasus Mountains and the Finno-Ugrics spreading west from the Ural Mountains who, in the end, succeeded in occupying the Russian plain.

I also mentioned in Chapter 4 the sudden spread of North Caucasian language across the plain of Central Asia. As you can see on the map, that too is perfectly logical once the extent of the flood is appreciated. Central Asia had been emptied of all life; it was there for the taking and, though many peoples may have tried, only the North Caucasians would succeed. At this distance it is generally impossible to understand fully why some groups succeeded while others failed, but the point is that it was clearly the after-effects of the flood that made such widespread change possible in the first place.

Elsewhere, all around the extensive flood-plains of Siberia, between the Ural Mountains and the river Yenisei, the map shows the various successful languages (and therefore peoples) that emerged into the post-flood world. Some of those shown are entirely non-controversial, such as Turkic and Samoyedic; some are no better than educated guesses, such as Yeniseian (now practically extinct);[13] some are distinctly controversial, notably Eskimo-Aleut.[14] However I do not propose to debate these issues

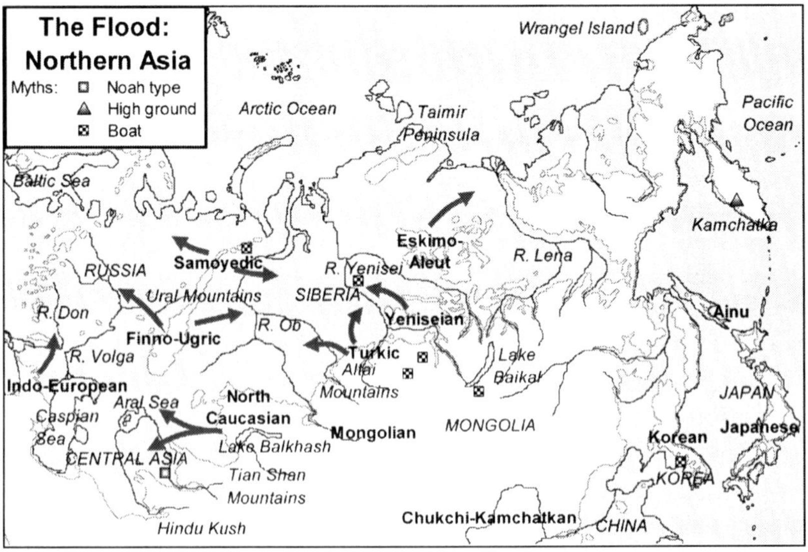

here; the point is that, if the language analysis is correct, the flood allowed these different peoples living on the edge of the flood-plain to take advantage of the misfortune of others. And I am happy to report that some of these peoples have tales that survive to this day, tales of the time many generations ago when their world turned upside down. Here is what the Yeniseians have to say.

> *Flood waters rose for seven days. Some people and animals were saved by climbing on floating logs and rafters. A strong north wind blew for seven days and scattered the people, which is why there are now different peoples speaking different languages.*[15]

By now you have probably noticed several tales that speak of a confusion of languages after the flood, and you may be slightly puzzled as to why that should be. I believe it to be quite logical however. Taking the case of the Yeniseians; before the flood there would have been a large area of Siberia hosting a spectrum of differing Yeniseian languages, although the differences would have been slight enough for each group still to have been able to communicate with their immediate neighbours. This situation is known as a 'language gradient'. But after the flood peoples who had previously lived hundreds of miles from each other would suddenly have come into contact as they moved to occupy the vacant land, peoples whose language, even if still Yeniseian, would have been too different to comprehend. And some will not have been Yeniseian at all, for example the Turkic tribes who would one day go on to dominate southern Siberia.

And the Turkic speakers too have their memories of these times.

The giant frog (or turtle) which supported the earth moved, which caused the cosmic ocean to begin flooding the earth. An old man who had guessed something like this would happen built an iron-reinforced raft, boarded it with his family and was saved. When the waters receded the raft was left on a high wooded mountain where, it is said, it remains today.[16]

Whether the reference to the earth moving is a genuine observation or not I could not say – but I know it did move! And I don't think we need worry too much about the mention of iron, which is surely a later addition to the tale.

I'll give the last word to the Samoyeds, who today live near the Arctic Ocean and who rode out the flood in the northern Ural Mountains.

Seven people were saved in a boat from a flood. A terrible drought followed the flood, but the people were saved by digging a deep hole in which water formed. However, all but one young man and woman died of hunger.[17]

In addition to the brief reference to the flood, this tale contains a very important truth indeed. If you remember, one of the legacies of the '8.2ka BP climatic event' in several parts of the world was reduced rainfall and, according to the findings of climatologists, it affected most of northern Asia.[18] The mention of drought in this story therefore makes excellent sense.

A MAMMOTH TALE

Very obviously, with thousand-mile-wide swathes of devastation, the natural world suffered very badly indeed. Nevertheless, life on earth is superbly adept at colonising and re-colonising, and so we see no obvious sign of this devastation today. After all, if there is less variety of fauna in Siberia than there otherwise might have been, that is not something that can easily be proved. Thus all we see are occasional clues. For example, the southward flow of Arctic water that reached the Black Sea and was then seen spilling into the Aegean by people on the island of Samothrace and the coast of Turkey was almost certainly responsible for bringing the Arctic fish species I spoke about in Chapter 5 south to the Caspian, species whose presence experts find so hard to explain. It seems quite plausible that the walrus who once owned the tusk discovered at the bottom of the Caspian Sea also made the journey south from the Arctic on this flood. The sudden appearance of the common cockle in the Caspian Sea is also explained, brought from the Black Sea during the early phase of the flood when the waters of the Black Sea rose high enough (about 50 metres) to cascade down into the Caspian.

However, what I consider to be one of the most noteworthy legacies of this flood is to be found much further to the east, and it doesn't involve extinction or inexplicable movement of a species; it involves a little-known survival. So far as we know, the woolly mammoth, once found right across northern Europe, northern Asia and North America, was restricted to one location and one location only in 6250BC, and a dangerously low-lying location at that. Yet the woolly mammoth survived. You may not have been aware of it but a mammoth population survived on a remote Arctic island called Wrangel Island down to as recently as 1700BC.[19] And the reason it survived is exactly the same reason that Charles Darwin was able to observe such a rich variety of species on the Galapagos Islands; it was all down to geographical good fortune. For the Galapagos salvation lay in a location on the equator; the mammoths of Wrangel Island were lucky enough to live almost 90 degrees from the longitude of Lake Agassiz. Their flood would have been less than 100 metres deep and Wrangel Island, though relatively low-lying, has plenty of ground 100 metres and more above sea level. If other mammoth populations still existed elsewhere in Siberia they were less fortunate.[20] Given that it would only take a single piece of irrefutable evidence to prove that the flood I am describing never actually happened, the fact that this unexpected survival took place in one of the limited number of low-lying locations where only a modest flood depth is predicted practically puts the last nail into the coffin of doubt.

SUMMARY

A number of puzzles are explained by the Great Flood in Europe and northern Asia, puzzles of archaeology in Hungary, of salinity change in the Black Sea and of Arctic fish in the Caspian. And in terms of validating the flood as described in this book, with depth varying from zero to many hundreds of metres, the evidence of the northern lands is very persuasive indeed. The way that human language spread out in so many directions across the low-lying plains of Russia, Central Asia and Siberia at just this time is so inexplicable given 'normal' conditions that it demands a catastrophe of some kind. Furthermore, we see the exceptions exactly where they should be. Western Europe had virtually no flood according to the predictions – and there we find just a single flood myth, from a people whose cultural ancestors inhabited the Caucasus region in 6250BC, and absolutely no evidence of any disaster. Lake Baikal is predicted to have escaped the flood – and its undisturbed ecosystem confirms it. Lake Balkhash too should have escaped – and this is supported by the lack of salt in the region. And finally there is the case of the mammoths of Wrangel Island. If there was ever an exception that proved the rule this is surely it.

Anyway; let's move on. South of the great Siberian plains lies the largest concentration of high ground on the planet, stretching from Mongolia through western China and Tibet to Afghanistan and Iran, lands which even this mighty flood could never touch. However, south and east of these upland areas lie some of the most densely populated regions on earth, the flood-plains of the Yellow River, the Yangtze and the Mekong. In 6250BC 'flood-plains' would be an apt description.

16

The Chinaman's Tale

A lot of people saw the flood in China and survived. Small mountain ranges are scattered throughout southern and central China, ranges that would have been transformed into an archipelago of islands during the Great Flood. In the north the population was less fortunate and untold thousands must have perished on the great plain of the Yellow River; nevertheless, the steeply-sloping hills to the west would have saved large numbers. You would expect these to be ideal conditions for both dramatic escape and tragic death, leading to stories that would be told and retold from generation to generation.

CHINESE FLOOD MEMORIES

And yet there are very few Chinese flood myths. Mainstream Chinese tradition tells us that the water god sent a flood as punishment for human misdeeds, requiring people to live in the mountains for 22 years,[1] and there are various supplementary tales of the actions of gods and mythical beasts. But the truth is that you have to look outside Chinese culture to the folklore of ethnic minority tribes to find anything more than this.

There is of course good reason for the lack of variety in Chinese memories of the flood. Although it may be 'politically incorrect' to say such a thing, the truth is that Chinese culture was not present over most of China in 6250BC. The valley of the Yellow River, the region which would later be the centre of classical Chinese civilisation, was home to a quite different culture in 6250BC. Whether my next map is correct in identifying the language family of this region as Chukchi-Kamchatkan may be debated[2] but, whoever the people were, they were not, in my opinion, speakers of any Chinese-related tongue. According to my language analysis Chinese culture arrived down the Yangtze River from India[3] and by 6250BC it had just about made its way through the Yangtze gorges. Speakers of ancestral Chinese had just begun to move out across the flat plain to the east. They were agriculturalists. Whether they had developed rice agriculture or whether they had picked up the idea from others I could not say, but the archaeological evidence is that the inhabitants of this very region, the lands just to the east of the Yangtze gorges, were the first to take up rice farming seriously as a way of life.

And then came the flood! The plains were inundated; the valley of the Yangtze would have flooded far upstream of the gorges, into what is now Sichuan Province; the rice paddies were destroyed. In Chapter 3 I pointed out that several early agricultural experiments in southern China seem to have been discontinued at this time for some reason – and we can now be pretty confident that the Great Flood was the reason. It seems that knowledge of the art was retained only in the middle Yangtze, the area where ancestral Chinese speakers lived, and also nearer to the coast, near modern Shanghai. And whatever the original language and culture of the Shanghai people it has now disappeared entirely, swamped by the more advanced Chinese culture from the middle Yangtze region. The result of all this is that all folk memories belonging to the culture which gave birth to those of modern China, whether Mandarin, Cantonese or even Taiwanese, must have come from one region and one region alone in 6250BC, namely the hills above the Yangtze gorges or other neighbouring hills to the east. That therefore is the setting for the various versions of the Chinese flood myth, a myth that goes on to tell us of a character named Yu, who is variously a god or a man, and who had the task of cutting channels to allow the floodwaters to escape back to the sea. He is supposed to have spent 13 years draining the land and to have gone on to found the first ever Chinese dynasty, the Hsia. Here is one version of the story, or at least part of it.

> *The inundating waters seemed to assail the heavens and in their extent embraced the hills and overtopped the great mounds so that the people were bewildered and overwhelmed. .... I opened passages for the streams*

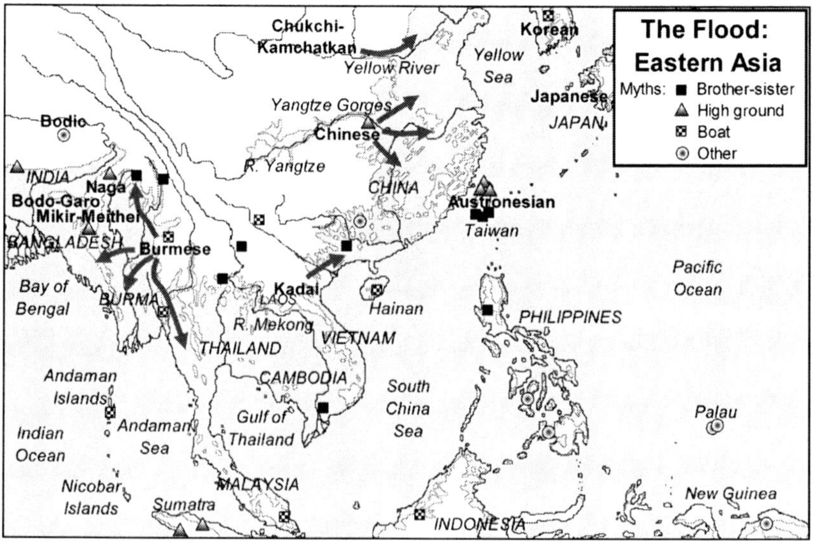

throughout the nine provinces and conducted them to the seas. I deepened the channels and conducted them to the streams.[4]

Now most commentators would simply take this as an exaggerated reference to the importance of hydraulic works in China since it deals with the subject of river control. However, take a look at the flood map. At the height of the flood the sea would have reached far up the Yangtze and across Sichuan province. Vast quantities of water had to pass through the famous gorges, both as the flood rose and then as it fell, and extensive erosion of the hills either side would have been the inevitable consequence. It is certain that great landslides would have occurred, sending enormous masses of debris down into the old Yangtze river channel. Some months later, when the ocean level began to subside, the Yangtze gorges would have been left with their own natural dams, rivalling those recently constructed by Chinese engineers! It is impossible to guess just how many or what size were the lakes that were created by these natural dams, but it is practically certain that they would have formed. With the technology available in 6250BC it is easy to understand why the task of restoring the land by draining the river valley would have taken Yu and his engineering colleagues 13 years of hard graft, even with a large labour force at their disposal. The story fits perfectly with the predicted flood and its inevitable consequences. It also finds its logical home exactly where ancestral Chinese culture was located in 6250BC.

THE OTHER PEOPLES OF CHINA

But as I said, you have to look outside Chinese tradition if you want to find a bit more variety. Two brother-sister stories survive from southern China and, if my interpretation was right back in Chapter 2, they are originally attributable to Austro-Asiatic-speaking tribes, even though in one case the people now telling the story speak a quite different language (Zhuang, related to modern Thai). The other southern Chinese tales shown on the map are told by the Sui and Lolo peoples of south-west China and the Li (or Hlai) people of Hainan Island. Here are brief extracts, concentrating on the flood-related elements of the stories.

Pelting rain fell from the sky and soon there was a vast flood. The evil man was helpless in his stone house, but the wooden houses of the others floated.[5]

In wrath, Tsegudzih locked the rain gates, and the waters mounted to the sky. Dumu was saved in a log hollowed out of a Pieris tree, together with his four sons, and otters, wild ducks and lampreys. The civilised peoples who can write are descended from the sons.[6]

In ancient times the Lis who lived by the banks of the Shihua River were hit by a great flood. Only one pair of lovers sitting in a big gourd ladle which floated to the Yanwo Hills survived the disaster.[7]

Now I suspect that the cultural ancestors of the Li people were not actually living on Hainan in 6250BC,[8] but experience has taught us not to take geographical landmarks too seriously. The Li language is of the Kadai family and in 6250BC my estimate is that it would have been spoken somewhere in Vietnam or Laos, as shown on the map.[9] The Sui and Lolo peoples have probably also moved during the eight millennia that have passed since the flood; presumably both were living somewhere on the edge of the flood zone shown on the map. But the point is that the experience contained in all three tales ("a vast flood"; "waters mounting to the sky"; "floating to the hills") is exactly consistent with the flood as predicted in Chapter 11 and experienced in America, Australia, Africa, Europe and northern Asia.

We should also check out the tale told by today's Chukchi-Kamchatkan speakers, now resident in the far north-east of Russia but, according to language analysis, probably living in northern China in 6250BC. You will recognise some very familiar themes – although I admit that there is nothing in the story to indicate a specifically north Chinese location.

> *A flood covered the whole land in the early days of the world. A few people saved themselves on rafts made from bound-together tree trunks. They carried their property and provisions and used stones tied to straps as anchors to prevent being swept out to sea. They were left stranded on mountains when the waters receded.*[10]

And look at the concentration of flood myths from Taiwan. Why should Taiwan be home to so many stories? Well, while the dominant culture of Taiwan today is Chinese, the flood myths all belong to the Austronesian-speaking tribes found scattered down the eastern side of the island. In fact, as I noted a couple of chapters ago, the people of Taiwan were the original Austronesians. It was from Taiwan that the first Austronesian seafarers set out in about 3500BC to colonise far and wide, and I suggested that many of the flood myths told throughout the Pacific probably find their true origin in Taiwan. On the other hand Taiwan was itself dramatically affected by the influence of Austro-Asiatic speakers, the bearers of the original brother-sister flood story, such that Austronesian culture is really a composite of indigenous 'Taiwanese' and Austro-Asiatic. So it is not at all surprising to find that three different versions of the brother-sister story survive on Taiwan, nor that another is found in the Philippines. I quoted one of the Taiwan stories back in Chapter 2; here is one of the other two together with the story from the Philippines.

> *In an earthquake, mountains tumbled down, the earth gaped and hot subterranean waters gushed out and flooded the whole earth. Two sisters and a brother escaped in a wooden mortar and floated south to Rarauran. They landed and climbed Mount Kaburugan to view the countryside; then the*

> *sisters searched south and the brother searched west for good land. Finding none, they returned and ascended to the mountain's summit again, but the older sister tired half way up and, when the other two returned for her, they found she had turned into a rock. .... They were uncertain whether it would be proper for them to marry, so they asked the sun as it rose the next morning. The sun answered immediately that they may marry.*[11]

> *A storm came, the river kept rising, and the elders advised people to run for the mountains, as the river gods were angry. Only two people made it to safety, a brother and a sister, Wigan and Bugan, on the separate mountains Amuyao and Kalawitan. Both had enough food on the summits, but only Bugan had fire. After 6 months the waters receded, creating the rugged terrain that exists today. Wigan travelled to his sister on Mount Kalawitan and they settled in the valley. The sister later found herself with child and ran away in shame, following the course of the river. The god Maknongan, appearing as an old man, assured her that her shame had no foundation, since she and her brother would repopulate the world.*[12]

The themes of rising water and escape to the mountains are all too familiar by now. And, as you know, almost all the brother-sister stories contain the additional ingredient that, being the only two people left alive, they are forced to marry so that the human race survives. Notice also the mention of earthquakes in the first tale.

The three non-brother-sister stories from Taiwan also tell of escape to the mountains and the hardships suffered by the survivors. Here is one example.

> *A giant crab caught and tried to eat a large snake, but the snake managed to escape into the ocean. Immediately a great flood covered the world. The ancestors of the Bunun escaped to Mount Usabeya and Mount Shinkan, where they lived by hunting until the waters receded. They returned to find their fields washed away, but a stalk of millet remained. They planted its seeds and subsisted on its produce.*[13]

These tales all describe nicely what would have in reality occurred as the waters began to rise. We need to remember that simply having dry land beneath your feet would not be enough to ensure survival. For hunter-gatherers and agriculturalists alike, the primary sources of food would have been cut off. Depending on the area of dry land, there may have been a supply of animals to hunt, but the vegetation might have been quite different from that down on the plain. The Philippines story (and one of the unquoted Taiwanese stories) makes the point that fire may have been 'lost'. The evidence from southern China is that in some previously rice-growing areas agricultural know-how was lost entirely.

Make no mistake; this was a very difficult time to live through over much of the face of the planet, but at least Taiwan had plenty of high ground and so every chance of survival. The same cannot be said for some of the lands to the south, where the third of the great rivers that flow east from Tibet, the Mekong, makes its tortuous way through Laos, Thailand, Cambodia and Vietnam to the sea.

PLAINS OF THE MEKONG

If you look back to the flood map you can see that a vast area of South-East Asia, including most of the Malaysian peninsula, was obliterated by this flood, up to a kilometre deep in places. Whoever the people were who occupied this land in 6250BC, their cultures have since sunk without trace. In fact northern Thailand and Laos had seen significant progress on the road to civilisation in the form of what is known as the 'Hoabinhiam' culture. These people had managed to cultivate gourds and were also using a relatively advanced 'toolkit' of stone artefacts. Yet it continues to surprise researchers that this advanced society seems to have vanished for no apparent reason and that there is so little evidence for human activity in the millennia between 6000BC and 4000BC; there seems to be almost nothing to bridge the gap between the Hoabinhiam people and the new cultures that appeared some time after 4000BC.[14] One glance at the flood map and the need for surprise evaporates.

The peoples that arrived from about 4000BC were different, and they came from two directions. From the north came Chinese-related tribes while Austro-Asiatic speakers pushed up from the south. And it would have been this latter group, the Austro-Asiatics, who brought with them the two versions of the brother-sister story shown on the previous map, one from Vietnam (quoted in Chapter 2), the other from northern Thailand. In the Thailand story[15] the brother and sister sealed themselves inside a drum while others made rafts for themselves – but lost their lives when the rafts overturned. As usual, when the brother and sister eventually reached dry land and left the drum they were the only survivors and had to marry each other.

The fact that the whole of this vast region is represented only by these two brother-sister stories, stories that almost certainly originated thousands of miles to the west, speaks volumes for the absolute nature of the collapse of civilisation that took place here in 6250BC. In fact the Li story from Hainan island, quoted three pages back, may be the only direct memory we have from those who were actually present on the northern edge of the Mekong plain when the Great Flood struck.

THE TRIBES OF BURMA

And across the mountains to the west a similar destruction took place throughout central Burma, wiping out all opposition to those who would inherit the land, the Burmese-speaking tribes who lived in the hills to the east. These people were the first to react when the waters receded and have since spread and subdivided into the plethora of different peoples that inhabit Burma today. And Burma's steep-sided mountains, combined with the fact that none of the peoples of Burma has moved any great distance over the last eight millennia,[16] provide the perfect recipe for the survival of flood stories. Here for example is a tale told by the Lushei people who live in the western hills, on the India-Burma border.

> *The king of the water demons fell in love with the woman Ngai-ti. She rejected him and ran away. He pursued and surrounded the whole human race with water on the hill Phun-lu-buk, said to be in the far north-east. Threatened by waters which continued to rise, the people threw Ngai-ti into the flood, which then receded.*[17]

Other similarly mythical tales are told by other Burmese hill tribes, the Jingpaw in the north and the Karen in the south, and always with the theme of the waters rising high over the land; "until they reached to heaven" according to the Karen.[18] And since the predicted depth across the Karen lands is around a kilometre, this description is certainly appropriate.

By the way, you might notice that there are two further brother-sister stories from Burma, one from the Jingpaw and the other from their eastern neighbours the Lisu (quoted in Chapter 2), both speakers of languages of the Burmese group. However these peoples have been dominated by Austro-Asiatic speakers[19] for much of the past 5000 years or so and the source is almost certainly the original Austro-Asiatic brother-sister story.

Language and myth are all that remain today to tell us of the year-long flood that destroyed ancient Burma. But immediately south of Burma lies a string of islands where we have every right to expect much more solid evidence. Today the Andaman and Nicobar Islands are hailed as an environmental paradise, a land full of endemic species found nowhere else on earth, and this claim is not restricted to the plant and animal life but also includes the human population. Yet if I am right in my calculations the entire island chain should have been submerged. I cannot, in all good conscience, avoid paying a visit.

THE ANDAMAN AND NICOBAR ISLANDS

Perhaps the first thing to do is to remind you that a year-long flood is no real problem to plant life, or at least not to survival of species in the form of seeds and roots. Within a century or two the vegetation of the islands would have looked just as rich and varied as it ever had. Next, turning to the wildlife, I am not aware of any species that is truly unique in the sense that there are no closely related species in adjacent regions on the mainland. The Andaman wild boar for example, though classified as a separate species from Burmese boars, surely descends from animals introduced relatively recently by man; the Nicobar crab-eating macaque, tree shrew and flying fox are all closely related to those found in Sumatra; the Nicobar pigeon is also found on islands off Sumatra. In short, much if not all of the fauna of these islands comprise recent divergences from mainland species that now specialise in island life.

The human population however is another matter entirely. I am not referring to the Nicobar Islanders, who are Austro-Asiatic speakers and whose culture (though not necessarily their genes) arrived a few thousand years ago, probably from Sumatra; my concern is with the inhabitants of the Andaman Islands, who have been labelled, perhaps unfairly, as one of the most primitive peoples on the planet, and who are isolated from the modern world by stringent laws. They still live in the Stone Age, caught in a time warp by the well-intentioned policies of the Indian government. Yet these people saw the flood and survived to tell the tale; here is their version of events.

> *Some time after their creation, men grew disobedient. In anger, Puluga, the Creator, sent a flood which covered the whole land, except perhaps Saddle Peak where Puluga himself resided. Of all creatures, the only survivors were two men and two women who had the fortune to be in a canoe when the flood came. The waters sank and they landed, but they found themselves in a sad plight.*[20]

The survival of the Andaman Islanders is a real challenge to my explanation of this flood and the associated calculation of flood depth. On the face of it they are living proof that the Andaman Islands were never totally submerged – and as if to rub salt into the wound they have a flood story to back this up. There, in black and white, I can read that Saddle Peak still had its head above water rather than about 50 metres beneath it, as predicted. This is more than a little embarrassing.

So let's take as close a look as we can at this mysterious people, a people who give endless fascination to anthropologists and linguists. They are physically and genetically quite different from all other races in that part of the world[21] and their language is also quite different, signs which almost everyone interprets as meaning they have been there for a very long time indeed – everyone that is except the archaeologists. Zarine Cooper spent many years investigating the archaeology of the islands, examining middens, fire hearths, animal bones etc., and her conclusion is clear; humans only arrived about 2000 years ago and they arrived already in possession of a knowledge of pottery and of pig domestication.[22]

Scanning the literature, this is something anthropologists find very difficult to accept. Linguists however might be a little more open to persuasion. Although the language of the islanders is quite different from any other in the region, several linguists have now pointed out that there are real similarities between their speech and that of the Papuan languages of western New Guinea and some of the neighbouring Indonesian islands.[23] Now I must admit that I have in the past been among those who have dismissed this connection as nothing more than coincidence – but I think I now have to humbly admit that there is truth in it after all! As I mentioned in Chapter 13, Papuan languages arrived in Indonesia some 35000-40000 years ago, and the implication is that related tongues were spoken in Sumatra and the Malaysian peninsula until the arrival of Austro-Asiatic speakers from the west in about 4000BC. The detailed movements of these Papuan-related peoples and cultures among the islands of Indonesia are, of course, completely unknown to us today. It could be, for example, that some technological or social advance – taro cultivation springs to mind – resulted in a 'wave' of culture (and speech) sweeping through the islands of Indonesia, bringing similar language from Sumatra in the west to the coasts of New Guinea in the east. And if this were the case the Andaman Islanders may be the last remnant of that Papuan-speaking people still living in the western part of the region. I am speculating of course but the Papuans were certainly able to travel by sea, and the lack of truly ancient archaeological finds on the Andaman Islands cannot simply be dismissed.

And it could be that even anthropologists may one day accept this connection. For a start there are real genetic similarities with populations in the New Guinea region,[24] matching the linguistic parallels. More generally, Andaman Islanders belong to a racial type known as 'Negritos', who can be found in remote areas of Malaysia, Sumatra, Borneo and all the major islands of Indonesia and the Philippines, as far as New Guinea. There is even evidence that they lived until recently in parts of Australia.[25] Most Negrito groups have adopted the languages of later arrivals in the area, Austro-Asiatic or Austronesian, but their cultures often retain memories of earlier times.[26] And one such culture is that of the Batak people of northern Sumatra, a people who are genetically related to other Negrito peoples.[27] Their language is Austronesian – but it's quite different from the other Austronesian languages of Sumatra; their religion is Christian – quite different from the Muslim majority. They are a distinct people with a distinct culture and they too have a memory of the flood, a memory which surely predates the arrival of Austronesian language (in about 1500BC). Here it is.

> *Debata, the creator, sent a flood to destroy every living thing when the earth grew old and dirty. The last pair of humans took refuge on the highest mountain, and the flood had already reached their knees when Debata repented his decision to destroy mankind. He tied a clod of earth to a thread and lowered it. The last pair stepped onto it and were saved.*[28]

Now compare this story with that of the Andaman Islanders. Both speak of an angry creator god who decided to destroy the world; admittedly the numbers of survivors (two and four) are different, as are the means of survival, but the threads of the two tales are really quite similar. It is far from inconceivable that they have a common root; in which case it is far from inconceivable that the Andaman Islanders arrived from Sumatra via the Nicobar Islands and that this occurred, as archaeology suggests, just 2000 years ago. They may even have been forced to flee the Nicobar Islands by the arrival of the Austro-Asiatic people who live there today.

The upshot of all this is that the presence of a flood story in a land which should have been totally inundated is not nearly so embarrassing as it first appeared. In fact I would say that the weight of evidence in support of the Great Flood as described in this book is so strong now that it can even be used as input into the Andaman Islands debate; it reinforces the message from archaeology that the Andaman Islanders were not living on the Andaman Islands in 6250BC, and northern Sumatra, where the Batak people live today, is the most likely place of origin.

SUMMARY

There has been no solid scientific evidence from the lands of eastern Asia, no unexplained salt deposits or puzzling transfer of fish species between river systems. Yet the human evidence, from both mythology and archaeology, has been highly persuasive. That the Chinese tale of Yu the great engineer should find such a plausible home amongst the gorges of the middle Yangtze river, in the very region that linguistics shows to be the location of Chinese culture in 6250BC, is as neat as it gets. When this is combined with the early history of rice agriculture, spreading out from this very region across the plain to the east in the 6th Millennium BC, then the pieces can be seen to fit together nicely.

However, the most significant archaeological puzzle from this region has been, in my opinion, the wholesale disappearance of the Hoabinhiam culture of Thailand and Laos. That such an advanced culture, including gourd cultivation, should vanish so suddenly when at the height of its power is an enigma for archaeologists, as is the lack of human evidence in that part of the world for the next two millennia or so. But when we read the Li tale, of a single pair of lovers who floated to the hills in a "gourd ladle" (whatever that is exactly), then we truly learn the fate of Hoabinhiam civilisation. Once more the pieces fit together perfectly.

In tale after tale from south-east Asia we read of waters that rose to the sky and of survivors who escaped to the highest hills, somehow enduring months of hunger and deprivation. Yet in the land we are about to visit the waters rose higher still. India lay exactly in the wrong place when the flood came. It is directly opposite Lake Agassiz, on the longitude of maximum tilt, and much of the continent lies between latitudes 10° and 30° north of the equator, where the worst effects would be felt. Few places would have got away with a sea level rise less than about 600 metres; over most of the subcontinent it would have been considerably deeper. Let me bring you something of the Indian experience.

17

The Indian's Tale

There are well over a billion citizens of India today; yet when the Great Flood struck, in about 6250BC, it would have left very few survivors. With the exception of a few scattered hills the entire subcontinent south of the Himalayas and east of the Iranian plateau, comprising almost all of modern Pakistan, India, Bangladesh and Sri Lanka, was under water. Those fortunate enough to have lived close to the towering Himalaya mountain range could readily escape, and in Chapter 2 I introduced the Hindu story of Manu, who survived the flood in a large boat which eventually came to rest among the mountains of the north. Another tale told of survival near the resort of Darjeeling in the foothills of the Himalayas. However for most Indians the year 6250BC (or thereabouts) would see their death. The hills of central and southern India slope relatively gently; it would not have been at all obvious in which direction to flee. The flood rose at up to 6 metres per day in central and southern India, 3 or 4 metres per day further north. Its progress across the plains would have been much too rapid for any escape. Even where there was a hill to escape to the chances are it wouldn't be high enough, and once a wrong choice had been made there would be no second chance. As you can see on the flood map, only a small archipelago of islands remained. The Vindya range in central India and the peaks of the Eastern and Western Ghats would still have held their heads above water; so would the Nilgiri hills in the far south and the highlands of central Sri Lanka. The other 97% of the land surface was under water. Here in India, more than anywhere else on earth, this flood truly deserves the title 'Great Flood'.

THOSE WHO LIVED

Quite obviously this event changed the pattern of human life utterly and it is no surprise at all to learn that archaeologists find very little evidence for the so-called Mesolithic period in the Indian subcontinent, the phase from around 6000BC to 4000BC.[1] In Chapter 3 I drew attention to the lack of settlement in the Indus valley of Pakistan during this period, but the same is true right across the subcontinent. Almost all the sites discovered so far have been in the mountains west of the Indus, in the Vindhya hills and neighbouring upland areas of central India, and in central Sri Lanka. It's not hard to see why wheat and barley based agriculture seems to have come to an abrupt halt on the edge of the Indus plain. Even once the land had recovered from the effects of saltwater inundation there may, understandably enough, have been some reluctance to risk long-term settlement so far from the safety of the hills.

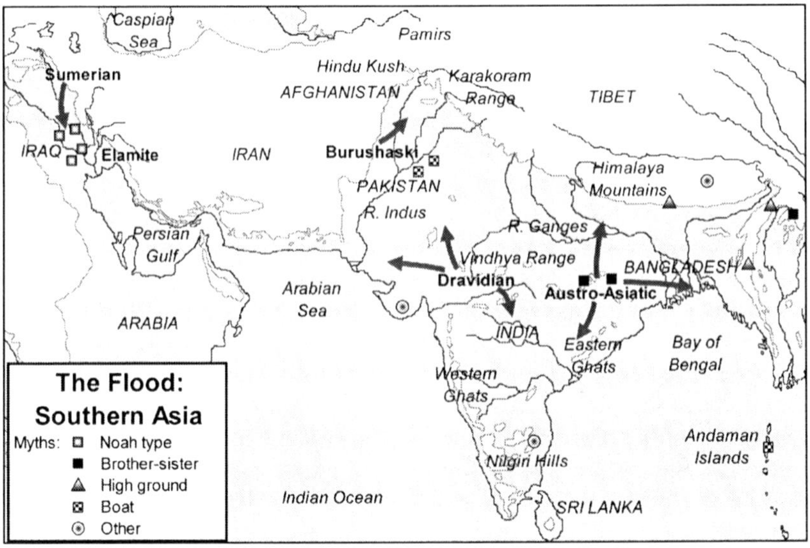

And this disaster almost certainly had a profound influence on the development of another sort of agriculture further east, on the plain of the river Ganges, namely rice farming. Although the world associates rice agriculture with China, wild rice actually grows naturally over a wide area including the southern slopes of the Himalayan foothills. And China was not the only place where some enterprising human had the idea of deliberately planting seeds to ensure supplies; this momentous step also occurred in India. The earliest evidence of which I am aware comes from the site of Lahuradewa on the low-lying land north of the Ganges, and it comes in the form of pollen grains found in lakebed deposits, pollen from both wild and cultivated strains of rice.[2] The oldest finds at Lahuradewa date to about 8000BC and they are entirely of wild rice – but there is a sudden change in about 6000BC when cultivated strains begin to appear alongside the wild varieties,[3] and this change approximately matches the earliest levels of occupation at the adjacent archaeological site. In fact the pollen record reveals a significant change some years previous to this when the quantity of wild rice pollen suddenly dropped to zero for no apparent reason, followed by a steady recovery. A zero pollen count implies a lack of flowering plants; yet there is no obvious explanation as to why rice should have suddenly refused to grow.

The evidence at Lahuradewa could never prove the flood – but it is most definitely compatible with it. Assuming it was the flood that led to the sudden scarcity of wild rice, presumably because rice found it less easy to cope with the soil conditions than other plants once the sea had retreated, then the generation of settlers who re-colonised the land after the flood (having journeyed about 75 miles from the Himalayan foothills) may have been almost forced into cultivation. If they were no longer able to gather enough of the wild rice they had previously relied on, then that would provide a powerful incentive to give nature a helping hand.[4] As they say, 'necessity is the mother of invention'.

Turning to the language evidence, it's now quite clear why two of India's language families went into overdrive starting in about 6250BC. In Chapter 4 I highlighted the Dravidian languages, then located in west central India. These languages and the culture that went with them had recently arrived from the west,[5] and there would have been a spread of similar culture right across the plain of the lower Indus; yet the evidence is that Dravidian started expanding back westwards across the plain from around 6250BC, something that would actually be very hard to explain under normal circumstances. But these circumstances were anything but normal. If my deductions are correct those few Dravidian speakers who survived spent several months marooned on a series of relatively small islands in the midst of a vastly expanded Indian Ocean. When the extent of the destruction caused by this flood is fully appreciated, it is easy to understand what happened to the language. For those fortunate enough to have survived, there was no competition at all; the whole land for hundreds of miles was theirs for the taking.

You might wonder about the lack of Dravidian flood myths but in truth the Hindu story of Manu is almost certainly Dravidian in origin, inherited by the Indo-European-speaking Aryan people when they reached India in the early 2nd Millennium BC. There is also a Tamil story, shown on the map in southern India, the region where Tamil is now spoken, which tells of the whole land of 'Kumari' sinking into the sea – which when you think about it is a different take on the phenomenon of the sea rising. In this tale a lone prince survived and made his way to the Indian state of Tamil Nadu.[6] Since Tamil is a Dravidian language the origin of this story is likely to lie in central India, where Dravidian speakers rode out the flood.

We know of course that there were survivors in the far west also, the agriculturalists of Mehrgarh and surrounding villages, practitioners of wheat and barley farming and keepers of sheep, goats and cattle. The evidence given in Chapter 4 highlighted the very significant change that occurred at Mehrgarh at this time, but the site was certainly reoccupied more or less straight away and the society continued to develop. And it is logical to suppose that the language of the agriculturalists of Mehrgarh would eventually have spread across the plains of northern Pakistan after the flood as survivors began to re-colonise the land. What that language was no-one really knows, but I am speculating that it was the ancestor of a minority Pakistani language known as Burushaski, a language that is only heard today in the high valleys under the shadow of the Karakoram Mountains. According to my analysis Burushaski spread north-east up the Indus at some stage during this general period[7] and so may well have been spoken in the Mehrgarh region in 6250BC, although today's Burusho people unfortunately can give us no further clue since they have no flood memory other than the story of Noah.

There were also survivors in southern India and Sri Lanka, survivors whose languages have since vanished without trace. There is archaeological evidence from Mesolithic times in central Sri Lanka, not to mention the fact that a physically and genetically distinct people known to anthropologists as the 'Veddas' makes up an element of the Sri Lankan and south Indian population today. Unfortunately we have lost whatever memories of the Great Flood they might have had, along with their languages.

However we know much more about the people who stood in the way of Dravidian expansion in the east. These were the Austro-Asiatic speakers, and they had survived in the ranges east of the Vindhya Hills, places where descendent languages (the Munda group) are still spoken today. Just as Dravidians were able to spread unchallenged across the Indus plain to the west, so Austro-Asiatic speakers spread east across the plain of the Ganges; and they went much further than that, as we have seen in previous chapters. In Chapter 4 I suggested that the evidence of modern Austro-Asiatic language strongly implies a 'pidginising' event, when speakers of Austro-Asiatic and Sino-Tibetan were forced together for some reason, giving rise to a sort of composite language. Since Sino-Tibetan speakers almost certainly occupied the lower Ganges plain in 6250BC,[8] and since the number of available refuges from the flood was extremely limited, it is highly likely that some of the hills of east central India provided sanctuary for speakers of both languages as the flood waters began to rise. The survival instinct is a powerful driver, and survival dictated that these two peoples would have to co-operate in their restricted island home over a period of months. Co-operation requires communication; communication in that sort of forced environment demands the creation of a pidgin. The rest is history. The resulting language is classified as Austro-Asiatic because the basic vocabulary remained the vocabulary of the original Austro-Asiatic language, but the grammar now much more closely resembled the grammar of Sino-Tibetan speech.

This band of flood survivors were so inspired by their narrow escape from the rising ocean that they went on to become world-class seafarers and to take their culture around the coasts of South-East Asia, colonising widely. They penetrated deep into Burma; they occupied Thailand and Cambodia and spread north into Vietnam. If my analysis is correct they also sailed their boats north along the Chinese coast, settling both on the mainland and in Taiwan, and I have already mentioned the profound influence they had on the Austronesian speakers of Taiwan.

And with their technological know-how they also brought their folk memories, one of which was the story of the flood, the event that had been instrumental in giving birth to their entire culture. And the particular story that they told was the story of a brother and sister who survived the flood while others perished and who then went on to marry each other. As you can see on the map, two such stories survive from the Austro-Asiatic-speaking region of eastern India. Here they are.

> *A fish told a dhobi (a pious man) that a great deluge was coming. The man prepared a large box in which he embarked with his sister and a cock. After the flood, a messenger of Rama sent to find the state of affairs discovered the box by the cock's crowing. Rama had the box brought to him and questioned the man. Facing north, east and west, the man swore that the woman was his sister; facing south, the man said she was his wife. Told that the fish gave the warning, Rama had the fish's tongue removed and fish have been tongueless ever since. Rama ordered the man to repopulate the world, so he married his sister, and they had seven daughters and seven sons.*[9]

> *A boy and a girl were born to the first man and woman. God sent a deluge to destroy a jackal that had angered him. The man and woman heard it coming, so they shut their children in a hollow piece of wood with provisions to last until the flood subsided. The deluge came and everything on earth was drowned. After 12 years God created two birds and sent them to see if the jackal had been drowned. They saw nothing but a floating log and, landing on it, heard the children inside, who were saying to each other that they had only three days of provisions left. The birds told God, who caused the flood to subside, took the children from the log, and heard their story. In due time they were married.*[10]

Just because eastern India was the true location of the original brother-sister story, it does not of course follow that either of these two tales is accurate! They will have changed through the millennia just as the other brother-sister stories have and, as you can see, they are quite unlike each other except for the essential ingredients, namely: a great flood; a brother and sister who survive; the fact that they marry. Whether there ever was a true set of events with all these ingredients I could not say; however I could most definitely say that the flood itself was a real occurrence and that there must certainly have been an original story.

The Great Flood changed India completely. It changed the language map; it acted as a brake on the spread of wheat and barley farming – yet at the same time it seems that it may well have kick-started rice agriculture in the Ganges region. In the archaeological record it appears as an unexplained lack of evidence for human settlement everywhere except on high ground. And in the tales of men and women it appears in just the same form as we have seen many times all around the globe, the memory of a time when the sea rose to cover the land – or, from the Tamil perspective, when the land sank beneath the sea.

And lying to the west of India is another large tract of land, almost large enough to be another 'subcontinent', much of which would, like India, have been nothing more than an extension of the Indian Ocean in the year the Great Flood struck.

ARABIA

Arabia was another land that suffered widespread devastation. For anyone caught out in the middle of what today is the Rub-al-Khali desert of eastern Arabia, but which in 6250BC was a land of grassy plains and lakes inhabited by hunter-gatherer tribes, the flood would have been very bad news indeed! It would have been a 400-mile walk in most directions to arrive at any ground high enough to escape the rapidly-rising waters. Unfortunately however we know almost nothing of the people of Arabia in those days. Humans were certainly present; this we know from scattered archaeological finds. Some doubtless escaped to tell the tale. But if they did tell of their experiences these tales are lost to us today. No-one knows what race or language lived in Arabia in those far-off times, although we know for sure that they were not the cultural ancestors of today's Arabs, who have only been there for some 2000 years. Nor were they the ancestors of the Sabeans, the previous inhabitants of southern Arabia; they only arrived in about 3000BC.[11] Whoever the flood survivors were – and there is little in the archaeological record to help us – they have since been overwhelmed by subsequent influxes of people and their culture has long since vanished, along with whatever stories they may have told.

IRAQ

However, while Arabia was a bit of a cultural backwater in those days, the land to the north was quite the opposite. Iraq, as I pointed out in Chapter 3, was one of the cradles of modern civilisation; and Iraq is where the story of Noah originated. Although it is true that no centres of population have been discovered out on the Iraqi plain dating from as far back as 6250BC, that does not mean that the plains were uninhabited. The archaeological site of Ali Kosh in south-west Iran lies right on the edge of the plain and Ali Kosh was one of the most up-to-date centres of civilisation in those days, supporting arable farming and livestock herding, and it is to be supposed that related peoples also inhabited the adjacent flat lands towards the Tigris river. As I said in Chapter 3, there may well be settlements waiting to be discovered, but they do not underlie the later settlements of the Sumerian people and so are not evident to today's archaeologists. Of course, once the destruction wrought by this flood is appreciated, then a complete cultural break between those who lived before and those who came after is only to be expected.

Anyway, if my reading of the language evidence is correct the southern Iraqi plain would, in 6250BC, have been inhabited by speakers of a language related to Elamite, one of the oldest written languages in the world. Elam, now a province in south-western Iran, was once a mighty nation, rivalling Babylon and the other great powers of the Middle East. The Elamite capital Susa lay right on the eastern edge of the plain of the Tigris and Euphrates rivers, and Susa is a very ancient city indeed, with a past revealed by archaeology to stretch way back into the 5th Millennium BC. Furthermore the culture of Susa clearly descends from a much older tradition, whose remains have been found at sites all over that part of the plain and dating as far back as 6000BC or shortly thereafter. And this 'Susiana' culture also has a clear ancestor, that of Ali Kosh, a town that somehow seems to have survived the flood.

Well perhaps that's a slight exaggeration. What I really mean is that the *culture* of Ali Kosh survived the flood, which is no surprise since the inhabitants would have had to do no more than spend an uncomfortable 9 months up in the adjacent Zagros foothills as the waters rose and fell. In fact Ali Kosh was perfectly placed to act as a springboard from which agricultural life could move out onto the Susiana plain. The degree of cultural continuity from Ali Kosh down to times when we genuinely know the people of Susa to have been Elamite implies that the direct ancestors of the Elamites lived in exactly the same region as their descendants. The fact that this ties in with the language evidence makes matters doubly certain.[12] It is a matter of great regret that the Elamite language has just failed to make it through to the 21st Century – by a few hundred years – and we have therefore lost whatever folk memories the people may have had. The Elamites wrote but, of those few inscriptions that have survived, none found so far tells us of the flood.

However someone on the Tigris-Euphrates plain obviously had a story to tell, a story that has gripped the world ever since. As we saw in Chapter 2, not only does the story of the flood form a key element in the Bible and the Koran but it also crops up in the *Epic of Gilgamesh*, the number one literary classic in the 2nd Millennium BC Middle East and a key product of Sumerian civilisation. Just as later Elamite culture can be traced back to Ali Kosh, so Sumerian culture can be traced back to settlements further north along the eastern edge of the plain, settlements such as Jarmo. And even though central Iraq is as bare of archaeology before 6250BC as is southern Iraq, it is logical to suppose that Sumerian-related peoples were already present. As was the case to the south, the flood wiped the land clean; it is no surprise that subsequent settlement took place in quite different locations and that no sign of a pre-6250BC population has therefore been found.

But the flood story in the *Epic of Gilgamesh* strongly suggests that Sumerian speakers had experienced the flood – or that they were directly in contact with a people who had experienced the flood, a people who must have lived on or around the central Iraqi plain. The story was clearly well known and, though it had doubtless gained various embellishments during the three and a half millennia that had passed between the time of the flood itself and the days of Gilgamesh, ruler of Uruk, it was a powerful enough story to stand the test of time. Like the brother-sister story now told from India to the Philippines, and the story of the wise man from North America who took with him on his raft a beaver, a muskrat, a duck and an otter, there would have been many variant versions told by the various peoples who had adopted the tale as their own. In this tale from the Middle East there are themes that we have seen many times already in flood myths from around the world; a man and his family told by God to build a boat, animals taken on board, waters rising to drown the land and everyone on it, survival and the repopulation of the earth. The flood that struck the Iraqi plain was the same flood that struck America, Australia, China, India and every other low-lying country on the planet, except for those lucky few favoured either by latitude (on the equator) or longitude (90 degrees from Lake Agassiz). Yet it is only the story of the flood in Iraq that most of the world knows anything about.

THE FLIGHT OF THE SOLITAIRE

But before I head back to Iraq and the story of Noah let me first take you on a journey far to the south, to a place where, so scientists might well argue, a fundamental objection to belief in the Great Flood once lurked in the natural history of the Indian Ocean. In Chapter 5 I called in on the island of Mauritius, making the point that the now-extinct dodo must have survived the flood and, therefore, that water could never have covered the whole island. As it happens the prediction is that no more than a few tens of metres of the tops of the mountain ranges of Mauritius would have remained above flood level,[13] so the dodo's survival was precarious to say the least. So was the survival of indigenous Mauritian ants in mountaintop locations. However the problem doesn't lie on Mauritius at all but on the much smaller island of Rodrigues, about 400 miles to the east, where another flightless bird known as the 'solitaire' once dwelt. And the problem is that, like the Andaman and Nicobar Islands, Rodrigues is predicted to have been fully submerged. The solitaire should never have survived.

This is a puzzle to which, frankly, I have no certain solution. Genetic material has been analysed suggesting that both the dodo and the solitaire were related to the Nicobar pigeon, but the reported genetic distances involved are enormous.[14] Separation could not therefore have occurred recently. I can offer only two solutions: either the flood described in this book has to be massively 'down-sized' – and this runs contrary to the weight of evidence so far – or the solitaire's flightlessness only developed over the millennia since the flood, i.e. it managed to fly to Rodrigues, probably from Mauritius. The fact that its cousins left behind on Mauritius no longer survive is not necessarily a big surprise. The Rodrigues flying fox was also once found on Mauritius but has since become extinct there; it too must have made the flight to Rodrigues at some date within the last 8000 years, probably carried unwillingly by the winds of a tropical storm. None of this proves the ancestry of the solitaire of course, but if the Great Flood was a real event then the ancestor of the solitaires eaten by 17th Century sailors could not have inhabited Rodrigues in 6250BC. However, if the truth about the solitaire's past is ever to be unearthed, I admit that I will not be the one to do it!

SUMMARY

I have deliberately ended this chapter with a crumb of comfort for those who still wish to doubt that this flood ever happened; but it is only a crumb. We have no way to view a live solitaire and so no way to judge how recently it may have had the power of flight, which means the only possible verdict is 'not proven'. All other indicators remain strongly supportive of the flood, even in India where predictions show that about 97% of the land was under water. Archaeology and linguistics both tell the story of small bands of survivors spreading out from the central Indian hills, and without a disaster on the scale of this flood there is absolutely no logical reason why this should have occurred, and no logical reason for the lack of subsequent archaeological evidence in lowland India.

But now, as I said, I want to head back to Iraq, and in Iraq the adventure will have come full circle. I started with the mystery of Noah's flood and it is with the flood of Noah that I shall finish. It is time to re-examine the most famous flood story of them all.

18

Noah's Tale

We now know pretty much what happened during the episode known to myth as the 'Great Flood', to some archaeologists as the 'great hiatus', and to climatologists as the '8.2ka BP climatic event'. We know why it happened (in terms of the physics of the Earth); we know it did indeed produce a near worldwide flood; we have a fair idea of just how deep it was at different locations around the globe; and we know how long it lasted. Given that the event that initiated the whole episode, the collapse of the ice dam that had been restraining Lake Agassiz, must surely have occurred during late summer or autumn in the northern hemisphere we can also take a pretty good guess at what time of year this flood occurred in different places.

We have also looked at myth after myth. I have drawn your attention to the common theme of the sea rising to cover the land and to those elements of the stories that are the most believable, such as escape to the mountains or in a boat. But in truth virtually all the tales contain elements that are either absurdly mythical, for example the concept of breathing on a lump of mud dredged up from the submerged ground in order to create dry land, or the disappearance of the flood waters being induced by the fiery tongue of a giant snake, or else they contain elements that are plainly incorrect. In this latter category are the many false geographical references, such as to Pacific Islands which were uninhabited in 6250BC or to floods covering peaks which are much higher than any possible upper limit on sea level rise. Admittedly I have quoted a few extracts that are so short that they could plausibly represent 100% truth, but that is usually because I have omitted other parts of the story that I considered 'unhelpful', often due to their inclusion of mythical beasts or malicious deities interfering with people's lives.

I don't wish to criticise these flood myths in the least. It is frankly amazing that they should have survived, most of them transmitted purely orally for more than eight millennia. I simply want to make the point that the years have taken their toll and that the stories we hear today are significantly altered from their original forms. This is in no way shameful; it is simply the usual way of things with human traditions.

But the story of Noah is different. It is much more than just a folk myth. It is a folk myth that has found its way into two of the great religious books of 21st Century Earth, the Bible and the Koran. It really matters to millions of people whether the story of Noah is true or not. If it is just one more version of the Iraqi tale referred to in the *Epic of Gilgamesh*, with no more credibility than any other version of that tale – or indeed any version of any of the many dozens of excellent flood myths from around the world – then this has serious implications for those who consider either the Bible or the Koran to be the 'word of God'. After all, you would expect an almighty God to keep major falsehoods out of his 'word'. One might accept copying errors or translation difficulties, but major falsehoods would be a serious disappointment. So the question here is: how does the flood of Noah match what we now know to be reality?

BEFORE THE FLOOD

Nowhere is it stated just where Noah lived, but the Bible does give a certain amount of geographical information about the Garden of Eden, the place where Noah's distant ancestors, Adam and Eve, are said to have lived. For a start, since *Eden* is the Sumerian word for *plain* this strongly suggests that Eden lay somewhere out on the plains of Iraq, where Sumerian would later be spoken. The Bible then reports that four rivers converged in Eden; they are the Tigris, the Euphrates, the Gihon and the Pishon.[1] The Tigris and Euphrates we know well enough – although not the exact route they took across the Iraqi plain in 6250BC. The Pishon is said to flow through the land of Havilah, and the name *Havilah* may plausibly be identified with the Wadi Hawrah, which flows into the Euphrates in central Iraq. Whether this identification is correct or not, there are other references to Havilah in the Bible and they seem to indicate this approximate location.[2] The Gihon I cannot identify[3] – nor the land of Cush through which it flowed[4] – but, with two rivers known and Havilah plausibly located, the approximate position of Eden is pretty clear. It was somewhere in central or southern Iraq. Of course we cannot be certain that Noah lived in the same general region as his forebears, but it has to be likely. The *Epic of Gilgamesh* informs us that Utanapishtim, Noah's *alter ego*, came from the city of Shuruppak which, though it would not be constructed for another 3000 years or so, lay right in the middle of southern Iraq.

I guess it isn't really vital exactly where Noah lived before the flood; the key point is that if it was somewhere out on the Iraqi plain it would most definitely have been flooded!

NOAH'S FLOOD

Let's take a look now at the story as it is given in the Bible, in Genesis chapters 6 to 8. I won't quote it in full; you can look it up for yourself if you wish. Here I shall just give you the essentials.

> *Now the earth was corrupt in God's sight and was full of violence. God saw how corrupt the earth had become, for all the people on earth had corrupted their ways. So God said to Noah: "I am going to put an end to all people, for the earth is filled with violence because of them. I am surely going to destroy both them and the earth. So make yourself an ark of cypress wood ...."*
>
> *............... In the 600th year of Noah's life, on the 17th day of the 2nd month – on that day all the springs of the great deep burst forth, and the floodgates of the heavens were opened. And rain fell on the earth for 40 days and 40 nights. On that very day Noah and his sons Shem, Ham and Japheth, together with his wife and the wives of his three sons, entered the ark. They had with them every wild animal according to its kind, all livestock according to their kinds, every creature that moves along the ground according to its kind and every bird according to its kind, everything with wings. ....*
>
> *............... For 40 days the flood kept coming on the earth, and as the waters increased they lifted the ark high above the earth. The waters rose and increased greatly on the earth, and the ark floated on the surface of the water. They rose greatly on the earth and all the high mountains under the entire heavens were covered. The waters rose and covered the mountains to a depth of more than 20 feet. Every living thing that moved on the earth perished – birds, livestock, wild animals, all the creatures that swarm over the earth, and all mankind. Everything on dry land that had the breath of life in its nostrils died. Every living thing on the face of the earth was wiped out; men and animals and the creatures that move along the ground and the birds of the air were wiped from the earth. Only Noah was left, and those with him in the ark. The waters flooded the earth for 150 days. ....*
>
> *............... The water receded steadily from the earth. At the end of the 150 days the water had gone down and on the 17th day of the 7th month the ark came to rest on the mountains of Ararat. The waters continued to recede until the 10th month, and on the 1st day of the 10th month the tops of the mountains became visible. ....*
>
> *............... By the 1st day of the 1st month of Noah's 601st year, the water had dried up from the earth. Noah then removed the covering from the ark and saw that the surface of the ground was dry. By the 27th day of the 2nd month the earth was completely dry. Then God said to Noah: "Come out of the ark ...."*

According to the Bible the flood arrived on the 17th day of the 2nd month, which would probably be some time in early May according to our present calendar.[5] Assuming that Lake Agassiz broke through its ice dam at the end of the northern hemisphere summer, in September, then, according to the calculation in Chapter 11, the flood should have reached the 100-metre mark in central Iraq by early May of the fifth year, about 1700 days later. As I said, we don't know where Noah actually lived, but the early agricultural community of Ali Kosh in the land of Elam for example lived close to the 100-metre contour.[6]

The Bible then reports that the waters flooded the land for 150 days and that the ark cleared the tops of the mountains by 20 feet (15 cubits in the original), which presumably means that during this 5-month period the keel (or perhaps the sea anchor) never, so far as Noah was aware, made contact with any land. However Noah's ark is reported to have run aground on the 17th day of the 7th month, which would be about 1850 days after Lake Agassiz emptied. According to Chapter 11 this would be very close to the high-point of the flood. This is logical. While the water was rising there was no possibility of any long-term grounding of the ark since the rising water would inevitably refloat it within hours. However as soon as the water started to recede it was equally inevitable that the ark would soon be left high and dry. The question is: where?

The location given in the Bible is the 'Mountains of Ararat' which, as I said in Chapter 1, should really be rendered 'Mountains of Urartu', Urartu being the name of the country around Lake Van, north of the Tigris plain, during the period of history when the majority of the so-called 'Old Testament' of the Bible was compiled.[7] The mountain known today as Mount Ararat is further north, just off the flood map.

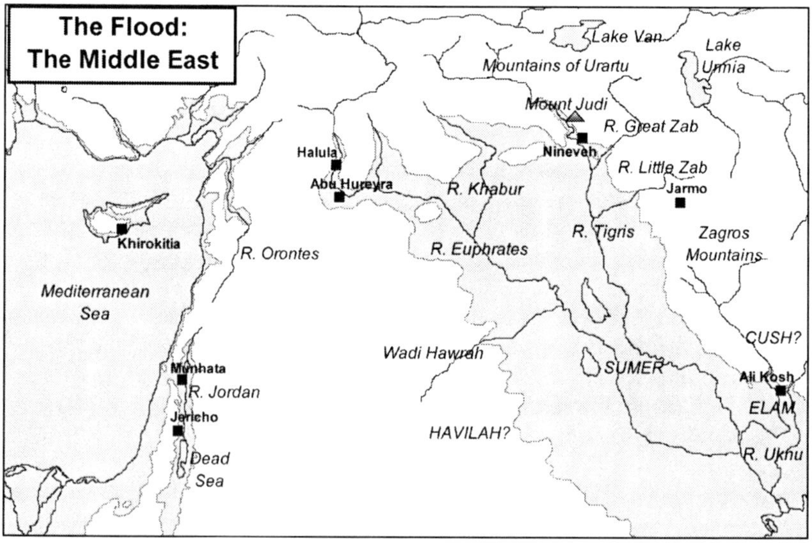

However I think we can be a little more specific about Noah's landfall, based on the Koran's report that the ark landed on a certain 'Mount Judi'.[8] Now one has to admit that there are several mountains named Mount Judi, an Arabian location being favoured by many Muslims, but there is certainly one Mount Judi located just north of the Tigris River on the edge of the mountains of Urartu and right on the predicted flood shoreline.[9] The location is just where it should be. The flood was being fed from the south, from the Persian Gulf; it would therefore tend to push whatever floating debris it picked up toward the north. If the wind were from the south as well, then this would be likely to drive Noah and his ark into one of the northern inlets. The slopes of Mount Judi would therefore be one of the most likely locations for the ark to come to rest, probably accompanied by all manner of flotsam and jetsam from the homes and businesses of those who had perished across the flooded plain. According to the prediction the high water mark in that part of the world should have been about 400 metres above normal ocean level, not too far up the mountainside but a long way above the plain.

The Bible tells us next that the tops of the mountains became visible on the 1st day of the 10th month, about 10 weeks after first running aground. According to Chapter 11 the water level would by then have fallen by about 70 metres from its peak so it is quite plausible that Noah and his family, looking out of their porthole, were beginning to see the tops of the hills on the other side of the flooded Tigris valley emerging from the water.

There then followed two months during which Noah is supposed to have released first a raven and then a dove, checking by this means whether there was enough solid ground for him and his family to live on. Eventually, some time in early March, with the flood now 200 metres below the ark and well out of sight to the south, the dove returned with an olive leaf in its beak, so Noah knew that plants were sprouting once more and that he could at last remove the covering from the ark. He was a cautious man however – and let's face it he had had a rather traumatic experience – and so he and his family only disembarked on the 27th day of the 2nd month, just over a year after climbing aboard, at which point the water level should have been not much more than 30 or 40 metres above normal ocean level; the shoreline would have been hundreds of miles away.

SUMMARY

Basically, my conclusion is that it all makes pretty good sense! The durations are right (bearing in mind the uncertainty involved in the flood prediction); the times of year are right. Even the geographical references to Mount Judi and to the Mountains of Ararat are right. If only Christians would stop insisting that nothing other than Mount Ararat in eastern Turkey will do and Muslims would stop looking for an Arabian location; if only the texts were simply read as they are, then the clear ring of truth is unmistakable. Once we look beyond the interpretations that generations of religious leaders, both Christian and Muslim, have come up with, it can fairly be said that the story of Noah, or at least the description of the flood which it contains, is indeed reliable. The statement that all creatures on the face of the earth perished is entirely accurate – once it is appreciated that the 'earth' referred to is not the entire planet but rather the earth known by Noah, i.e. lowland Iraq.[10] The reference to all the high mountains being covered is also absolutely true – once it is appreciated that the mountains referred to are the hills that Noah saw vanishing beneath the rising water, not the Himalayas or the Andes of which he had no knowledge. You may wish to question some of the other elements of the story, notably the reference to Noah living for over 600 years, but that is a matter beyond the scope of this book!

The bottom line is that this particular flood myth, unlike all the many others from across the globe, contains real truth, not only in essence (waters rising to cover the land) but also in detail, and that is remarkable indeed. Is it sheer coincidence that it was this flood myth rather than the 7-day flood of the Babylonian hero Atrahasis for example that was incorporated into the Bible, and later endorsed by the Koran? Was it pure luck that those who first put pen to paper and created the written scriptures chose to believe this particular story?

These are questions that cannot be answered here of course but I hope that you now have increased respect for the age-old story of Noah and, possibly, that you have increased respect for the accuracy of the oral tradition which was first set down in writing thousands of years after the event, possibly by Moses himself, and which is now part of that international best-seller, the Bible. And if the story of Noah's flood, just about the most unlikely story in the entire Bible, is basically true, then isn't the rest of the book worth a look?

Appendix: Calculations

This appendix is included to assist any reader who would like to replicate the predictions presented in this book. The intention is that sufficient information is given to set up the necessary computation procedures.

1. Elastic Rebound following Draining of Lake Agassiz

Assumptions

a) Volume of Lake Agassiz = 163000km^3 (Teller, 2003) = $163\times10^{12}\text{m}^3$
b) Lake surface area = 1000000km^2 (estimated from plan)
c) Density profile of the mantle-crust layer is as shown in diagram (Robertson, 1966)
d) Density of surface rock = 2700kg/m^3
e) Density of liquid iron outer core = 9700kg/m^3
f) Thickness of mantle-crust layer = 2883km
g) Stiffness modulus of mantle-crust in compression = 100GPa (= 1×10^{11}Pa)
h) Radius of Earth = 6368km
i) The total mass of the Earth = 5.9742×10^{24}kg
j) The mantle shears as required to allow the layer to rise or fall in response to the addition or loss of mass from the surface.
k) Gravity at the Earth's surface = 9.81ms^{-2}

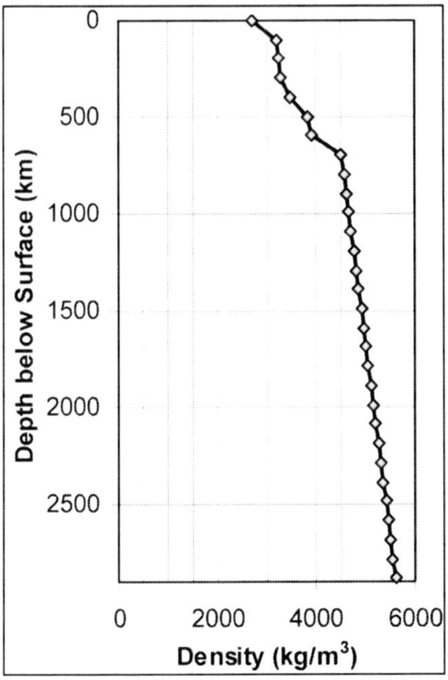

Calculation steps

1) Average lake depth = 163000/1000000 km = 163m
2) Sum mass of mantle-crust layer in 100km layers: total mass = 4.02×10^{24}kg
3) Therefore mass of core = $(5.9742 - 4.02) \times 10^{24}$ = 1.9486×10^{24}kg

4) Radius of core = 6368 – 2883 = 3485km
5) Therefore gravity at core-mantle boundary = 9.81 × (1.9486/5.9742) × (6368/3485)^2 = 10.69ms^{-2}
6) Each 1m^2 at the surface overlies (3485/6368)^2 m^2 at the core-mantle boundary = 0.2995m^2
7) Weight of water in Lake Agassiz = 163 × 10^{12} × 1000 × 9.81 = 1.60 × 10^{18}N
8) This is balanced by 1.60 × 10^{18} ÷ 10.69 ÷ 9700 = 15.42 × 10^{12}m^3 of liquid iron core
9) This is distributed over an area of 1000000 × 0.2995 = 299500km^2 = 2.995 × 10^{11}m^2
10) The 163m depth of Lake Agassiz is therefore balanced by 15.42 × 10^{12} ÷ 2.995 × 10^{11} = 51.49m of liquid iron core
11) When (this idealised version of) Lake Agassiz drained, the mantle-crust layer would have rebounded by 51.49m due to pressure from the liquid iron core
12) The entire mantle-crust layer also experienced a reduction in vertical compressive stress due to draining of Lake Agassiz = 163 × 1000 × 9.81 = 1.60 × 10^{6}Pa
13) The resulting extensile strain = 1.60 × 10^6 ÷ 1 × 10^{11} = 1.6 × 10^{-5}
14) This gives an additional rebound of 1.6 × 10^{-5} × 2883 × 1000 = 46.13m at the surface

2. Overturning Moment induced by Draining of Lake Agassiz

Assumptions

a) Region of mantle-crust beneath Lake Agassiz rises by 51.49m and expands by 46.13m (Section 1)
b) Adjacent mantle-crust regions are unaffected (note: this assumption is clearly incorrect but allows a reasonable estimate of overturning moment to be made)
c) Dimensions, densities etc. are as in Section 1
d) Lake Agassiz was centred at latitude 52 degrees north of the equator

Calculation steps

1) Work out mass (m) of each 100km layer of mantle-crust underlying Lake Agassiz
2) Angular velocity of the Earth (ω) = 1 revolution every 23.93 hours (a sidereal day) = 2π/(23.93×3600) = 7.29×10^{-5} rads per second
3) Work out centrifugal force due to each 100km mantle-crust layer (= mrω^2 where r is the distances to axis of spin); multiply by change in distance (z) north of the centre of the Earth to obtain contributions to overturning moment

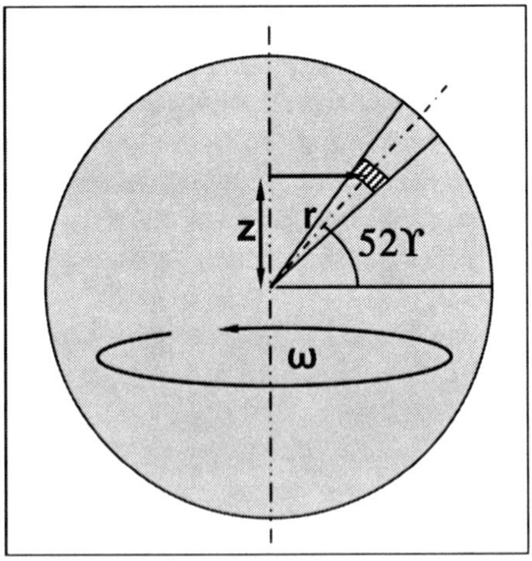

4) Also work out change in centrifugal force due to change in position of each 100km mantle-crust layer (= $m[r_1\text{-}r_1]\omega^2$ where r_1 and r_2 are initial and changed distances to axis of spin); multiply by distance (z) north of the centre of the Earth to obtain contributions to overturning moment
5) Also work out centrifugal force lost due to loss of mass of Lake Agassiz water; multiply by distance (z) north of the centre of the Earth to obtain contribution to overturning moment
6) Also work out centrifugal force gained due to additional liquid iron core thickness; multiply by distance (z) north of the centre of the Earth to obtain contribution to overturning moment
7) Sum all components of overturning moment = $\underline{+3.9\times10^{21}\text{Nm}}$

3. Moment of Inertia of the Earth

Assumptions

a) The density profile of the mantle crust layer is as given previously
b) The core of the Earth does not contribute to the Moment of Inertia relating to true polar shift (i.e. it is assumed not to move with the mantle)

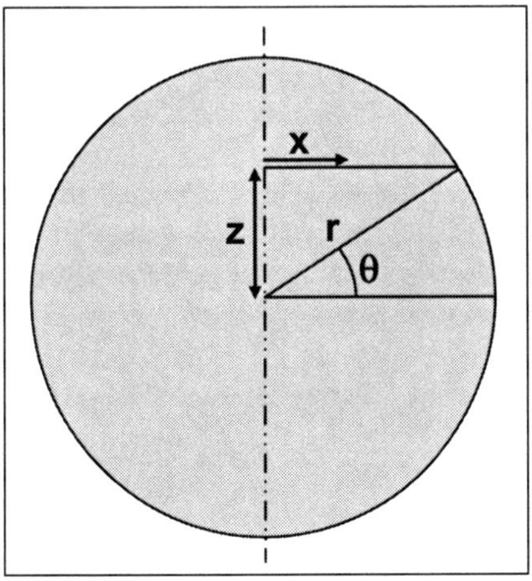

Calculation steps

1) Work out the 2nd moment of area (I) of a solid sphere rotating about any diameter

$I = 2\int \{\int 2\pi x\ x^2\ dx\}\ dz$

$= 2\int\ (\pi/2)\ r^4\cos^4\theta\ dz$

(integrating x between 0 and r cosθ)

$= \pi r^4 \int \{1 - 2\sin^2\theta + \sin^4\theta)\ dz$

But $z = r\ \sin\theta$, therefore

$I = \pi r^4 \int \{1 - 2z^2/r^2 + z^4/r^4)\ dz$

$I = \pi r^4 [z - (2/3)z^3/r^2 + (1/5)z^5/r^4]$ *between 0 and r*
$I = \pi r^4 [r - (2/3)r + (1/5)r] = (8/15)\pi r^5$

2) Work out the 2nd moment of area of each 100km layer of mantle-crust by subtracting the value for one sphere from another
3) Multiply each 2nd moment of area by the average density of that layer to give the moment of inertia
4) Sum throughout the mantle-crust layer = $\underline{7.06 \times 10^{37} kgm^2}$

4. The Detailed Shape of the Earth

Assumptions

a) Acceleration due to gravity at the surface = $9.81ms^{-2}$
b) Acceleration due to gravity at the core-mantle boundary = $10.69ms^{-2}$ (Section 1)
c) The angular velocity of the Earth = 7.29×10^{-5} rads per second (Section 2)
d) The mean radius at the surface = 6368km
e) The mean radius at the core-mantle boundary = 3485km

Calculation steps

1) Centripetal acceleration on the equator at the surface = $6368 \times 1000 \times (7.29 \times 10^{-5})^2 = 0.0338ms^{-2}$
2) Centripetal acceleration on the equator at the core-mantle boundary = $3485 \times 1000 \times (7.29 \times 10^{-5})^2 = 0.0185ms^{-2}$
3) Additional radius on the equator at the surface ≈ $(0.0338/9.81) \times 6368 = 21.9$km note: this is not strictly accurate; the real value is $\underline{21.3km}$ and is due to a summation of effects throughout the thickness of the Earth]
4) Additional radius on the equator at the core-mantle boundary ≈ $(0.0185/10.69) \times 3485 = 6.0$km note: again this is not strictly accurate; factor in line with real value of additional surface radius: $= 6.0 \times 21.3/21.9 = \underline{5.8km}$]
5) Mantle thickness = 21.3 – 5.8 = 15.5km greater at the equator than the poles
6) At latitude θ centripetal acceleration = $r\cos\theta \times \omega^2$; the effect perpendicular to the surface = $r\cos^2\theta \times \omega^2$; the effect therefore varies linearly from $r\omega^2$ at the equator to zero at the poles since $\cos^2\theta$ is a linear function; mantle thickness therefore also varies linearly

5. Level Change due to a 1 degree True Polar Shift

Assumptions

a) The mantle-crust layer is 15.5km thicker at the equator than at the poles (Section 4)

b) The thickness decreases linearly with latitude
c) The mean radius at the surface = 6368km
d) The mean thickness of the core-mantle layer = 2883km
e) Densities are as given previously
f) Acceleration due to gravity varies as shown on the plot (calculated using the approach outlined in Section 1)
g) Acceleration due to gravity at the core-mantle boundary = $10.69ms^{-2}$ (Section 1)
h) Each $1m^2$ at the surface reduces to $0.2995m^2$ at the core-mantle boundary (Section 1)

Calculation steps

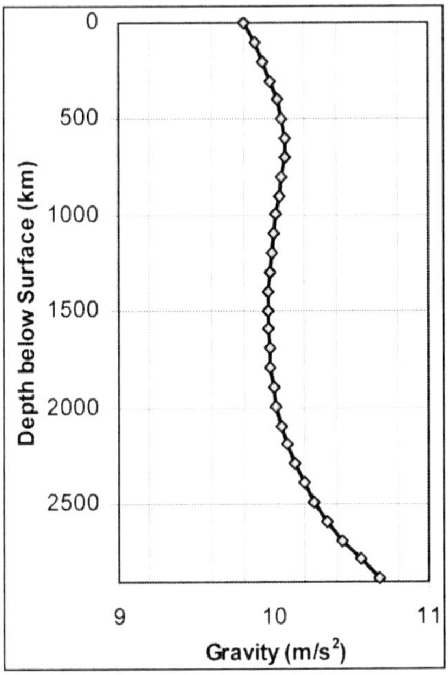

1) 1 degree represents 1/90 of the distance from the equator to the pole
2) Each location on the longitude of tilt (other than very close to the equator or the pole) will therefore have a mantle-crust thickness more (or less) than it would be if the planet were to be in gravitational equilibrium, by 15.5/90 km = 172.2m
3) Sum the weights of 100km thick mantle-core layers beneath a $1m^2$ area on the surface multiplying mass by acceleration due to gravity for each layer = $7.933\times10^{10}N$
4) Each $1m^2$ on the surface therefore applies more (or less) force than it would if the planet were to be in gravitational equilibrium, by $7.933\times10^{10} \times 172.2/(2.883\times10^6) = 4.74\times10^6N$
5) It will therefore displace $4.74\times10^6/(9700\times10.69\times0.2995)$ = 152.6m more (or less) of liquid iron core
6) The result at the surface is a rise (or fall) in level by 172.2 – 152.6 = <u>19.6m</u>
7) On average, the mantle-crust layer sinks (or rises) by (152.6 – 19.6)/2 = <u>66.5m</u>

6. Bending and Shearing of the Earth's Mantle

Assumptions

a) Each strip of the mantle-crust layer can be treated as a uniform beam on a dense liquid foundation [note: this is increasingly untrue with increasing distance from the equator – see diagram]

b) While one hemisphere tries to rise by 66.5m for each 1 degree true polar shift, the other tries to sink by 66.5m (Section 5)

c) There is a transition zone near the equator of width equal to the amount of true polar shift between regions where the mantle-crust tries to rise and sink

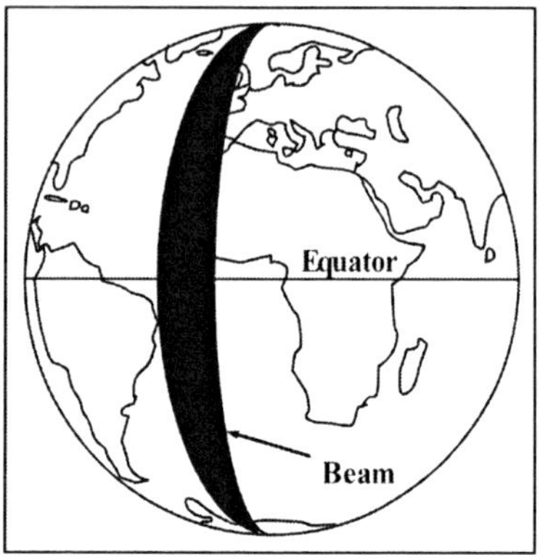

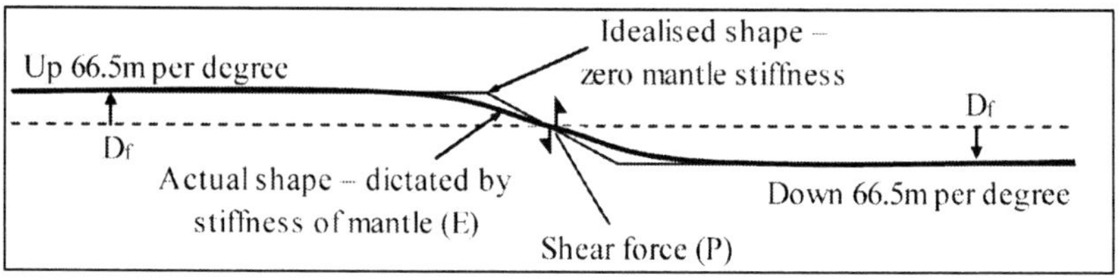

Calculation steps A – key quantities

1) The neutral axis of the mantle is obtained by considering it as a trapezium in section; the result is that it occurs at a radius of 5067km

2) The dense liquid foundation would provide a modulus of subgrade reaction (k) of $9700 \times 10.69 = 1.037\times10^5 N/m^3$ if this were a standard rectangular beam; reduce by the ratio of area at the core-mantle boundary to area at the neutral axis $= 1.037\times10^5 \times (3485/5067)^2 =$ <u>$4.905\times10^4 N/m^3$</u>

3) The 2nd moment of area (I) is found by integrating over the trapezium section:

$$I = \int ((6368-x)/6368)(6368-5067-x)^2\,dx$$
$$= \int (1-x/6368)(1301-x)^2\,dx$$
$$= \int 1301^2 - ((1301^2/6368)+2602)x + (1+2602/6368)x^2 - (1/6368)x^3\,dx$$

Integrate between 0 and 2883km

$I = 1301^2 \times 2883 - ((1301^2/6368)+2602) \times 2883^2/2 + (1+2602/6368) \times 2883^3/3 - (1/6368) \times 2883^4/4$

$= \underline{1.501\times10^9\ km^4}$ per kilometre width at the surface

Calculation steps B – bending

1) Standard beam on dense liquid foundation equation: $y = (P\lambda/2k)\ e^{-\lambda x}(\sin\lambda x+\cos\lambda x)$ where y = deflection, P = applied load, $\lambda = (k/4EI)^{0.25}$, E = stiffness modulus, x = distance from load
2) Mantle-crust in bending is modelled using the part of the beam beyond the inflexion point, where $d^2y/dx^2 = 0$
3) Double differentiate equation: $d^2y/dx^2 = (P\lambda^3/k)\ e^{-\lambda x}(\sin\lambda x-\cos\lambda x)$
4) $d^2y/dx^2 = 0$ when $x = \pi/4\lambda$; at which point $y = (P\lambda/2^{0.5}k)\ e^{-\pi/4}$
5) Shear force (F) is given by $EI\ d^3y/dx^3 = EI\ (2P\lambda^4/k)\ e^{-\lambda x}\cos\lambda x$
6) When $x = \pi/4\lambda$, $F = EI\ (8^{0.5}P\lambda^4/k)\ e^{-\pi/4}$; but $\lambda^4 = k/4EI$ therefore $F = (P/2^{0.5})\ e^{-\pi/4}$
7) Thus, at point of inflexion $\underline{y_{bending} = F_{bending}\lambda/k}$

Calculation steps C – shear

1) Standard shear beam on dense liquid foundation equation: $y = y_{shear}\ e^{\sqrt{(k/hG)}\ x}$ where y = deflection, y_{shear} = deflection at end of beam, h = beam (i.e. mantle-crust) thickness, G = shear modulus, x = distance from end of beam
2) Shear force (F) is given by $hG\ dy/dx = hG\ y_{shear}\sqrt{(k/hG)}\ e^{\sqrt{(k/hG)}\ x}$
3) When $x = 0$, $F = hG\ y_{shear}\sqrt{(k/hG)} = y_{shear}\sqrt{(khG)}$
4) Thus, at end of beam $\underline{y_{shear} = F_{shear}/\sqrt{(khG)}}$

Calculation steps D – ratio of deflections due to bending and shear

1) The same shear force at the point of inflexion between northern and southern hemispheres of the Earth induces both bending and shear; Thus $F_{bending} = F_{shear} = F$
2) Therefore $y_{bending}/y_{shear} = (\lambda/k)/(1/\sqrt{(khG)}) = \lambda\sqrt{(hG/k)}$
3) But $\lambda^4 = k/4EI$; also assume $E = 3G$ (i.e. zero volume change)
4) Therefore: $y_{bending}/y_{shear} = (k^{0.25}h^{0.5}E^{0.5})/(4^{0.25}E^{0.25}I^{0.25}3^{0.5}k^{0.5}) = 0.408\ (h^2E/Ik)^{0.25}$

7. Accounting for the Transition Zone near the Equator

Assumptions

a) It is acceptable to carry out the calculation for shear only and to rely on the ratio of bending and shear deflections in Section 6
b) In the transition zone the pressure from the liquid iron core decreases linearly to zero

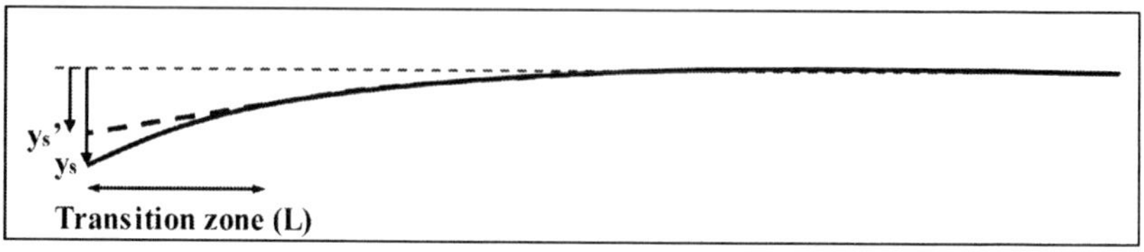

Calculation steps

1) Deflection change ($y_{shear}-y_{shear}'$) due to pressure drop-off in transition zone works out as $ky_{shear}'L^2/6hG$
2) Therefore, outside transition zone $y = y_{shear}'\ (1+\ kL^2/6hG)\ e^{\sqrt{(k/hG)}\ x}$; inside assume a linear slope [note: this is not correct but the error involved is not considered significant]

8. Calculation of True Polar Shift

Assumptions

a) The entire mantle-crust layer acts as a series of beams at each longitude
b) The fact that each beam becomes thinner toward the poles and therefore has less 2nd moment of area (I) is compensated by a proportional reduction in modulus of subgrade reaction (k).
c) The amount of true polar shift decreases according to the cosine of the angle from the longitude of tilt

Calculation Steps

1) Sum numerically the effects of a 1 degree true polar shift ignoring bending and shearing of the mantle-crust layer, i.e. just due to a thickening or thinning of the layer together with a rise or fall of 66.5m per 1 degree of shift together with a linear transition zone; the result in terms of mass times radius squared = 1.213×10^{12}kgkm^2 per square metre at the surface
2) Sum numerically the effects of a further 1m displacement in level of the mantle-crust layer due to effects either side of the equator (and the poles); the result in terms of mass times radius squared = 1.153×10^{11}kgkm^2 per square metre at the surface
3) Sum numerically the contributions to overturning moment from each degree of latitude on each line of longitude [too complex to express here]
4) Set up an incremental computation such that:

In step 1 the moment due to the draining of Lake Agassiz (Section 2) generates an angular acceleration $d^2\phi/dt^2$, depending on the moment of iner-

tia of the Earth (Section 3), giving angular velocity $d\phi/dt$ and angle of shift ϕ at the end of the increment

Shift ϕ causes deformation of the mantle (rising, sinking, bending and shear), which generates a resisting moment

In step 2 the Lake Agassiz moment is reduced by the value of the resisting moment from Step 1 – and so the process is repeated in discrete time increments

Additionally, the Lake Agassiz moment is allowed to decay with a half-life of about 2000 years (based on the known response of land following Ice Age glacier melt)

9. Modelling the Chandler Wobble

Assumptions

a) The natural amplitude of motion is ±6m, which is about $\pm 5\times10^{-5}$ degrees
b) The natural frequency is 430 days
c) The Chandler Wobble is due to an imbalance of mass of a similar nature to that created when Lake Agassiz drained but which dissipates within a few weeks

Calculation

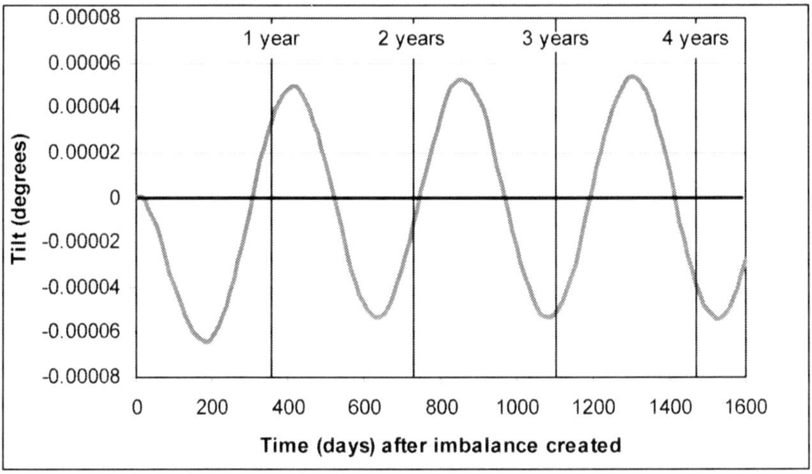

1) The prediction is only correct when the imbalance in mass is equivalent to 0.05% of that of Lake Agassiz (equal to about 3cm of snow over Canada and the United States)
2) The prediction is only correct when the mantle-crust stiffness modulus = 64GPa

10. Modelling the Great Flood

Assumptions

a) The stiffness modulus of the mantle-crust layer is 64 GigaPascals at small angles of tilt (<0.1 degrees)

b) Above 0.1 degrees of tilt the stiffness modulus of the mantle-crust layer obeys the following formula: $E = 64 \div (k \times \text{tilt})^n$ GigaPascals where *n* is a coefficient describing the tendency of stiffness to fall as deformation increases and *k* is a constant

c) Constant *k* is chosen such that E = 64 GigaPascals at a tilt of 0.1 degrees

Calculation steps

1) Compute the response of the Earth with different levels of coefficient *n*

2) Select n = 0.036 giving 20 degrees of tilt [allowing the stiffness modulus of the mantle-crust layer to reduce from 64 to 52.3 GigaPascals at maximum tilt] – see Chapter 11 for result

3) Calculate flood depth considering the following:

each 1 degree of tilt generates 19.6m reduction in land surface level (Section 5)

to this is added the difference between the calculated shape of the mantle-crust layer and the simple assumption of 66.5m rise/fall per degree (Section 5)

total sea level rise at any given longitude depends on the tilt at that longitude which is given (approximately) by the maximum tilt × the cosine of the angle by which the chosen longitude differs from the longitude of maximum tilt

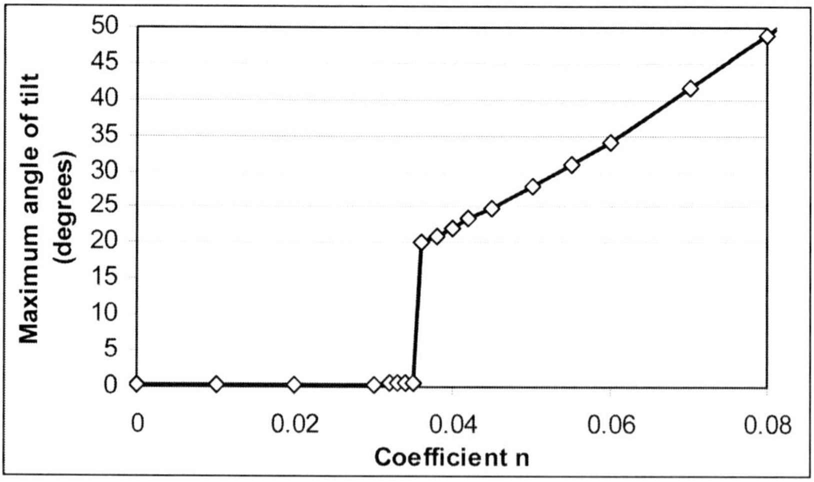

Notes

Chapter 1. Introduction

1. Although there were many before Darwin who held similar views, he was the first to formulate a serious theory as to how the natural world had developed through the ages.
2. The date conventionally given for creation was 4004BC, based on a summing of various time periods given in the Bible, although scholars now realise that the numbers concerned differ between different source documents.
3. For a full explanation of the data to be obtained from ice cores I recommend Richard Alley's book, *The Two-mile Time Machine* (Alley, 2000). A core from Vostok, East Antarctica, has given discernible data over 420000 years, covering four great glacial periods – i.e. 'ice ages' (Petit et al, 1999).
4. The most commonly quoted estimate of sea level rise was formulated by Fairbanks (1989). This shows a steady rise from about 18000BC, accelerating to a maximum rate of around 2 centimetres per year by 8000BC, and then flattening off by about 4000BC, by which time levels were just 10 metres lower than today. Other researchers, e.g. Cronin et al (2002), have deduced significantly different rates for particular locations (Chesapeake Bay in this case), but the Fairbanks curve is treated as a reasonable estimate for the global average.
5. The lake emptied in several stages over the course of a few thousand years. The volume quoted relates to the final massive release of water (Teller, 2003). The giant lake that covered western Siberia may have been even bigger (Lioubimtseva et al, 2003) but no evidence of any comparable sudden emptying has yet come to light.
6. Ryan and Pitman's flood seems to have caught the popular imagination. In particular it has been associated with theories on the spread of Indo-European language since these languages are believed to have originated just north of the Black Sea at about this time (see Chapter 4).
7. Woolley, 1929.
8. This is my own estimate; others may be a couple of hundred years different either way.

Chapter 2. Legend and Myth

1. Experts agree that Middle Eastern civilisation collapsed at the end of the Bronze Age and that Level VI at Troy was one of those cities

destroyed at around this time. There is, however, no consensus regarding date. Most would opt for a date in the 1250-1150BC range (e.g. Murray, 1993); my own estimate is around 1070BC (Thom, 2008).

2. The principal reference to the name *Arthur* comes from a 12th Century manuscript in the British Museum dealing with the calculation of the date of Easter. However the manuscript incorporates 9th Century text from Nennius, which is thought to be authentic. Original sources are clearly much older still. A 'King of the Britons' named Arthur is reported to have fought in a 'Battle of Badon' in the year 518 and to have died at a 'Battle of Camlann' in 539. The context makes it certain that this king was a leader of the Romano-Celtic part of Britain, in which case he is presumed to have been fighting the Anglo-Saxon invaders.
3. Laing, 1979.
4. The Rigveda contains numerous references to identifiable geographical locations, notably the rivers of the Punjab, including the Sarasvati river which no longer exists today. Roy (1989) has analysed the texts in detail and the name Harappa (Hariyupiya) stands out as the seat of a powerful king, who was defeated by the so-called 'Devas'. Several battles are mentioned, first the capture of Harappa and then the attempts of the Harappans to retake their city. Roy dates these events by reference to astronomical observations to 1735BC. The picture given in the texts accords well with the findings of archaeology and linguistics.
5. George (1999) gives an excellent translation.
6. The principal source here is the Babylonian priest Berosus, who lived approximately 330-260BC. He describes Mount Nisir as being in the 'Gordyan' (Kurdish?) Mountains of Armenia. There have been various opinions over the centuries regarding the intended location but most settle for somewhere just east of the river Tigris, either in northern Iraq or southern Turkey.
7. The city of Kish is known from archaeology to have been founded during the Jemdet Nasr period, i.e. during the two centuries immediately preceding the Early Dynastic period (Leick, 2001).
8. The *Sumerian king list* is a most useful document, compiled from 15 different fragments of cuneiform tablet and relating the history of Sumer from semi-mythical times through to the 2nd Millennium BC. It tells of times (the Early Dynastic period) during which supremacy in Iraq swapped regularly from city to city, and Kish, Uruk and Ur were three of the chief contenders.
9. George (1999) presents each of these tales.

10. Assyrian kings can be dated confidently back to the year 911BC (plus or minus 1 year), the coronation year of Adad Nirari II. This is based on a king list, the 'Limmu' list (a list of high officials) and astronomical observations which have been correlated with modern retro-calculation. This gives reliable dates for references to kings Ahab, Jehu, Pekah and Hoshea of Israel and to the capture of Samaria in 722BC. See Roux (1966) for an overview of Assyrian history and Wilson (1999) for correlations to the Bible.
11. The key historical reference given in the Bible during Abraham's life is to the so-called 'battle of the kings' (Genesis 14). The confederation of eastern kings described, from Shinar (Sumer), Elam, Ellasar (Ashur?) and Goiim (Gutium?), could only have come together at a very specific time in history, namely the 3rd Dynasty of Ur. Experts differ on the dating of this dynasty; the dates suggested here reflect my own assessment (Thom, 2008).
12. The oldest extant manuscripts of the Septuagint translation date from the 4th Century AD while those of the Masoretic text date to the 9th Century.
13. My principal source here is Mark Isaak's website (Isaak, 2004), in which he presents a collation of flood stories from around the world, abstracted from a number of other authors.
14. There is ample evidence that much of Hindu culture stems from the Indus Valley civilisation, including some of the iconography found on Indus Valley seals. Manu himself is mentioned in the Rigveda as the king of a country called 'Dravida'. Although there is ongoing debate as to the relative influence on ancient Indian society of the Indo-European-speaking and Dravidian-speaking elements of the population, it is quite clear that the Dravidian element, which has always been staunchly Hindu and which most believe was the dominant force in Indus Valley culture, has contributed strongly. Recently discovered parallels between Indus Valley pottery decoration motifs and those of early Tamil culture emphasise the point.
15. Gaster (1969), Kelsen (1988) and Brinton (1876), reproduced by Isaak (2004).
16. Miller (1994), Howey (1955) and Frazer (1919), reproduced by Isaak (2004).
17. Gaster (1969) reproduced by Isaak (2004).
18. Gaster (1969) reproduced by Isaak (2004).
19. Gaster (1969) reproduced by Isaak (2004).
20. Gaster (1969) reproduced by Isaak (2004).
21. Miller (1994) reproduced by Isaak (2004).
22. Frazer (1919) reproduced by Isaak (2004).

23. See Frazer (1919) reproduced by Isaak (2004). Cape Cleveland is on the coast of Queensland near Townsville.
24. See Frazer (1919) reproduced by Isaak (2004). Encounter Bay is off the South Australian coast just south of Adelaide.
25. Gaster (1969) reproduced by Isaak (2004).
26. La Haye and Morris (1976) reproduced by Isaak (2004).
27. This date lies around the average of the different estimates made by various experts.
28. Although there is no agreement on the origin of the whole group of peoples whose languages are of the Eskimo-Aleut family, it can be demonstrated from archaeology (e.g. Dumond, 1987) that Inuit culture originated on the Asian side of the Bering Strait and then crossed to Alaska.
29. For arguments that there may have been further input of Old World culture into America, see Thom (2007).
30. Clark (1953) reproduced by Isaak (2004).
31. Frazer (1919) reproduced by Isaak (2004).
32. Vitaliano (1973) reproduced by Isaak (2004).
33. Frazer (1919) reproduced by Isaak (2004).
34. Horcasitas (1953) reproduced by Isaak (2004).
35. Gaster (1969) reproduced by Isaak (2004).
36. Kelsen (1988) and Roheim (1952), reproduced by Isaak (2004).
37. Frazer (1919) reproduced by Isaak (2004).
38. Gaster (1969) reproduced by Isaak (2004).
39. Frazer (1919) reproduced by Isaak (2004).
40. Wilbert (1977) reproduced by Isaak (2004).
41. Lithuanian is an Indo-European language; the figure of 2000 years is highly approximate and is based principally on the difference between Lithuanian and Latvian (Thom, 2007). The origin of the Indo-European language family is discussed in Chapter 4.
42. Gaster (1969) reproduced by Isaak (2004).
43. Gaster (1969) and Dixon (1916) reproduced by Isaak (2004).
44. The date at which Austronesian speakers left Taiwan is only approximately known of course, derived from genetic studies (Sykes, 2001) and linguistics (e.g. Dalby, 1998), with significant support from archaeology, namely the spread of 'Lapita' pottery styles across Indonesia and then Polynesia.
45. See Thom (2007). This interpretation is certainly not 'mainstream' but there are no detailed interpretations of which I am aware developed by mainstream linguists. However an important point with which most linguists would agree is the connection to Taiwan, since similarities have been noted between the Austro-Asiatic and Austronesian language families, Austronesian having originated on Taiwan – see note 44.

Chapter 3. The Archaeologist's Report

1. I have summarised in a few paragraphs a vast body of archaeological knowledge which can be found in numerous reports and papers, too many to detail here. There are undoubtedly differences in interpretation between experts, but there is a consensus nowadays that the mountains of the northern Zagros and eastern Turkey saw the earliest development of Middle Eastern agriculture and that 'civilisation' has radiated out from there, including a move south onto the Iraqi plain as evidenced by the culture of Hassuna. Zeder (2005) discusses the inter-relationships between many of the sites of western Iran and the course of animal domestication in the region.
2. The deduction that Sumerian culture arrived from the north is made here on the basis of archaeology; however I believe it also ties in with the language evidence (Thom, 2007).
3. Both Halula and Abu Hureyra were centres of the Pre-pottery Neolithic B culture (discussed in the main text in relation to Jericho) in the 7th Millennium BC.
4. Kenyon, 1970.
5. Grains of both domesticated wheat and barley have been found in Pre-pottery Neolithic A levels at Jericho (Kenyon, 1970).
6. Ancient cities are often evidenced today by mounds (or 'tells'). These grew up over the millennia of occupation from the accumulation of debris left by each generation, much of it often consisting of the remains of mud brick construction.
7. Yakar (1998) discusses the various centres of Pre-pottery Neolithic B culture, emphasising the magnitude of the cultural break that occurred after its collapse. Several researchers comment on the lack of archaeological evidence relating to the next 500 years or so in that part of the Middle East.
8. Rollefson, 1992.
9. The error margin on this date is probably no more than about 200 years. At individual sites the possibility of error is much greater, reflecting the uncertainty in interpretation of Carbon 14 dating evidence; however, when the cumulative evidence from many sites where Pre-pottery Neolithic B culture came to a sudden end is taken into account, the uncertainty is greatly reduced.
10. Cyprus was first settled in the 10th Millennium BC (Simmons, 2001) and agriculture and cattle farming had been developed (or introduced) by the 8th Millennium BC (Guilaine and Briois, 2001). The succeeding 7th Millennium BC culture of Khirokitia had strong similarities to Pre-pottery Neolithic B (Peltenburg et al, 2001) and reached its height just before its sudden and total collapse in the late 7th Millennium BC.

11. See for example Bard (1994).
12. The earliest levels at Jericho date from well before 9000BC and the culture of the time, known as Natufian, has been discovered at several sites in the region. The people were mainly hunters and gatherers, although many believe that some primitive agriculture was being practised. Pre-pottery Neolithic A culture, which had appeared by 9000BC, certainly included arable farming (see Note 5).
13. See Barich (1998) and Grimal (1992). Most of the evidence for primitive agriculture comes from around 9000BC and it seems to have been abandoned for some reason over succeeding millennia in favour of a return to the hunter-gatherer lifestyle.
14. Keita and Boyce (2005) refer to this gap in the archaeological record as well as dealing with the genetic make-up of the ancient Egyptian population. That the gap was not a complete one is evidenced by seasonal occupation of sites like El Kab adjacent to the Nile.
15. The site of Nabta Playa, about 50 miles west of the Nile and just downstream from the second cataract, provides evidence for occupation by a pastoralist people from around 6000BC. See Wendorf and Close (1992) and Malville et al (1998). Several researchers have now identified the Sahara as the source of classical Egyptian civilisation.
16. The 'oracle bones' are ox scapulae that were used in ancient Chinese culture to record the results of consultations with divine oracles. The language of those from Shang dynasty times is poorly understood with the exception of calendrical terms and the names of some of the early Chinese kings (Hay, 1973).
17. This is admittedly a gross oversimplification of the Neolithic cultures of northern China. Strictly 'Peiligang' refers to a much more limited time period and locality, but I am including a series of differing millet-growing cultures in northern China under this general heading. The culture named after the well-preserved site of Xinglongwa in Inner Mongolia is one of the earliest of all.
18. It is clear that belief in the reliability of the evidence for this extremely early cultivation of rice is now widespread (e.g. Xu, 1998) although some researchers continue to question the interpretation of the evidence (Liu, 2000).
19. Gong et al (2007) present a full description of the evidence.
20. Yi (2000) discusses each in turn.
21. Some studies (Normile, 1997) have provided dates as early as 9500BC from grain samples from the middle Yangtze, providing further evidence that this was the region where the idea of rice cultivation first took hold.
22. See for example Piggott (1950).

23. The earliest texts from Iran date from about 3000BC. The language is usually known as proto-Elamite (although relationship with subsequent Elamite language is still conjectural) and inscriptions have been found right across Iran and parts of Afghanistan (Robinson, 2002). The most likely inference is that it accompanied Elamite traders since archaeology attests to the fact that precious stones from Afghanistan were in use at that time in Iran and Iraq (Hinz, 1972).
24. Dating of layers at Mehrgarh is problematic because widely differing Carbon 14 dates have been reported from the same occupation phase (Jarrige et al, 1995). Thus the age of the transition from Period IA, the pre-pottery phase, to Period IB, the first phase with pottery, which is usually put at around 6000BC, cannot in reality be accurately known. The real date could be at least 500 years either way.
25. Biagi, 2003.
26. See note 24.

Chapter 4. The Linguist's Report

1. In his fascinating book *Genes, Peoples and Languages* Professor Cavalli-Sforza explores the similarities between the findings of genetics, archaeology and linguistics regarding the relationships between different peoples and races, and the parallels are sometimes impressive.
2. Duridanov (1976) argued the link between Slavonic and Thracian strongly. The most extreme disagreement with this position of which I am aware is that expounded by Alinei (2003), who sees Slavonic language as having been spoken throughout much of its current range since Palaeolithic times.
3. This statement is chiefly based on the massive cultural change that took place in Greece in the late 3rd Millennium BC at sites such as Lerna (Hood, 1967) and links with cultures to the north, notably the Tripolye culture of western Ukraine.
4. This is a subject that has attracted a great deal of debate and there is still much opposition in India to the idea that the Aryan invasion deduced by early archaeologists (e.g. Piggott, 1950) ever took place. Agarwal (2005) gives a well-balanced summary of the evidence.
5. The first known Iranian language speakers in Iran were the Medes and the Persians, who appear in records dated to the Assyrian king Shalmaneser III (859 to 824BC).
6. A particular type of grey pottery appears in north-western Iran in the Late Bronze Age (1300-1100BC) associated with a culture which looks very Indo-European (militaristic; warrior burials). There are references to 'Armens' in Assyrian annals from about 1100BC and, perhaps of greatest significance, modern Armenians trace their

history back to the kingdom known to the Hittites of the 2nd Millennium BC as 'Azzi-Hayasa', located around the source of the Euphrates river.

7. Renfrew, 1987.
8. Gimbutas (1970) is the best known champion of this widely-held view.
9. Thom, 2007.
10. Few researchers look further back in time than the date of the common Indo-European ancestor. However the analysis in Thom (2007), which implies a distant link to the Afro-Asiatic language family, demands that the ancestor of Indo-European was taken north through the Middle East and across the Caucasus.
11. In fact there is widespread agreement regarding both the location (Ural Mountains somewhere) and date (4000-7000BC) for 'proto' Finno-Ugric.
12. The rather unexpected nature of this supposed expansion of Finno-Ugric speech across plains that should have been inhabited by people of a similar culture and technological ability has led several linguists to doubt that the generally accepted history of this language family can be correct.
13. It is clear from the literature that there is no agreement on the point of origin of Dravidian language, with most researchers content to admit that it is unknown.
14. For example see Blench (2005).
15. A typical estimate appears to be 4000-3000BC. However there seems to be a tendency to underestimate the degree of difference between North and South Semitic, and the picture is confused by the fact that the most commonly quoted family tree for Semitic shows so-called 'East' Semitic (basically Akkadian) as an even earlier branch than South Semitic, something with which I could not possibly agree.
16. Ancient Egyptian is most closely related to the Berber languages of North Africa. The statement that Egyptian language reached Egypt from the Sahara is based on the analysis in Thom (2007) but also agrees with the archaeological history of Egyptian society. The cultural superiority of the Semites is based on the assumption that they were responsible for the early agricultural experiments of the Qadan culture as far back as the 9th Millennium BC – see Chapter 3.
17. The Australian evidence is most interesting. No-one doubts that Homo Sapiens was in Australia from about 35000 to 40000 years ago; there is plenty of evidence. However, at Nauwalabila rockshelter a layer bearing manufactured stone artefacts has been dated to between 53000 and 60000 years ago, and this, many believe, signals the first appearance of humans on the continent. However there are even claims that pollen evidence shows that fire was being used to control the environment up to 130000 years ago!

18. Fernández-Armesto (2001) suggests that taro farming may have started in New Guinea up to 10000 years ago.
19. The same rockshelter (Nauwalabila) that produced evidence for hominid presence at least 53000 years ago has also produced evidence for a very significant change in technology about 6000 years ago (4000BC) with the introduction of nicely-finished stone spear points.
20. The analysis in Thom (2007) implies that a wave of language and culture spread from Egypt into the Middle East in about 15000BC, fanning out in different directions. To the north, one version of the language became Indo-European; in the east, two more versions became Dravidian and Austro-Asiatic; and in the north-east, Uralic and Altaic. The constraints imposed by geography and the passage of time demand that the ancestor of Mongolian had reached the Lake Balkhash region of eastern Kazakhstan by 6250BC. Incidentally this whole group of language families approximately coincides with the super-family known as 'Nostratic', first proposed by Pedersen (1962) and taken up more recently by others (Dolgopolsky, 1998; Bomhard and Kerns, 1994).
21. For example Watson (1966) and Hay (1973) both draw attention to striking parallels between Yangshao pottery and that found at Anau (particularly Level Ib) and other sites in Turkmenistan. I suggest that Yangshao culture was Mongolian speaking, ancestral Chinese then being spoken further south, in the Yangtze river region.

Chapter 5. The Biologist's Report

1. The point is that there are two different indicators used to establish divergence between species. Given the opportunity (new habitat) or necessity (new predators) there may be very rapid changes in appearance or lifestyle, driven by the 'survival of the fittest' maxim. There is also a steady ongoing change in DNA. Rapid speciation, whatever the driving force, means that physical changes occur with very little time for DNA divergence. The result is a closely related 'species flock' such as the cichlids of Lake Victoria.
2. Johnson et al, 1996.
3. Mayr, 1970.
4. This is a very approximate figure, based on the difference between *Eretmodus* fish species from Lake Tanganyika and Lake Victoria cichlids. See Won et al (2006).
5. Sturmbauer et al, 2001.
6. Sturmbauer et al, 2001.
7. Sediment analysis shows a continuous record stretching back at least 78000 years in Lake Malawi (Scholz and Finney, 1994).

8. For example Won et al (2005) suggest between 1000 and 17000 years for speciation of the genus *Tropheops*, a particular cichlid fish type.
9. McClanahan and Young (1996) suggest either a recent episode of high salinity or else a complete drying out of the lake.
10. Candle fish are unique to Lake Baikal. Their name stems from their high oil content, meaning that they burn like candles when dried!
11. For example Kantula et al (2003) studied the 33 species of cottoid fish found in Lake Baikal and found that, although they were all related, they had been diversifying for millions of years. A similar study by Väinölä and Kamaltynov (1999) came to similar conclusions with regard to the 1000 or so species of amphipod.
12. Palo and Väinölä (2006) suggest about 2 million years while Sasaki et al (2003) go for around 0.4 million years.
13. Dumont (1998) gives a full description of Caspian Sea species and their origins.
14. Aladin et al (2008) describe the various theories on this subject.
15. This comment does not include the Caspian seal which, like the Baikal seal, is related to the Arctic ringed seal, but whose genetic code implies hundreds of thousands of years of separate development.
16. Zenkevitch, 1963.
17. Starobogatov (1994) suggested that the lack of deep water species implies there has been a period of anoxia in the recent past, but no cause for this was identified.
18. Väinölä (1995) investigated three Caspian open-water species and noted how unusual it was to find that speciation had occurred so recently. He also noted a clear relationship with species in lakes to the north. Audzijonyte et al (2005) give a broader picture and also emphasise the low genetic diversity even where species are quite different in appearance.
19. Vermeij, 2004.
20. The North Pacific waters circulate clockwise, moving north past Japan, crossing to America, and then returning south past Mexico. Thus western species are more likely to drift north than eastern species. However, at the Bering Strait the current drifts south, which means that it is hard to see any possibility of entry from the Pacific – as Vermeij (2004) proposes. A more likely scenario might be a rounding of Cape Horn at the southern tip of South America, crossing to Africa and then re-crossing the Atlantic to reach the Caribbean. Either way the journey appears impossibly long.
21. Kornfield and Nevo, 1976.
22. A full report on the colonisation of Long Island can be found in Thornton et al (2003).

23. Burton, 2004.
24. Barnosky (2005) estimates that 10000 years is commonly required for subspecies to develop, based on a study of lemmings, moose, deer and marmots. However, this is for 'normal' conditions; island life appears to accelerate the process considerably because of the opportunities for specialisation.
25. Stanley, 1979.
26. United Nations, 2008.
27. Fisher (2005) discusses the question as to why native Mauritian ants are only found near the mountain tops, but admits that there is no clear answer.
28. Zhao et al (2004) demonstrated that hatching of land snail eggs delayed from the usual 2-3 days at 20-25°C to over 30 days at 5°C.
29. For example Andrews et al (1997) studied *Sceloporus* lizards from America and found delays in embryo development when the eggs were subjected to periods of low temperature. As well as carrying out their own study on *Sceloporus* lizards, Christian et al (1986) also reported studies by other researchers that low temperature delayed hatching, by several weeks in the case of an Australian tortoise. In a similar vein, Darken et al (1998) report that eggs of the California Grunion fish, which are laid in beach sand, will lie dormant for many weeks if necessary until 'activated' by the next ultra-high tide.
30. The only bird eggs which could conceivably have survived a short period of inundation are those of the 'megapode' species of Australasia and surrounding islands. These remarkable birds bury their eggs in large mounds of earth. However one has to doubt whether even megapode eggs could have survived for long. Besides, there is much evidence of recent speciation amongst today's island megapodes, suggesting recent expansion from much reduced populations.
31. Palkovacs et al, 2002.
32. For example the Aldabra rail is flightless but is otherwise very similar to the Madagascar species; its flightlessness is likely to be a recent phenomenon. The Aldabra drongo is very similar to the crested drongo of Madagascar; and the sacred ibis of Aldabra really is almost indistinguishable from the Madagascan variety. The fody occurs in several subspecies across the islands of the western Indian Ocean, but these subspecies can still readily interbreed.
33. Jones et al (2008) describe the Henderson Island crake and its relationship to the various other flightless rails of the Pacific.
34. Slikas et al (2002) make the case for rapid evolution of flightlessness.
35. Tosi and Coke, 2007.

Chapter 6. The Geologist's Report

1. The investigation carried out by Harvey and Grove (1982) included Carbon-dating of ancient shoreline features and their conclusion was that Lake Turkana overspilled into the Nile between about the 9th Millennium BC and the 6th Millennium BC, and again between the 5th Millennium BC and the 2nd Millennium BC.
2. McClanahan and Young, 1996.
3. Davies and Walker, 1986.
4. Gasse et al, 2004.
5. Powers et al (2005) used an indicator known as TEX86, an index based on the tetraethers found in sediment layers. These tetraethers are produced by certain aquatic organisms (*crenarchaeota*) and production is known to be temperature-dependent.
6. Aladin et al (2008) include reference to various indirect salinity indicators, notably the detailed shapes of different mollusc shells.
7. For example Caspian Sea levels are known to have been much lower during the days of the Sassanid Empire of Iran, when a great wall was built across the northern frontier, a wall that extends beneath the current Caspian Sea at its western end.
8. The ancient Caspian Sea from about 50000 to 8000 years ago is known as the 'Khvalyn' reservoir and it included periods of outflow to the Black Sea. Salinity indicators give values ranging from 0.4% to 1.25% during this period. The next phase, from about 6000BC, produced salinity values of 1.5% to 2%. See Aladin et al (2008).
9. I assume here that outflow to the Black Sea would have run to a maximum of 100 cubic kilometres per year and that the enlarged Caspian Sea would have held about 120000 cubic kilometres of water.
10. Aladin et al (2008) estimate that the annual outflow through the Kara Bogaz Gol was 20-25km^3 in 1900.
11. Garrett (2001), quoting other sources, lists three layers. Karpychev (2007) identifies four.
12. The upper salt layer is assumed to be 3 metres thick (Garrett, 2001) over an area of 18000 square kilometres. The rate of inflow into the Kara Bogaz Gol is taken as 10-20 cubic kilometres per year.
13. See note 7.
14. Karpychev (2007) suggests that three of the four salt layers he identifies date either from the 'New Caspian' period (since about 4000BC) or the late 'Khvalyn' period (the previous few thousand years).
15. I assume an average of 10-20 metres of salt across the 18000-square-kilometre Kara Bogaz Gol (Garrett, 2001). The volume of the Caspian Sea is taken as 78000 cubic kilometres and the specific gravity of salt as 2.165.

16. See note 8 for salinity evidence. River inflow at current rates would increase salinity by about 0.15% in a millennium if there was no outflow.
17. There is certainly plenty of evidence for the common cockle from 4000BC (e.g. Ferronskii et al, 2003). The true date of its first entry into the Aral Sea can have been only slightly earlier.
18. Salinity evidence is very hard to come by. Niemi et al (1997) deduced a low salinity value based on the conductivity of sand grain coatings.
19. Enzel et al (2006) present a useful summary of the evidence, including their view that the salt content would have prevented the level falling beyond 510 metres below sea level.
20. According to Enzel et al (2006), the signs are that this salt deposit was laid down under deep-water conditions and an arid climate.
21. The dates are from inclusions of wood in the debris layer and the problem with wood is that it can survive for thousands of years after the death of the parent tree – hence the availability of the samples for testing. The range of dates may therefore indicate that the debris had been eroded from various different original locations.
22. This is the interpretation given by Niemi et al (1997).
23. Frumkin et al, 1991.
24. This explanation is offered by Niemi et al (1997).
25. The calculation uses an idealised shape for the basin of the Dead Sea and the whole Jordan valley. Evaporation is assumed to be constant at 1500mm per year; rainfall reaching the Dead Sea is assumed to be that required to maintain balance (i.e. unchanging water level) with the surface at 400 metres below sea level. Salt deposit thickness is calculated assuming a specific gravity of 2.165 for salt.
26. The maximum salt layer thickness shown in the figure (14 metres) would in reality be substantially reduced due to salts leaching into underlying soil strata. The actual thickness present is up to about 6.5 metres (Enzel et al, 2006).
27. It is now widely recognised that the Black Sea was once at a much lower level. For example Popescu et al (2004) have investigated the under-sea valley which once carried the river Danube far out across the continental shelf to an estimated sea level 110 metres below that of today. Other evidence has come from the presence of wind-blown soils across the sea bed, implying that it was once dry land.
28. Ryan et al, 1997.
29. There is anecdotal reference (e.g. Wilson, 2001) to a spread of debris having been noted over a wide area of seabed north of the Bosphorus channel. However as far as I can see this is not supported by anything in the scientific literature.

30. There is no doubt that the old shoreline features are well preserved and that this suggests a relatively rapid sea level rise. An alternative explanation to that of Ryan and Pitman is that this was due to the Caspian Sea overflowing into the Black Sea, perhaps combined with a change in the course of the river Don, which may previously have spilled down the Manych channel and into the Caspian. If so this would have dramatically altered the water balance in both seas.
31. Ryan and Pitman, 1998.
32. Görür et al (2001) examined deposits at various levels beneath the Sakarya River flood plain in northern Turkey and discovered the remains of fresh-water fauna dating from the millennium prior to Ryan and Pitman's proposed Black Sea flood date. The nature of these remains indicated that they had lived in a large body of water, not a river; hence their deduction regarding the level of the Black Sea.
33. The sediment delta was reported by Aksu et al (2002) and was of a form suggesting that the Bosphorus channel was, at the time the delta was created, effectively the mouth of a large river, flowing out into the Sea of Marmara and forming a river delta like that of the Mississippi.
34. Aksu et al, 2002.
35. Aksu et al, 2002.
36. There is little dispute that the climate north of the Black Sea was very dry during the Ice Age. However there is evidence to show (e.g. Harrison et al, 1996) that it had become much wetter by 8000BC.
37. This is an inexact point since it is hard to have full confidence in a fluid dynamics model of anything on the scale of the proposed Black Sea flood. Kerr (1998) reports the issue as a possible cause for concern regarding the dating of Ryan and Pitman's flood.
38. Ryan et al, 1997.
39. Degens and Ross (1972) suggest this should have taken nearly 2000 years based on their predictive model.
40. Cordova (2002) dates this sudden arrival of new Mediterranean-originating species in the Crimea to 5480BC (uncalibrated), i.e. about 6000BC (calibrated).
41. See Zielinski et al (1994), who also note that there are numerous undated volcanoes, many of them in Africa, that are known to be of 'Holocene' age, i.e. since about 9000BC.

Chapter 7. The Climatologist's Report

1. The data shown is taken from Alley et al (1993) and is one of several published interpreted temperature records based on central Greenland ice cores. The numbers differ from interpretation to interpretation but the principal features are agreed by all.

2. The 'BP' system was introduced partly to avoid having to add two thousand years or so to a date in the 'BC' system, particularly for dates many tens of thousands of years in the past, and partly to detach science from religion. Since the 'present' is a continually changing reference point it was an unfortunate necessity to agree to fix it so that dates could be compared with confidence, and the agreed reference date was 1950 – now many decades in the past!
3. Wiersma and Renssen (2006) collected a database of references to anomalies around 8200 years ago. Many of the examples quoted in this chapter are taken from their paper.
4. Jouzel et al, 1987.
5. Wang et al, 2002.
6. Klitgaard-Kristensen et al, 1998.
7. Calvo et al, 2002; Dolven et al, 2002.
8. Duplessy et al, 1992.
9. O'Reilly et al, 2004.
10. de Menocal et al, 2000.
11. The South China Sea evidence is found in Wang et al (1999); numerous researchers have reported on records from the Mediterranean, for example Cacho et al (2001); Gagan et al (2002) report a cooling of the western Pacific near Indonesia, as do Yu et al (2008) for the Okinawa trench region.
12. von Grafenstein et al, 1998.
13. Rousseau et al, 1998.
14. McDermott et al, 2001.
15. Bar-Matthews et al, 1999.
16. See Gasse and van Campo (1994) for the Lake Chad evidence. Gasse (2008) identifies a brief dry spell between 6500BC and 6000BC across northern Africa, suggesting a link to the 8.2ka BP event.
17. Thompson et al, 2002.
18. Fleitmann et al, 2003.
19. Staubwasser et al, 2002.
20. Davis and Stevenson, 2007.
21. Alley et al, 1997.
22. Wagner at al (2002) report an 8% fall in Carbon dioxide over a 300 year period.
23. See for example Doumange (1996).
24. Hughen et al, 1996.
25. Birks and Koç, 2002.
26. Bond et al, 1997.
27. Kerwin, 1996.
28. The possibility that the landscape west of Missoula had been created by a giant flood was dismissed by the scientific community for

decades, despite the evidence being no less clear then than it is today, betraying a deep prejudice against 'catastrophism'. Benito and Connor (2003) give a relatively recent assessment of what scientists now believe.

29. Teller, 2003.
30. Incidentally, I have to wonder whether the much more significant climatic shift represented by the Younger Dryas cooling might be related to outflow of water from the giant glacial lake that once covered western Siberia. The water volume was probably at least twice that in Lake Agassiz and, although no evidence of any sudden release of water has been found, a series of smaller outflows would still have been sufficient to affect ocean circulation dramatically. The period during which this lake met its end is not known exactly, but it was probably during the 12000-10000BC range (Lioubimtseva et al, 2003), which is about right for the Younger Dryas event.
31. See for example Wiersma and Renssen (2006).

Chapter 8. Newton's Law

1. Water vapour is the most effective greenhouse gas in our atmosphere today. A large increase in atmospheric water content would mean a much more efficient 'greenhouse', as is the case under the carbon dioxide clouds of Venus.
2. The view that the flood was brought about by massive geological upheaval is strongly associated with the works of Henry Morris, expressed in Whitcomb and Morris (1961), who argued that the preflood world was destroyed by the release of water and then reshaped as it is today. As far as I know this is not a view that is supported by any mainstream geologists.
3. The Chandler Wobble (e.g. Munk and MacDonald, 1960) is an oscillation of the Earth relative to its axis of spin with a maximum amplitude of ± 6.5 metres. It has two interacting frequencies of motion. The dominant one gives one oscillation every 14 months; the secondary one, with a 12 month oscillation period, means that the amplitude of motion varies significantly and repeats about every 7 years.
4. The view that the driving force behind the Chandler Wobble is variation in seabed pressure has been put forward very confidently by the Jet Propulsion Laboratory in the United States.
5. The regular motion of the Chandler Wobble suddenly changed in December 2004, curtailing the normal 7-year cyclic change in amplitude to just over 6 years. The Indian Ocean earthquake of December 26th 2004 is the most obvious cause.

6. The loss of the water mass from Lake Agassiz creates an 'overturning moment', namely the centrifugal force lost multiplied by distance north of the equatorial plane. This generates an overturning motion, resisted by the 'moment of inertia' of the Earth. As the Earth starts to overturn, the equatorial bulge is displaced, which soon leads to a cancelling out of the Lake Agassiz effect and a 'restorative' moment, bringing the overturning motion to an end.

Chapter 9. Archimedes' Law

1. The change at about 670km depth shows up as a pronounced discontinuity to seismic waves.
2. This is a calculated figure (see Appendix). Just as the 21-kilometre equatorial bulge has occurred in response to the centrifugal forces at the surface generated by the Earth's spin, so the lower centrifugal force at the base of the mantle demands a much reduced bulge – about 6 kilometres. Hence the thickness of the mantle is predicted to be about 15 kilometres (21 minus 6) greater at the equator. The change in gravitational pull at the base of the mantle also has to be taken into account.
3. I have broadly followed Robertson (1966), assuming a surface density of 2700kg/m^3, rising rapidly to 3200kg/m^3 at the crust-mantle interface. At the minor discontinuity at 400 kilometres depth I assume it reaches almost 4000kg/m^3, jumping to 4500kg/m^3 at the 670-kilometre discontinuity. I then assume a steady rise to 5600kg/m^3 at the base of the mantle. Opinions on the density of the core are more varied; I have adopted what appears to be a typical view and taken 9700kg/m^3 for the outer part of the outer core. I have not specifically referred to densities of materials closer to the centre of the Earth but have based the necessary calculations on the known approximate mass of the Earth, namely 5.97×10^{24} kilograms.

Chapter 10. Hooke's Law

1. Quoted stiffness values for small elements of igneous rock tend to be between 30 and 100 GigaPascals (e.g. Turcotte and Schubert, 1982), with peridotite near the top end of the range. By way of comparison, steel comes out at 205 GigaPascals while concrete stiffness is generally 30-40 GigaPascals.
2. Despite the current world-wide rise in sea levels, the Scandinavian land mass continues to rise even faster, at up to a centimetre per year, due to the rebound following the melting of the ice cap some 10000 years ago. Another sign of ongoing redistribution of material within the mantle

may be the fact that the poles are actually shifting relative to the continents by about 10 centimetres per year, a rate which is much too fast to be explained by plate tectonics.

3. Bevis et al (2004), who carried out this study, suggested that the low stiffness they deduced was due to the reservoir being located in a volcanically active region with inclusions of molten or semi-molten rock within the underlying crust-mantle material.
4. Despite the apparent logic behind this value of 64 GigaPascals it is quite different from the 'official' conclusion based on the Chandler Wobble, which is that the Earth is actually stiffer than steel. Personally I believe the reason for this is a misunderstanding of the cause of the Chandler Wobble. The standard explanation originated with a theory proposed by Leonhard Euler in 1755, 136 years before Seth Chandler made his discovery, and that theory was based on the possibility that the axis of spin was actually not quite the same as the axis of symmetry of the Earth. At that time the Earth was thought to be a solid spheroid. Euler theorised that, if the two axes did not coincide, there should be a motion with a return period of 10 months, assuming the planet was perfectly rigid. When the Chandler Wobble was discovered Euler's theory was adjusted to account for the non-rigid nature of the Earth and it was deduced (from the measured return period of 14 months) that the actual stiffness was still greater than that of steel. However it is the contention in this book that the dominant 14-month cycle of the Chandler Wobble is not in reality due to Euler's predicted motion at all. The Euler effect may still be present but, if 64 GigaPascals is a realistic estimate for the stiffness of the mantle-crust layer, then it can only form a secondary or even tertiary effect.
5. The fact that the Chandler Wobble comprises two frequencies (see note 3 of Chapter 8) is important. The dominant one (one oscillation every 14 months) is the natural frequency of small amplitude true polar shift. However the secondary frequency (one oscillation every 12 months) is clearly related to an annual effect on the Earth. A snow cover of 3 centimetres more across the United States and Canada than across Siberia, lasting a few weeks, would just about provide the impulse needed to sustain the Chandler Wobble – according to the calculation in the Appendix. I do not deny however that other causes such as changes in ocean floor pressure are also possible.

Chapter 11. Murphy's Law

1. For example Kaufmann and Lambeck (2000) estimate a viscosity between 5×10^{20} and 10^{21} Pascal seconds down to the 670-kilometre discontinuity and between 3×10^{22} and 8×10^{22} Pascal seconds beneath

this level. This is deduced from the observed 'rebound' of Canada and Scandinavia following the melting of the ice sheets that once covered them.

2. To produce a tilt of 20 degrees the crust-mantle stiffness has to reduce from 64 GigaPascals to a minimum of 52.3 GigaPascals at maximum deformation (see Appendix).
3. Only a tale from Washington State and another from Oregon mention more than one flood (two and three respectively) – see Vitaliano (1973) and Clark (1953) reproduced by Isaak (2004).
4. Historically there have been other catastrophic releases of water, including many earlier but much smaller outflows from Lake Agassiz. The Missoula floods are well known – but the volumes were small by comparison. Lake Bonneville in Utah, now famous as the salt flat where land speed records are attempted, suffered a 10000 cubic kilometre discharge at one point when it overtopped and then rapidly cut its way down through the hillside. The other location where one might have expected a large release of water was the great glacial lake that once covered western Siberia (see note 30 of Chapter 7), but it seems that it managed to empty in a much more controlled manner than Lake Agassiz.

Chapter 12. The Native American's Tale

1. Erdoes and Ortiz (1984) reproduced by Isaak (2004).
2. I am relying on the analysis presented in Thom (2007) which shows a gradual spread of language from west to east across the continent. I am not aware of other attempts to build up such a detailed picture of these prehistoric language movements.
3. Frazer (1919) reproduced by Isaak (2004).
4. Gaster (1969) reproduced by Isaak (2004).
5. Gaster (1969) reproduced by Isaak (2004).
6. Gaster (1969) reproduced by Isaak (2004).
7. Frazer (1919) reproduced by Isaak (2004).
8. I should stress that when I refer to language analysis, I refer once more to the analysis in *The Origin of Tongues* (Thom, 2007). Almost all linguists have followed the line proposed by Joseph Greenberg in the 1980s that the family known as Na Dené, which includes Athapaskan, represents a separate influx of population from Asia, in which case it should be quite distinct from Algonquian and the other North American families. The evidence of these shared flood myths would seem to count very strongly indeed against Greenberg's proposal.
9. Gaster (1969) reproduced by Isaak (2004).
10. Clovis culture, which is identified by a particular and very distinctive type of stone spear point, was once thought to be the very first human

culture in the Americas, although many now accept that there is evidence for the earlier presence of humans (see for example Gruhn, 2000). Clovis culture seems to have been adopted right across the United States within a very short period, which means that experts are divided on its true place of origin. However the western United States is most commonly proposed.

11. These rates are based on the analysis in Thom (2007).
12. Field (1992) is among those who note the widespread deduction of a cultural hiatus across the great plains, giving dates of 6000-3500BC. Frison et al (1996) report evidence from Arkansas that, while occupation continued up in the hills, there is very little evidence for human activity on the lower-lying plains during this time window. The term 'Great Hiatus' was coined by Tuck (1984) to mark the abrupt end of 'Paleo-Indian' evidence in the north-eastern United States and, while the term is not in favour these days, all agree that this point in prehistory marks a significant change in settlement pattern in that region also. Foster at al (2002) report an excavation from Long Island dating to the 6th Millennium BC, thereby supplying evidence that some human life continued in the region, but they nevertheless refer to the general low density of sites across eastern North America during this period.
13. Faught (2004) has reported these undersea investigations. Apart from his specific findings off the Florida coast, he also remarks on the significant change in stone tool technology that took place in Florida from about 6000BC.
14. For example documents on the archaeology of Missouri refer to the concentration of evidence in the Ozark Plateau region in what is known as the Middle Archaic period (from about 6000BC in this part of the continent) while those from Tennessee acknowledge the apparent decrease in population and that evidence seems to be restricted to a few sites in the east, in the Appalachian Mountains.
15. I am following Walthall (1990) here, who contrasts the vigorously expanding population evident during the first half of the 7th Millennium BC right across the eastern United States with the "little known, little studied" Archaic period that followed.
16. Both Frison et al (1996) and Wykoff (1992) refer to the decline in the bison population from about 6000BC and relate this to a change in climate.
17. Clark (1953) reproduced by Isaak (2004).
18. Clark (1953) reproduced by Isaak (2004).
19. Frazer (1919) reproduced by Isaak (2004).
20. Frazer (1919) reproduced by Isaak (2004).
21. Merriam (1910) reproduced by Isaak (2004).

22. Frazer (1919) reproduced by Isaak (2004).
23. Gaster (1969) and Horcasitas (1953) reproduced by Isaak (2004).
24. Gaster (1969), Horcasitas (1953) and Vitaliano (1973) reproduced by Isaak (2004).
25. Horcasitas (1953) reproduced by Isaak (2004).
26. Again, these language deductions rely on Thom (2007). I am not aware of similarly detailed analysis by other researchers.
27. This finding was reported by Araujo et al (2005).
28. All language deductions continue to be taken from Thom (2007).
29. Chagnon (1977) reproduced by Isaak (2004).
30. Gaster (1969) and Miller (1994) reproduced by Isaak (2004).
31. Gaster (1969) reproduced by Isaak (2004).
32. Bierhorst (1988) reproduced by Isaak (2004).
33. Human-related remains from numerous archaeological sites in Argentina have been Carbon-dated to between 9000 and 8000BC, rather less between 8000 and 7000BC, less again between 7000 and 6000BC and comparatively few thereafter (Baker, 2004). Garvey et al (2008) refer specifically to the remarkable lack of archaeological sites in Mendoza Province, Argentina, in the middle Holocene period (roughly 6000-4000BC) compared to both earlier and later times.
34. Gaster (1969) reproduced by Isaak (2004).
35. Vitaliano (1973) and Frazer (1919) reproduced by Isaak (2004).
36. Wilbert (1977) reproduced by Isaak (2004).

Chapter 13. The Australian Aborigine's Tale

1. This follows the analysis presented in Chapter 4. I have not come across any other detailed analysis of Pama-Nyungan language history although most linguists would agree that the family had its origin at this approximate time.
2. Dixon (1916) reproduced by Isaak (2004).
3. Smith (1930) reproduced by Isaak (2004).
4. These estimates can be found in Kotwicki (2008), although his figures do not differ significantly from those of others. Warren (2006) admits that "one would perhaps expect large volumes of salt ..." and goes on to discuss the way that groundwater can 'recycle' the salt.
5. Lake Torrens has only a very thin salt veneer, while parts of Lakes Gairdner and Frome can have up to 20 or 30 centimetres in certain locations but nothing elsewhere.
6. Today the Lake Bonneville salt crust is reducing rapidly due to brine extraction (Mason and Kipp, 1998) but records show a thickness of over 2 metres during the 1960's and 1970's.

7. Gillespie et al (1991) interpret the buried halite strata in parts of Lake Eyre as a former saltpan that was partially dissolved in the early Holocene (i.e. around the date proposed for the Great Flood) and then rapidly overlain by clay deposits (which could have been brought in by an inrush of ocean waters since Lake Eyre is below sea level).
8. Johns (1962) reports that the composition of Lake Eyre salts (and those of the other great salt lakes of Australia) implies that the original source was the ocean.
9. The actual seawater volumes involved are difficult to judge accurately since the land barriers between the ocean and Lake Torrens and between Lake Torrens and Lake Eyre are very low and have been subject to changes in elevation over the millennia. It is also the case that as the planet tilted for a second time, raising Australia well above the level of the ocean, the entire region would have been inclined to the south, emptying a significant proportion of the newly-created saltwater lakes out into the ocean again.
10. The Flores evidence is still hotly disputed but it is suggested, based on the circumstantial evidence of stone tools and fire hearths, that the dwarf-size Flores people probably lived between 95000 and 13000 years ago (Brown et al, 2004).
11. Gaster (1969) reproduced by Isaak (2004).
12. Gaster (1969) and Kelsen (1943) reproduced by Isaak (2004).
13. Eliot (1976) reproduced by Isaak (2004).
14. Gaster (1969) reproduced by Isaak (2004).
15. Gaster (1969) reproduced by Isaak (2004).
16. There is plenty of evidence that the population of New Guinea has been occupying its current home for tens of thousands of years. Genetically the people are quite distinct from the inhabitants of most of Indonesia; linguistically Papuan languages are highly diverse, implying a long and relatively undisturbed passage of time; culturally little has changed for millennia according to archaeological evidence (e.g. in taro cultivation).
17. This statement would attract fairly general agreement amongst linguists – see note 44 of Chapter 2.
18. The reason for suspecting that Papuan language was once spoken on Borneo lie in the self-evident truth that *homo sapiens* must have reached New Guinea via the islands of Indonesia, including Borneo. The relationship between the pre-Austronesian speech of Borneo and the modern Papuan languages of New Guinea may have been a very distant one but it is logical to suppose that a relationship would have existed.
19. These dates, though approximate, can be determined from archaeological evidence (e.g. human remains, pottery).
20. Gaster (1969) and Kelsen (1943) reproduced by Isaak (2004).

21. Barrère (1969) reproduced by Isaak (2004).
22. Cogger et al, 1987.
23. Dawson (2005) makes the point that large differences in appearance and behaviour of different Palau jellyfish species have arisen over a period of time that he estimates as 12000 years, while the genetic difference between lake species and those of the ocean are still very slight.

Chapter 14. The African's Tale

1. This is entirely non-controversial. Archaeology attests the spread of agriculture and associated pottery forms across southern Africa from about 500BC, commencing somewhere south-west of Lake Victoria (e.g. Phillipson, 1977), and this is nicely matched by the observed distribution of Bantu language.
2. This statement on South Cushitic speech is a little controversial – or at least goes beyond what is generally agreed. It reflects the analysis in Thom (2007) and also matches the spread of an archaeological culture known as the 'Kenya Capsian' (Phillipson, 1977).
3. Frazer (1919) reproduced by Isaak (2004).
4. Gasse et al, 2004.
5. See Joyce et al (2005) for a full description of the evidence.
6. The reason for the greater tilting of the land in the tropics is that the equatorial belt marks the boundary between quadrants of the Earth; while the mantle in one quadrant would have found itself excessively thick as the planet tilted and it would have sunk down into the liquid iron core, the adjacent quadrant would have been pushed up. The equatorial region would therefore have seen a bending of the mantle-crust layer between the two quadrants, as illustrated in Chapter 10.
7. Joyce et al (2005) admit that there must have been connections in the past between the various river systems involved but they offer no explanation as to how this could have come about.
8. Only in the case of the Chott el Djerid and surrounding playas in Tunisia and Algeria is a marine origin for the salt generally accepted, although the date at which this region was last connected to the sea is usually given as at least 30000 years ago. At this date sea levels were approximately as they are today according to some researchers although others maintain that they were still several tens of metres lower. The reason for the disagreement is that the land surface has also been rising and falling in different locations around the world.
9. Based on fossilised corals, Bonatti et al (1971) have estimated the age of the uppermost salt layer in the Danakil depression, which is known to be of marine origin, as no more than 32000 years.

10. Osiris is said to have been a great early king of Egypt, murdered by Seth and then placed in a coffin which was cast into the flooded river Nile. As a god, he was then associated with the Nile flood. Some later versions of the story link the death of Osiris to a 'Great Flood'.
11. The difference between the various Khordofanian languages today suggests a time depth of much more than 8000 years (Thom, 2007), which means they were almost certainly already present in the Nuba Hills region in 6250BC.
12. Climate modellers consistently suggest that the climate became considerably drier right across northern Africa following the 8.2ka BP event (e.g. Wiersma and Renssen, 2006).
13. Today most speakers of Nubian languages are to be found about 400 miles north of the Nuba Hills around the 'big bend' of the Nile. However Hill Nubian remains in the Nuba Hills region.
14. Hausa, the principal language of northern Nigeria, is much the most widely spoken Chadic language today. However according to Thom (2007) the closest relatives to the Chadic languages (members of the Afro-Asiatic family) are to be found far to the east, in Ethiopia and Kenya. Chadic language and culture made the journey west across central Africa over the course of several millennia.
15. Kahler-Meyer (1971) reproduced by Isaak (2004).
16. Courlander (1996) reproduced by Isaak (2004).
17. The most likely reason for the lack of species in Lake Turkana is that the lake underwent a period of significantly reduced level and therefore significantly increased salinity.
18. See for example Maley (1981) and Thiemeyer (2000).
19. Davies and Walker, 1986.
20. Davies and Walker, 1986.
21. Davies and Walker (1986) acknowledge that, in their words, "Holocene changes must have occurred" but they offer no explanation as to how these changes were accomplished.

Chapter 15. The Northerner's Tale

1. Gaster (1969) reproduced by Isaak (2004).
2. Sproul (1979) reproduced by Isaak (2004).
3. This tale is taken from James Frazer's translation of the writings of Apollodorus.
4. Frazer (1919) reproduced by Isaak (2004).
5. Gaster (1969) reproduced by Isaak (2004).
6. Frazer (1919) reproduced by Isaak (2004).
7. Baldia (2004) discusses the evidence and suggests that, on balance, there probably was a hiatus of some sort between Starčevo-Körös-Criş

culture and that of the succeeding Linear Band Pottery period and he dates it to the first half of the 6th Millennium BC. This is based on a comparison of Carbon dates for the two cultures on the Hungarian plains and also on interpretation of cave deposits in the Czech Republic.

8. That some relationship existed between Starčevo-Körös-Criş and Linear Band is proved by the fact that they planted the same crops and kept the same farm animals. The Linear Band people also inherited the practice of using Mediterranean shells as ornaments. Their villages and building construction techniques however are quite different, suggesting input from a culture other than Starčevo-Körös-Criş (e.g. Piggott, 1965).
9. Linear Band Pottery culture can be seen to break into several descendant cultures from about 5000BC. By around 4000BC the pottery type known as 'funnel beakers' was in use from the Netherlands to Poland and the name is used to describe the whole range of agricultural societies in these areas. By the late 4th Millennium BC pottery known as 'corded ware' reached as far east as the Baltic states and Russia, where its arrival heralded the first use of agriculture. Many see continuity between Linear Band, Funnel Beakers and Corded Ware, although the interaction between the various different sub-groups was clearly complex, and Indo-European influence certainly emerged in many eastern Corded Ware societies during the 3rd Millennium BC.
10. This may seem a very strange location to propose for ancestral Basque. However the analysis in Thom (2007) suggests that Basque's nearest relatives are actually the modern Finno-Ugric languages (Finnish etc.) and that they separated in about 9000BC somewhere just north of the Caspian Sea in southern Russia. By 6250BC the leading edge of the westward 'language wave' had just about reached the Carpathian Mountains.
11. We know enough of Etruscan from bilingual Greek-Etruscan texts to see what type of language it was and to give us some of the basic vocabulary, but not enough to read the great majority of the available texts.
12. Etruscan is shown by Thom (2007) to have separated from the Finno-Ugric languages at approximately the same time as Basque, i.e. about 9000BC.
13. Today a single Yeniseian language, Ket, remains. However historical records tell us of others spoken until recently in western Siberia. According to Thom (2007) Ket's closest relative is Ainu, a recently extinct language of northern Japan and Sakhalin Island, and the suggestion is made that they both descend from the advanced culture of the Lena river valley in eastern Siberia, which thrived throughout the last Ice Age.

14. This placement again follows Thom (2007) in which Eskimo-Aleut languages are found to be related to the Turkic group, diverging in about 7500BC.
15. Holmberg (1927) reproduced by Isaak (2004).
16. Holmberg (1927) reproduced by Isaak (2004).
17. Holmberg (1927) reproduced by Isaak (2004).
18. Wiersma and Renssen, 2006.
19. Vartanyan et al, 1993.
20. The next most recent mammoth remains of which I am aware were found in the Taimir Peninsula of northern Russia and were dated to about 7600BC.

Chapter 16. The Chinaman's Tale

1. Walls and Walls (1986) reproduced by Isaak (2004).
2. Today's Chukchi-Kamchatkan languages are spoken in the far north-east of Russia and in the Kamchatka Peninsula. The deduction that they were spoken in northern China in 6250BC is based on proposed relationships with other language families, notably Dravidian, Uralic and Altaic (see Thom, 2007).
3. There is no agreement amongst linguists as to the point of origin of the Sino-Tibetan language family, the family that includes Chinese. Thom (2007) argues for eastern India based on a reconstructed language family tree. Others have proposed southern China or the Yellow river region.
4. Yap and Cotterell, 1975.
5. Miller (1994) reproduced by Isaak (2004).
6. Gaster (1969) reproduced by Isaak (2004).
7. This tale has been taken from a website dealing with the customs of the Li people. In this case the flood story lies behind the Li's 'Love Festival', a celebration (held on March 3rd each year) of the two lovers who survived the flood.
8. The earliest archaeological evidence for human occupation found to date on Hainan is from about 4000BC.
9. This statement reflects my own view (Thom, 2007) based on a link between the Kadai language family and Sino-Tibetan.
10. Holmberg (1927) and Gaster (1969) reproduced by Isaak (2004).
11. Frazer (1919) reproduced by Isaak (2004).
12. Demetrio (1968) and Dixon (1916) reproduced by Isaak (2004).
13. Frazer (1919) reproduced by Isaak (2004).
14. In a recent article on this subject (White, 2008) the period from 6000BC to 2000BC is described as the "missing Holocene" in South-East Asia due to the paucity of the evidence.

15. Lindell et al (1976) reproduced by Isaak (2004).
16. The lack of movement is deduced from the fact that several branches of the Sino-Tibetan language family are present in the Burma region, yet the differences between those branches imply a separation date well over 8000 years ago. It is hard to conceive of circumstances which would have led to all these branches being carried independently from a point of origin elsewhere.
17. Gaster (1969) reproduced by Isaak (2004).
18. Frazer (1919) reproduced by Isaak (2004).
19. The Lisu and the Jingpaw live just across the Nu Shan mountains from the Salween river valley, and the Salween valley is still home to several Austro-Asiatic-speaking tribes. In the past Austro-Asiatic territory was much more extensive than it is today.
20. Gaster (1969) reproduced by Isaak (2004).
21. The Andaman islanders belong genetically to Mitochondrial haplogroup M, which is found throughout southern Asia as far as New Guinea and Australia. Their Y chromosome affinities are also with other southern Asian populations. However in both cases the differences are very significant, suggesting some thousands of years of separation.
22. Cooper (2002) reports extensive archaeological studies. Her earliest Carbon 14 date related to human occupation is 162AD.
23. The connection between Papuan and Andamanese was proposed by the famous linguist Joseph Greenberg, the man who also tried to rationalise the language families of Africa and America. The clearest similarities are seen in the pronouns (*I*, *you*, *we* etc.), rather like the similarities between many Indo-European pronouns. See Ross (2005).
24. One particular variation in the Mitochondrial DNA sequence is shared with populations in New Guinea and adjacent islands. See Thangaraj et al (2003).
25. Windshuttle and Gillin, 2002.
26. Negrito languages are often different from those of more recent colonists. In southern Thailand and Malaysia they speak Austro-Asiatic languages rather than Thai or Malay; on Sumatra they speak a longer-established Austronesian language than those of surrounding peoples. The evidence therefore clearly points to their being the remnant of a pre-existing culture.
27. Cavalli-Sforza et al (1993) sampled genetic material from peoples around the world and created a map of the interrelationships between them. They grouped the Batak with the Negrito peoples, whereas the surrounding Sundanese were genetically closer to the Austronesians of Borneo, Bali and Taiwan.
28. Gaster (1969) reproduced by Isaak (2004).

Chapter 17. The Indian's Tale

1. Misra (2001) highlights the restricted distribution of Mesolithic archaeological sites in India, concentrated in the upland regions (Kashmir, Vindhya hills, north-east India and southern India), whereas sites from the subsequent Chalcolithic period are much more widespread. The recent excavation of caves at Bastar in Madhya Pradesh (Yadava et al, 2007) provides an example, with millennia of occupation coming to an end in the 7th Millennium BC.
2. Saxena et al (2006) detail the rice evidence at Lahuradewa.
3. The earliest Carbon 14 date for cultivated rice at Lahuradewa is actually 6400BC (although Carbon 14 dating can never be seen as precise).
4. Rice cultivation also took off in the Vindhya Hills to the south of Lahuradewa although the dating evidence is disputed. Extremely early dates have been claimed for the site of Koldihwa, but these are not generally accepted (e.g. Misra, 2001). Pokharia (2008) describes the botanical evidence relating to Vindhya Hills sites.
5. The claim that Dravidian had arrived in India from the west is based on Thom (2007). However several linguists link Dravidian with the ancient language known as Elamite, once spoken in south-western Iran, so the claim is far from being controversial.
6. Adigal (1965) reproduced by Isaak (2004).
7. Burushaski is thought by most to be unrelated to the other languages of India. However the evidence in Thom (2007) is that it diverged from ancestral Dravidian in southern Iran some time before 10000BC. It has since made the journey across Iran, into Pakistan and up the Indus valley to the far north of the country; hence my suggestion that its ancestor was spoken in the hills to the west of the Indus valley in 6250BC.
8. This statement is based on the finding that Sino-Tibetan language stems from eastern India – see note 3 of Chapter 16.
9. Gaster (1969) reproduced by Isaak (2004).
10. Gaster (1969) reproduced by Isaak (2004).
11. Sabean was a South Semitic language, descended from the original Semitic tongue spoken somewhere on the Egypt-Palestine border in about 6000BC (refer to Chapter 4).
12. Elamite is another language with no recognised affiliation. However the analysis in Thom (2007) traces its roots back to around 13000BC in southern Iraq, almost exactly the same location in which it was spoken in historical times. The likely implication is that it never moved far, and this is supported by a slow rate of language change deduced for the intervening millennia.

13. With a 20-degree tilt the flood is predicted to come just about level with the tops of Mauritius' mountains. However, lying just over 20 degrees south of the equator, the location is very sensitive to the planet's exact angle of tilt. If it had only tilted 19 degrees for instance the flood level would have been about 100 metres lower.
14. There is actually considerable disagreement as to whether the reported connection between the dodo, the solitaire and the Nicobar pigeon is real or not, and this seems to be related to which particular genetic sequence is investigated.

Chapter 18. Noah's Tale

1. It is not clear from Genesis 2:10 whether the four rivers flowed in or out of Eden.
2. The expression "from Havilah to Shur" is used on two occasions in the Bible. The first (Genesis 25:18) describes the area settled by the descendants of Ishmael son of Abraham; the second (I Samuel 15:17) relates to the territory of a people known as the Amalekites. Shur is identified as being just to the east of Egypt but Havilah is not clearly located. However the expression "toward Ashur" is added in the Genesis passage, and Ashur lay about 60 miles south of Nineveh in northern Iraq.
3. This is the only reference to a river Gihon in the Bible; elsewhere the Gihon refers to a famous spring in Jerusalem. On grounds of phonetic similarity, the river known in ancient times as the Uknu, now the Karun, which flows west from the Zagros Mountains of Iran to join the Shatt al Arab waterway south of Basra, would be a reasonable proposal. The Shatt al Arab is the name for the 90 mile stretch from the confluence of the Tigris and Euphrates rivers to the Persian Gulf.
4. Apart from this reference, the Bible (and a multitude of other ancient texts) consistently applies the name Cush to the land south of Egypt, now northern Sudan, and for this reason the Gihon river is sometimes equated with the Nile. However, in the context of Iraq/Iran, the Zagros Mountains through which the river Karun flows are known as the 'Kuhha' in Persian; it is therefore possible that the name Cush applied to the Zagros region.
5. This assumes a calendar similar to today's Jewish calendar and to that used by the ancient Babylonians, which was probably inherited from the Sumerians.
6. I should admit here that the prediction is sensitive to the various assumptions made and so a small change could make a significant difference to the predicted flood dates in Iraq.

7. The kingdom of Urartu flourished during the 8th Century BC before being subjugated by the Assyrians. It is generally thought that most of the Old Testament of the Bible was compiled (from texts already in existence) during the time of the exile of the Israelites in Babylonia in the 6th Century BC.
8. This is found in the Houd Sura 11:44.
9. I am indebted to Fashold (1990) for this information. The mountain in question lies close to the town of Şirnak in southern Turkey, just north of the Iraqi and Syrian borders.
10. The word used for 'earth' here is the same word that is regularly used in the Bible when speaking of individual lands.

Bibliography

The Holy Bible, New International Version, Hodder & Stoughton, 1979.

The Koran, translated by N.J. Dawood, Penguin Books, London, 1974.

Prince Ilango Adigal, *Shilappadikaram (The Ankle Bracelet)*, translated by Alain Danielou, New Directions, New York, 1965.

D P Agrawal, *The Indus Civilisation = Aryans equation: Is it really a problem?*, http://www.infinityfoundation.com/mandala/h_es/h_es_agraw_indus.htm, accessed August 2005.

A.E. Aksu, R.N. Hiscott, P.J. Mudie, A. Rochon, M.A. Kaminski, T. Abrajano and D. Yasar, "Persistent Holocene outflow from the Black Sea to the eastern Mediterranean contradicts Noah's Flood hypothesis", *GSA Today*, 2002, pp.4-10.

N. Aladin, I. Plotnikov, A. Bolshov and A. Pichugin, *Biodiversity of the Caspian Sea*, Caspian Sea Biodiversity Project, http://www.zin.ru/projects/caspdiv/biodiversity_report.html, accessed July 2008.

Mario Alinei, "Interdisciplinary and linguistic evidence for Paleolithic continuity of Indo-European, Uralic and Altaic populations in Eurasia, with an excursus on Slavic ethnogenesis", Conference on Ancient Settlers in Europe, Kobarid, Slovenia, 2003.

Richard Alley, *The Two-Mile Time Machine*, Princeton University Press, 2000.

Richard Alley, D.A. Meese, C.A. Shuman, A.J. Gow, K.C. Taylor, P.M. Grootes, J.W.C. White, M. Ram, E.D. Waddington, P.A. Majewski and G.A. Zielinski, "Abrupt increase in Greenland snow accumulation at the end of the Younger Dryas event", *Nature*, Vol.362, 1993, pp.527-528.

Richard Alley, P.A. Mayewski, T. Sowers, M. Stuiver, K.C. Taylor and P.U. Clark, "Holocene climatic instability: a prominent widespread event 8200yr ago", *Geology*, Vol.25, No.6, 1997, pp.483-486.

Robin Andrews, Cari Qualls and Barbara Rose, "Effects of low temperature on embryonic development of Sceloporus lizards", *Copeia*, No.4, 1997, pp827-833.

Apollodorus, *The Library*, translated by James Frazer, Harvard University Press, 1921 and 1976.

Astolfo Araujo, Walter Neves, Luis Piló and João Paulo Atui, "Holocene dryness and human occupation in Brazil during the 'Archaic gap"', *Quaternary Research*, Vol.64, No.3, 2005, pp.298-307.

Asta Audzijonite, Jacob Damgaard, Sirkka-Liisa Varvio, Jouni Vainio and Risto Väinölä, "Phylogeny of Mysis (Crustacean Mysida): history of continental invasions inferred from molecular and morphological data", *Cladistics*, Vol.21, Issue 6, 2005, pp.575-596.

Tony Baker, *Late Pleistocene and early Holocene hunter-gatherers of the Pampas and Patagonia, Argentina and Chile*, http://www.ele.net/LaBelle/pampas/pampas.htm, accessed April 2004.

Maximilian Baldia, *The Earliest Bandkeramik (LBK): The Central and North European Neolithic/Copper Age Chronology*, http://www.comp.archaeology.org/Bandkeramik.htm, accessed March 2004.

Kathryn Bard, "The Egyptian predynastic: a review of the evidence", *Journal of Field Archaeology*, Fall, 1994.

Barbara Barich, *People, Water and Grain: the beginnings of domestication in the Sahara and the Nile Valley*, L'Erma di Brettschneider, 1998.

M. Bar-Matthews, A. Ayalon, A. Kaufman and G.J. Wasserburg, "The Eastern Mediterranean paleoclimate as a reflection of regional events: Soreq cave, Israel", *Earth and Planetary Science Letters*, Vol.166, 1999, pp.85-95.

Anthony Barnosky, "Effects of quaternary climate change on speciation in mammals", *Journal of Mammalian Evolution*, Vol.12, Nos.1/2, 2005, pp.247-264.

Dorothy Barrère, "The Kumuhonua Legends: a study of oate 19th Century Hawaiian stories of creation and origins", *Pacific Anthropological Records*, No.3, Bishop Museum, Honolulu, 1969.

Gerardo Benito and Jim Connor, "Number and size of last-glacial Missoula floods in the Colombia river valley between the Pasco Basin and Portland, Oregon", *GSA Bulletin*, Vol.115, No.5, 2003, pp.624-638.

Michael Bevis, Eric Kendrick, Americo Cser and Robert Smalley, "Geodetic measurement of the local elastic response to the changing mass of water in Lago Laja, Chile", *Physics of the Earth and Planetary Interiors*, Vol.141, 2004, pp.71-78.

Paolo Biagi, "The Mesolithic settlement of Sindh (Pakistan): a preliminary assessment", *Praehistoria*, Vol.4-5, 2003, pp.195-220.

John Bierhorst, *The Mythology of South America*, William Morrow, New York, 1988.

C.J.A. Birks and N. Koç, "A high-resolution diatom record of late Quaternary sea-surface temperatures and oceanographic conditions from the eastern Norwegian Sea", *Boreas*, Vol.31, 2002, pp.323-344.

Roger Blench, *Language, Archaeology and the African Past*, http://homepage.ntlworld.com/roger_blench/RBOP.htm, 2005, accessed September 2005.

Alan Bomhard and John Kerns, *The Nostratic Macrofamily: A Study in Distant Linguistic Relationship*, Mouton de Gruyter, Berlin, 1994.

Enrico Bonatti, Cesare Emiliani, Göte Ostlund and Harold Rydell, "Final dessication of the Afar rift, Ethiopia", *Science*, Vol.172, No.3982, 1971, pp.468-469.

G.C. Bond, W. Showers, M. Cheseby, R. Lotti, P. Almasi, P. de Menocal, P. Priore, H. Cullen, I. Hajdas and G. Bonani, "A pervasive millennial-scale cycle in North Atlantic Holocene and glacial climates", *Science*, Vol.278, 1997, pp.1257-1266.

Daniel Brinton, *The Myths of the New World*, Greenwood Press, New York, 1876 and 1969.

Peter Brown, T Sutikna, M J Morwood, R P Soejono, Jatmiko, E Wayhu Saptomo and Rokus Awe Due, "A new small-bodied hominin from the late Pleistocene of Flores, Indonesia", *Nature*, No.431, 2004, pp.1055-1061.

Frederic Burton, "Revision to species of *Cyclura nubile lewisi*, the Grand Cayman blue iguana", *Caribbean Journal of Science*, Vol.40, No.2, 2004, pp.198-203.

I. Cacho, J.O. Grimalt, M. Canals, L. Sbaffi, N.J. Shackleton, J. Schönfeld and R. Zahn, "Variability of the western Mediterranean Sea surface temperature during the last 25,000 years and its connection with the Northern Hemisphere climatic changes", *Paleoceanography*, Vol.16, 2001, p.40.

E. Calvo, J. Grimalt and E. Jansen, "High resolution U^{K}_{37} sea surface temperature reconstruction in the Norwegian Sea during the Holocene", *Quaternary Science Reviews*, Vol.21, 2002, pp.1385-1394.

Luigi Luca Cavalli-Sforza, *Genes, Peoples and Languages*, Allen Lane, The Penguin Press, 2000.

Luigi Luca Cavalli-Sforza, Paolo Menozzi and Alberto Piazza, *The History and Geography of Human Genes*, Princeton University Press, 1993.

Napoleon Chagnon, *Yanomamö, The Fierce People*, Holt, Rinehart & Winston, 1977.

Keith Christian, Richard Tracy and Warren Porter, "The effect of cold exposure during incubation of Sceloporus Undulatus eggs", *Copeia*, No.4, 1986, pp.1012-1014.

Ella Clark, *Indian Legends of the Pacific Northwest*, University of California Press, Berkeley, 1953.

Harold Cogger, Harold Heatwole, Yuji Ishikawa, Michael McCoy, Nobuo Tamiya and Toshiyuki Teruuchi, "The status and natural history of the Rennell Island Sea Krait, Laticauda crockeri (Serpentes: Laticaudidae)", *Journal of Herpetology*, Vol.21, No.4, 1987, pp.255-266.

Zarine Cooper, *Archaeology and History: early settlements in the Andaman Islands*, New Delhi, 2002.

Carlos Cordova, "Abrupt vegetation and soil changes in south-western Crimea during the Holocene", *Proceedings of the International Conference on Environmental Catastrophes and Recoveries in the Holocene*, London, 2002.

Harold Courlander, *A Treasury of African Folklore*, Marlowe & Co, New York, 1996.

T.M. Cronin, P.R. Vogt and D.A Willard, *Rapid sea level rise at 8.0-7.5ka and Antarctic ice sheet thinning*, EOS Transactions, AGU Fall Meeting Supplement, Vol.83, No.47, 2002.

Andrew Dalby, *Dictionary of Languages*, Bloomsbury, London, 1998.

Willi Dansgaard, "Stable isotopes in precipitation", *Tellus*, Vol.16, 1964, pp.436-468.

R.S. Darken, K.L. Martin and M.C. Fisher, "Metabolism during delayed hatching in terrestrial eggs of a marine fish, the grunion Leuresthes Tenuis", *Physiological Zoology*, Vol.71, No.4, 1998, pp.400-406.

Charles Darwin, *On the Origin of Species by means of Natural Selection*, John Murray, London, 1859.

Bryant Davies and Keith Walker, *The Ecology of River Systems*, Springer, 1986.

Basil Davis and Anthony Stevenson, "The 8.2ka event and early Holocene facets, fires and flooding in the central Ebro desert, NE Spain", *Quaternary Science Review*, Vol.26, Issue 13-14, 2007, pp.1695-1712.

Michael Dawson, "Five new subspecies of Mastigias (Scyphozoa: Rhizostomeae: Mastigiidae) from marine lakes, Palau, Micronesia", *Journal of the Marine Biological Association of the United Kingdom*, Vol.85, No.3, 2005, pp.679-694.

E.T. Degens and D.A. Ross, "Chronology of the Black Sea over the last 25,000 years", *Chemical Geology*, Vol.10, 1972, pp.1-16.

P. de Menocal, J. Ortiz, T. Guilderson and M. Sarnthein, "Coherent high- and low-latitude climate variability during the Holocene warm period", *Science*, Vol.288, 2000, pp.2198-2202.

Francisco Demetrio, *The Flood Motif and the Symbolism of Rebirth in Filipino Mythology*, 1968, in Alan Dundes (editor), *The Flood Myth*, University of California Press, Berkeley, 1988.

Roland Dixon, "Oceanic", in L.H. Gray (editor), *The Mythology of All Races*, Marshall Jones Co., Boston, 1916.

Aharon Dolgopolsky, *The Nostratic Macrofamily and Linguistic Palaeontology*, McDonald Institute for Archaeological research, Cambridge, UK, 1998.

J.K. Dolven, G. Cortese and K.R. Bjorklund, "A high-resolution radiolarian-derived paleotemperature record for the late Pleistocene-Holocene in the Norwegian Sea", *Paleoceanography*, Vol.17, 2002, p.1072.

François Doumange, *The Mediterranean Crises*, Lecture to UNU HQ, July 1996.

Don Dumond, *The Eskimos and Aleuts*, Thames & Hudson, London, 1987.

H.J. Dumont, The Caspian lake: history, biota, structure and function", *Limnology and Oceanography*, Vol.43, No.1, 1998, pp.44-52.

J.C. Duplessy, L. Labeyrie, M. Arnold, M. Paterne, J. Duprat and T.C.E. Van Weering, "Changes in surface salinity of the north Atlantic Ocean during the last deglaciation", *Nature*, Vol.358, 1992, pp.485-488.

Ivan Duridanov, "Ezikyt na Trakite" (The Language of the Thracians), *Nauka i izkustvo*, Sofia, 1976.

Alexander Eliot, *The Universal Myths*, Truman Talley Books/Meridian, New York, 1976.

Yehouda Enzel, Amotz Agnon and Mordechai Stein, *New Frontiers in Dead Sea Palaeoenvironmental Research*, Geological Society of America, 2006.

Richard Erdoes and Alfonso Ortiz, *American Indian Myths and Legends*, Pantheon Books, New York, 1984.

R.G. Fairbanks, "A 17,000-year-old glacioeustatic sea level record", *Nature*, Vol.342, 1989, pp.637-642.

David Fashold, *The Discovery of Noah's Ark*, Sidgwick & Jackson, London, 1990.

Michael Faught, "Submerged Paleoindian Archaic sites of the big bend, Florida", *Journal of Field Archaeology*, Vol.29, 2002-2004, pp.273-290.

Felipe Fernández-Armesto, *Civilisations*, Pan Books, London, 2001.

V.I. Ferronskii, V.A. Polyakov, V.S. Brezgunov, L.S. Vlasova, Y.A. Karpychev, A.F Bobkov, V.V. Romaniovskii, T. Johnson, D. Ricketts and K. Rasmussen, "Variations in the hydrological regime of Kara-Bogaz-Gol gulf, Lake Issyk-Kul and the Aral Sea, assessed based on data from bottom sediment studies", *Vodnye Resursy* [Water Resources], Vol.30, No.3, 2003, pp.281-288.

Stuart Field, *Prehistory of the Americas*, Cambridge University Press, 1992.

Brian Fisher, "A new species of Discothyrea Roger from Mauritius and a new species of Proceratium Roger from Madagascar (Hymenoptera: Formicidae)", *Proc. California Academy of Sciences*, Vol.56, No.35, 2005, pp.657-667.

D. Fleitmann, S.J. Burns, M. Mudelsee, U. Neff, J. Kramers, A. Mangine and A. Matter, "Holocene forcing of the Indian monsoon recorded in a stalagmite from southern Oman", *Science*, Vol.300, 2003, pp.1737-1739.

Donald Foster, Victoria Kenyon and George Nicholas, "Ancient lifeways at the Smyth site", in T. Piotrowski, *The Indian Heritage of New Hampshire and Northern New England*, McFarland, 2002.

James Frazer, *Folklore in the Old Testament*, Vol. 1, Macmillan & Co, London, 1919.

G.C. Frison, D. Schwab, L.A. Hannus, P. Winham, D. Walter and R. Mainfort, in *Archaeological and Bioarchaeological Resources of the Northern Plains*, Arkansas Archaeological Research Series, No.47, 1996, pp.8-40.

A. Frumkin, M. Magaritz, I Carmi and I. Zaki, "The Holocene climatic record of the salt caves of Mount Sedom, Israel", *The Holocene*, Vol.1, 1991, pp.191-200.

M.K. Gagan, L.K. Ayliffe, H. Scott-Gagan, W.S. Hantoro and M.T. McCulloch, "Coral reconstruction of abrupt tropical cooling 8,000 years ago", *Geochimica et Cosmochimica Acta*, Vol.66, 2002, p.A255.

Donald Garrett, *Sodium Sulphate: Handbook of Deposits, Processing, Properties and Use*, Academic Press, 2001.

Raven Garvey, Adolfo Gill and Gustavo Neme, "Middle Holocene behavioural strategies in the Americas", *Before Farming*, Vol.2, 2008.

Françoise Gasse, "Holocene hydrological changes in North Africa", *Proc. 20th Conference on Climatic Variability and Change*, New Orleans, 2008.

Françoise Gasse and E. van Campo, "Abrupt post-glacial climatic events in West Asia and North Africa monsoon domains", *Earth and Planetary Science Letters*, Vol.126, 1994, pp.435-456.

Françoise Gasse, Philip Barker and Thomas Johnson, *A 24,000 year diatom record from the northern basin of Lake Malawi*, in E.O. Odada and D.O. Olago (editors), *The East African Great Lakes: Limnology, Palaeolimnology and Biodiversity*, Springer Netherlands, 2004.

Theodor Gaster, *Myth, Legend and Custom in the Old Testament*, Harper & Row, New York, 1969.

Andrew George, *The Epic of Gilgamesh: a new translation*, Penguin Press, London, 1999.

R. Gillespie, J.W. Magee, J.G. Luly, E. Dlugokencky, R.J. Sparks and G. Wallace, "AMS radiocarbon dating in the study of arid environments: examples from Lake Eyre, South Australia", *Palaeogeography, Palaeoclimatology, Palaeoecology*, Vol.84, 1991, pp.333-338.

Marija Gimbutas, *Proto-Indo-European Culture: the Kurgan Culture during the 5th to the 3rd Millennia BC*, in G Cordona, H M Koenigswald and A Senn (editors), *Indo-European and Indo-Europeans*, University of Pennsylvania Press, Philadelphia, 1970.

Zi Tong Gong, Hong Zhao Chen, Da Gang Yuan, Yu Guo Zhao, Yun Jin Wu and Gan Lin Zhang, "The temporal and spatial distribution of ancient rice in China and its implications", *Chinese Science Bulletin*, Vol.52, No.8, 2007, pp.1071-1079.

N. Görür, N.M. Çagatay, Ö. Emre, B. Alpar, M. Sakinç, Y. Islamoglu, O. Algan, T. Erkal, M. Keçer, R. Akkök and G Karlik, "Is the abrupt drowning of the Black Sea shelf at 7150 yr BP a myth?", *Marine Geology*, Vol.176, 2001, pp.65-73.

Nicolas Grimal, *A History of Ancient Egypt*, translated by Ian Shaw, Blackwell, Oxford, 1992.

R.S. Gross, "The excitation of the Chandler wobble", *Geophysical Research Letters*, Vol.27, 2000, pp.2329-2332.

Ruth Gruhn, "The South American twist: Clovis first doesn't fit the rich prehistory of the southern continent", *Scientific American Discovering Archaeology*, Jan/Feb, 2000, pp.51-53.

Jean Guilaine and François Briois, "Parekklisha Shillourokambos: an early Neolithic site in Cyprus", in Stuart Swiny (editor), *The Earliest Prehistory of Cyprus: from Colonisation to Exploitation*, American Schools of Oriental Research, 2001.

S.P. Harrison, G. Yu and P. Tarasov, "Late Quaternary lake level record from northern Eurasia", *Quaternary Research*, Vol.45, 1996, pp.138-159.

C.P.D. Harvey and A.T. Grove, "A prehistoric source of the Nile", *The Geological Journal*, Vol.148, No.3, 1982, pp.327-336.

John Hay, *Ancient China*, The Bodley Head, 1973.

Walther Hinz, *The Lost World of Elam: recreation of a vanished civilisation*, translated by Jennifer Barnes, Sidgwick & Jackson, 1972.

Uno Holmberg, *Finno-Ugric, Siberian*, in C.J.A McCulloch (editor), *The Mythology of All Races*, Vol IV, Marshall Jones Co, Boston, 1927.

Homer, *The Iliad*, translated by Robert Foyles, Viking Penguin, 1990.

Sinclair Hood, *The Home of the Heroes*, Thames & Hudson, London, 1967.

Fernando Horcasitas, *An Analysis of the Deluge Myth in Mesoamerica*, 1953, in Alan Dundes (editor), *The Flood Myth*, University of California Press, Berkeley, 1988.

M.O. Howey, *The Encircled Serpent*, Arthur Richmond Company, New York, 1955.

K.A. Hughen, J.T. Overpeck, L.C. Peterson and S. Trumbore, "Rapid climate changes in the tropical Atlantic region during the last deglaciation", *Nature*, Vol.380, 1996, pp.51-54.

Mark Isaak, *Flood stories from around the world*, http://home.earthlink.net/(misaak/floods.htm, accessed March 2004.

Catherine Jarrige, Jean-François Jarrige, Richeard Meadow and Gonzague Quivron (editors), *Mehrgarh: Field Reports 1974-1985 – from Neolithic times to the Indus Civilisation*, Department of Culture and Tourism, Sindh, Pakistan, 1995.

R.K. Johns, *Investigation of Lake Eyre Part 1: the sediments of the Lake Eyre evaporates and brines, their constitution and age*, Report of Investigations No.24, Geological Survey of South Australia, 1962.

T.C. Johnson, C.A. Scholz, M.R. Talbot, K. Kelts, R.D. Ricketts, G. Ngobi, K. Beuning, I. Ssemmanda and J.W. McGill, "Late Pleistocene desiccation of Lake Victoria and rapid evolution of cichlid fishes", *Science*, No.273, 1996, pp.1091-1093.

P. Jones, S. Schubel, J. Jolly, M. de L. Brooke and J. Vickery, "Behaviour, natural history and annual cycle of the Henderson Island rail *Porzana atra* (*aves: rallidae*)", *Biological Journal of the Linnean Society*, Vol.56, Issue 1-2, 2008, pp.167-183.

J. Jouzel, C. Lorius, J.R. Petit, C. Genthon, N.I. Barkov, V.M. Kotlyakov and V.M. Petrov, "Vostok ice core: a continuous isotope temperature record over the last climatic cycle (160,000 years)", *Nature*, Vol.329, 1987, pp.403-408.

Domino Joyce, David Lunt, Roger Bills, George Turner, Cyprian Katongo, Nina Duftner, Christian Sturmbauer and Ole Seehausen, "An extant cichlid fish radiation emerged in an extinct Pleistocene lake", *Nature*, No.435, 2005, pp.90-95.

Emmi Kahler-Meyer (1971), "Myth motifs in flood stories from the grasslands of Cameroon", in *The Flood Myth*, Alan Dundes (editor), University of California Press, Berkeley and London, 1988.

T. Kantula, S.V. Kirilchik and R. Väinölä, "Endemic diversification of the monophyletic cottoid fish species flock in Lake Baikal explored with DNA sequencing", *Molecular Phylogenetics and Evolution*, No.27, 2003, pp.143-155.

Y.A. Karpychev, "Variations in the sedimentation in the Kara Bogaz Gol bay related to sea level fluctuations during the Novocaspian time", *MAIK Nauka*, Vol.47, No.6, 2007, pp.857-864.

Georg Kaufmann and Kurt Lambeck, "Mantle dynamics, post-glacial rebound and the radial viscosity profile", *Physics of the Earth and Planetary Interiors*, Vol.121, Nos.3-4, 2000, pp.303-327.

S.O.Y. Keita and A.J. Boyce, "Genetics, Egypt and history: interpreting geographical patterns of Y-Chromosome variation", *History in Africa*, Vol.32, 2005, pp.221-246.

Hans Kelsen, *The Principle of Retribution in the Flood and Catastrophe Myths*, 1943, in Alan Dundes (editor), *The Flood Myth*, University of California Press, Berkeley, 1988.

Kathleen Kenyon, *Archaeology in the Holy Land*, 3rd Edition, Earnest Benn, London, 1970.

Richard Kerr, "Black Sea deluge may have helped spread farming", *Science*, Vol.279, 1998.

M.W. Kerwin, "A regional stratigraphic isochron (ca. 8000 ^{14}C yr B.P.) from final deglaciation of Hudson Strait", *Quaternary Research*, Vol.46, 1996, pp.89-98.

D. Klitgaard-Kristensen, H.P. Sejrup, H. Haflidason, S. Johnsen and M. Spurk, "A regional 8200 cal.yr BP cooling event in northwest Europe, induced by final stages of the Laurentide ice-sheet deglaciation?", *Journal of Quaternary Science*, Vol.13, 1998, pp.165-169.

I.L. Kornfield and E. Nevo, "Likely pre-Suez occurrence of a Red Sea fish *Aphanius dispar* in the Mediterranean", *Nature*, No.264, 1976, pp.289-291.

Vincent Kotwicki, *Floods of Lake Eyre*, http://www.k26.com/eyre/The_Lake/Papers/Lake_Eyre_basics/lake_eyre_basics.html, accessed September 2008.

Tim La Haye and John Morris, *The Ark on Ararat*, Thomas Nelson Inc and Creation-Life Publishers, Nashville/New York, 1976.

Lloyd Laing, *Celtic Britain*, Routledge & Kegan Paul, 1979.

Gwendolyn Leick, *Mesopotamia*, Penguin Books, 2001.

Kristina Lindell, Jan Ojvind Swahn and Daonrong Tayanin, "The flood: three northern Kammu versions of the story of creation", 1976, in Alan Dundes (editor), *The Flood Myth*, University of California Press, Berkeley, 1988.

E.U. Lioubimtseva, S.P. Gorshkov and J.M Adams, *A giant Siberian lake during the last glacial: evidence and implications*, http://www.esd.ornl.gov/projects/qen/lake.html, accessed April 2003 (otherwise unpublished).

Zhiyi Liu, "Were 'rice paddies' near Pengtoushan and Jiahu sites", *Agricultural Archaeology*, 2000, pp.70-72.

J. Maley, *Etudes palynologiques dans le basin du Tchad et paléoclimatologie de l'Afrique nord-tropicale de 30000 ans à l'époque actuelle*, Doctoral Thesis, ORSTOM, 129: 586 S, Paris, 1981.

J.McK. Malville, F. Wendorf, A.A. Mazar and R. Schild, "Megaliths and Neolithic astronomy in southern Egypt", *Nature*, Vol.392, 1998, pp.488-491.

James Mason and Kenneth Kipp, *Hydrology of Bonneville Salt Flats, Northwestern Utah, and Simulation of Water Flow and Solute Transport in the shallow-brine Aquifer*, U.S. Geological Survey, Professional Paper 1585, 1998.
E. Mayr, *Population, Species and Evolution*, Harvard University Press, 1970.
T.R. McClanahan and T.P. Young, *East African Ecosystems and their Conservation*, Oxford University Press, 1996.
F. McDermott, D.P. Mattey and C. Hawkesworth, "Centennial-scale Holocene climatic variability revealed by high-resolution speliothem delta ^{18}O record from SW Ireland", *Science*, Vol.294, 2001, pp.1328-1331.
C.H. Merriam, *The Dawn of the World*, University of Nebraska Press, Lincoln and London, 1910 and 1993.
Lucien Miller, *South of the Clouds: Tales from Yunnan*, University of Washington Press, Seattle, 1994.
V.N. Misra, "Prehistoric human colonisation of India", *Journal of Bioscience*, Indian Academy of Sciences, Vol.26, No.4, Supplement, 2001, pp.491-531.
W.H. Munk and G.J.F. MacDonald, *The Rotation of the Earth*, Cambridge University Press, 1960.
Oswyn Murray, *Early Greece*, 2nd Edition, Fontana Press, 1993.
Tina Niemi, Zvi Ben-Avraham and Joel Gat, *The Dead Sea: the lake and its setting*, Oxford University Press, 1997.
Dennis Normile, "Archaeology: Yangtze seen as earliest rice site", *Science*, Vol.275, No.5298, 1997, pp.309-310.
B.M. O'Reilly, P.W. Readman and P.M. Shannon, "Cold-water coral mounds: evidence for early Holocene climate change and slope failure", *Geophysical Research Letters*, Vol.31, 2004.
Eric Palkovacs, Justin Gerlach and Adalgisa Caccone, "The evolutionary origin of Indian Ocean tortoises", *Molecular Phylogenetics and Evolution*, Vol.24, No.2, 2002, pp.216-227.
J.U. Palo and R. Väinölä, "The enigma of the landlocked Baikal and Caspian seals addressed through phylogeny of phocine mitochondrial sequences", *Biological Journal of the Linnean Society*, No.88, 2006, pp.61-72.
Holger Pedersen, *The Discovery of Language*, translated by J W Spargo, Indiana University Press, 1962.
Edgar Peltenburg, Paul Croft, Adam Jackson, Carole McCartney and Mary Anne Murray, "Well-established colonists: Mylouthkia I and the Cypro-pre-pottery Neolithic B", in Stuart Swiny (editor), *The Earliest Prehistory of Cyprus: from Colonisation to Exploitation*, American Schools of Oriental Research, 2001.
J.R. Petit, J. Jouzel, D. Raynaud, N.I. Barkov, J.M Barnola, I. Basile, M. Bender, J Cappellaz, M. Davis, G. Delaygue, M. Delmotte, V.M. Kotlyakov, M. Legrand, V.Y. Lipenkov, C. Lorius, L. Pepin, C. Ritz, E Slatzman and M. Stievenard, "Climate and atmospheric history of the past 420,000 years from the Vostok ice core, Antarctica", *Nature*, Vol.399, 1999, pp.429-436.
David Phillipson, *The Later Prehistory of Eastern and Southern Africa*, Heinemann, London, 1977.
Stuart Piggott, *Prehistoric India*, Penguin, London, 1950.
Stuart Piggott, *Ancient Europe*, Edinburgh University Press, 1965.

Anil Pokharia, "Palaeoethnobotanical record of cultivated crops and associated weeds and wild taxa from Neolithic site, Tokwa, Uttar Pradesh, India", *Current Science*, Indian Academy of Sciences, Vol.94, No.2, 2008, 248-255.

Irina Popescu, Gilles Lericolais, Nicolae Panin, Alain Normand, Cornel Dinu and Eliane Le Drezen, "The Danube submarine canyon (Black Sea): morphology and sedimentary processes", *Marine Geology*, Vol.206, 2004, pp.249-265.

Lindsay Powers, Thomas Johnson, Josef Werne, Isla Castañeda, Ellen Hopmans, Jaap Sinninghe Damsté and Stefan Schouten, "Large temperature variability in the southern African tropics since the last glacial maximum", *Geophysical Research Letters*, Vol.32, 2005.

Colin Renfrew, *Archaeology and Language*, Jonathan Cape, 1987.

Eugene Robertson, *The Interior of the Earth: an elementary description*, US Geological Survey Circular 532, 1966.

Andrew Robinson, *Lost Languages*, Nevraumont Publishing Company, New York, 2002.

Geza Roheim, *The Flood Myth as Vesical Dream*, 1952, in Alan Dundes (editor), *The Flood Myth*, University of California Press, Berkeley, 1988.

Gary Rollefson, Alan Simmons and Zeidan Kafafi, "Neolithic cultures at 'Ain Ghazal, Jordan", *Journal of Field Archaeology*, Vol.19, 1992, pp.443-470.

Malcolm Ross, "Pronouns as a preliminary diagnostic for grouping Papuan languages", in A. Pawley, R. Attenborough, R. Hide and J. Golson (editors), *Papuan Pasts: Cultural, Linguistic and Biological Histories of Papuan-speaking Peoples*, Pacific Linguistics, Canberra, 2005.

D.D. Rousseau, R. Preece and N. Limondin-Lozouet, "British late glacial and Holocene climatic history reconstructed from land snail assemblages", *Geology*, Vol.26, 1998, pp.651-654.

George Roux, *Ancient Iraq*, Pelican Books, 1966.

S.B. Roy, *The Early Aryans of India*, New Delhi, 1989.

W.B.F Ryan, W.C Pitman, C.O. Major, K. Shimkus, V. Moskalenko, J.A. Jones, P. Dimitrov, N. Görür, M. Sakinç and H. Yüce, "An abrupt drowning of the Black Sea shelf", *Marine Geology*, Vol.138, 1997, pp.119-126.

William Ryan and Walter Pitman, *Noah's flood; the new scientific discoveries about the event that changed history*, Simon & Schuster, New York, 1998.

Hiroyuke Sasaki, Ken-ichi Numachi and Mikhail Grachev, "The origin and genetic relationships of the Baikal seal, *Phoca sibirica*, by restriction analysis of Mitochondrial DNA", *Zoological Science*, Vol.20, 2003, pp.1417-1422.

A. Saxena, V. Prasad, I.B. Singh, M.S. Chauhan and R. Hasan, "On the Holocene record of phytoliths of wild and cultivated rice from Ganga plain: evidence for rice-based agriculture", *Current Science*, Indian Academy of Sciences, Vol.90, No.11, 2006, pp.1547-1552.

Christopher Scholz and Bruce Finney, Late quaternary sequence stratigraphy of Lake Malawi (Nyasa), Africa", *Sedimentology*, Vol.41, No.1, 1994, pp.163-179.

Alan Simmons, "The first humans and last pygmy hippopotami of Cyprus", in Stuart Swiny (editor), *The Earliest Prehistory of Cyprus: from Colonisation to Exploitation*, American Schools of Oriental Research, 2001.

Beth Slikas, Storrs Olsen and Robert Fleischer, "Rapid, independent evolution of flightlessness in four species of Pacific island rails (rallidae): an analysis based on mitochondrial sequence data", *Journal of Avian Biology*, Vol.33, No.1, 2002, pp.5-14.

William Ramsay Smith, *Aborigine Myths and Legends*, Senate, London, 1930 and 1996

Barbara Sproul, *Primal Myths*, Harper Collins, New York, 1979.

S. Stanley, *Macroevolution: Pattern and Process*, W H Freeman & Co, San Francisco, 1979.

Y.I. Starobogatov (1994), "Systematics and palaeonthology of Dreissena polymorpha", in N. Aladin and I. Plotnikov (editors), *The Caspian Sea*, Lake basin management initiative, 2004.

M. Staubwasser, F. Sirocko, P.M. Grootes and H. Erlenkeuser, "South Asian monsoon climate change and radiocarbon in the Arabian Sea during early and middle Holocene", *Paleoceanography*, Vol.17, 2002, p.1063.

Christian Sturmbauer, Sanja Baric, Walter Salzbutger, Lukas Rüber and Erik Verheyen, "Lake level fluctuations synchronize genetic divergences of cichlid fishes in African lakes", *Molecular Biology and Evolution*, Vol.18, No.2, 2001, pp.144-154.

Bryan Sykes, *The Seven Daughters of Eve*, Bantam Press, 2001.

James Teller, "Glacial Lake Agassiz: a 5000-year history of change", *Proceedings of the 16th Congress of the International Union for Quaternary Research (INQUA)*, Reno, 2003.

Kumarasamy Thangaraj, Lalji Singh, Alla Reddy, Raghavendra Rao, Subhash Sehgal, Peter Underhill, Melanie Pierson, Ian Frame and Erika Hagelberg, "Genetic affinities of the Andaman Islanders: a vanishing human population", *Current Biology*, Vol.13, No.2, 2003, pp.86-93.

Heinrich Thiemeyer, "From Megachad to Microchad – environmental changes during the Holocene", *Berichte der Sonderforschungsbereichs*, No.268, Vol.14, Frankfurt am Main, 2000, pp.11-19.

Nick Thom, *The Origin of Tongues*, 2nd Edition, Grosvenor House Publishing, 2007.

Nick Thom, *History Rewritten*, Grosvenor House Publishing, 2008.

L.G. Thompson, E. Mosley-Thompson, M.E. Davis, K.A. Henderson, H.H. BrecherV.S. Zagorodnov, T.A. Mashiotta, P-N. Lin, V.N. Michalenko, D.R. Hardy and J. Beer, "Kilimanjaro ice core records: evidence of Holocene climatic change in tropical Africa, *Science*, Vol.298, 2002, pp.589-593.

Ian Thornton, Rhett Harrison, Roy Banka, Mike Shanahan, Ruby Yamuna, Clinton Schipper, Simon Cook, R. Singidan, W. Boen, John Edwards, "Colonisation of an island volcano, Long Island, Papua New Guinea, and an emergent island, Motmot, in its caldera lake", *Journal of Biogeography*, Vol.28, No.11-12, 2003, pp.1299-1408.

Anthony Tosi and Cathryn Coke, "Comparative phylogenetics offer new insights into the biogeographic history of *Macaca fascicularis* and the origin of the Mauritian macaque", *Molecular Phylogenetics and Evolution*, Vol.44, No.2, 2007, pp.498-504.

James Tuck, *Maritime Provinces Prehistory*, Canadian Prehistory Series, National Museum of Man, Ottawa, 1984.

D. Turcotte and G. Schubert, *Applications of Continuum Physics to Geological Problems*, Wiley, New York, 1982.

United Nations, *Island Directory Tables: Islands by Total Terrestrial Endemic Species*, http://www.islands.unep.ch/Tiendot.htm, accessed July 2008.

Risto Väinölä, "Origin and recent endemic divergence of a Caspian Mysis species flock with affinities to the 'glacial relict' crustaceans in boreal lakes", *Evolution*, Vol.49, No.6, 1995, pp.1215-1223.

R. Väinölä and R.M. Kamaltynov, "Species diversity and speciation in the endemic amphipods of Lake Baikal: molecular evidence", *Crustaceana*, No.72, 1999, pp.945-956.

Sergei Vartanyan, V.E. Garatt and A.V. Sher, "Holocene dwarf mammoths from Wrangel Island in the Siberian Arctic", *Nature*, No.362, 1993, pp.337-340.

Geerat Vermeij, *Nature: an Economic History*, Princeton University Press, 2004.

Dorothy Vitaliano, *Legends of the Earth*, Indiana University Press, Bloomington, 1973.

U. von Grafenstein, H. Erlenkeuser, J. Müller, J. Jouzel and S. Johnsen, "The cold event 8200 years ago documented in oxygen isotope records of precipitation in Europe and Greenland", *Climate Dynamics*, Vol.14, 1998, pp.73-81.

Friederike Wagner, Bent Aaby and Henk Visscher, "Rapid atmospheric CO2 changes associated with the 8,200 years BP cooling event", *Proceedings of the National Academy of Science*, USA, Vol.99, No.19, 2002, pp.12011-12014.

Jan Walls and Yvonne Walls, *Classical Chinese Myths*, Spring Publications, Dallas, Texas, 1986.

John Walthall, *Prehistoric Indians of the Southeast*, University of Alabama Press, 1990.

L. Wang, N. Sarnthein, H. Erlenkeuser, J. Grimalt, P. Grootes, S. Heilig, E. Ivanova, M. Kienast, C. Pelejero and U. Pflaumann, "East Asian monsoon climate during the late Pleistocene: high-resolution sediment cores from the South China Sea", *Marine Geology*, Vol.156, 1999, pp.245-284.

N. Wang, Yao Tandong, L.G. Thompson, K.A. Henderson and M.E. Davis, "Evidence for cold events in the early Holocene from the Guliya ice core, Tibetan plateau, China", *Chinese Science Bulletin*, Vol.47, 2002, pp.1422-1427.

John Warren, *Evaporites: Sediments, Resources and Hydrocarbons*, Birkhäuser, 2006.

William Watson, *Early Civilisation in China*, Thames & Hudson, 1966.

Fred Wendorf and A.E. Close, Early Neolithic food-economies in the eastern Sahara" in R. Friedman and B. Adams (editors), *The Followers of Horus: Studies dedicated to Michael Allen Hoffman*, Oxbow Monograph 20, Egyptian Studies Publication Association No.2, Oxford, 1992, pp.155-162.

John Whitcomb and Henry Morris, *The Genesis Flood*, Presbyterian and Reformed Publishing, Philadelphia, 1961.

Joyce White, "Bronze and rice: digging in the middle Mekong basin", *Current World Archaeology*, Issue 30, Vol.3, No.6, 2008, pp.51-55.

Ane Wiersma and H. Renssen, "Model-data comparison for the 8.2ka BP event: confirmation of a forcing mechanism by catastrophic drainage of Laurentide lakes", *Quaternary Science Reviews*, Vol.25, 2006, pp.63-88.

Johannes Wilbert, *Folk Literature of the Yamana Indian*, University of California Press, Berkeley, 1977.

Ian Wilson, *The Bible is History*, Weidenfeld & Nicolson, London, 1999.

Ian Wilson, *Before the Flood*, Orion, London, 2001.

Keith Windschuttle and Tim Gillin, "The extinction of the Australian pygmies", *Quadrant*, June 2002.

Yong-Jin Won, Arjun Sivasundar, Yong Wang and Jody Hey, "On the origin of Lake Malawi cichlid species: a population genetic analysis of divergence", *Proceedings of the National Academy of Science*, No.102, Supplement No.1, 2005, pp.6581-6586.

Yong-Jin Won, Yong Wang, Arjun Sivasundar, Jeremy Raincrow and Jody Hey, "Nuclear gene variation and molecular dating of the cichlid species flock of Lake Malawi", *Molecular Biology and Evolution*, Vol.23, No.4, 2006, pp.828-837.

Leonard Woolley, *Ur of the Chaldees: seven years of excavation*, Penguin Books, 1929.

Don Wyckoff, "Archaic cultural manifestations on the southern plains", *Journal of American Archaeology*, Vol.5, 1992, pp.167-199.

Yun Feng Xu, "Origin and distribution of rice", *Agricultural Archaeology*, 1998, pp.246-254.

M.G. Yadava, K.S. Sarswat, I.B. Singh and R. Ramesh, "Evidences of early human occupation in the limestone caves of Bastar, Chhattisgarh", *Current Science*, Vol.92, N0.6, 2007.

Jak Yakar, "The socio-economic structure of prehistoric communities in the southern Levant, ca. 13,000-8,000 B.P.", *Proc. 5th Neolithic Seminar on the Neolithization of Europe and Asia – Regional Approaches*, Lubljana, 1998.

Yong Yap and Arthur Cotterell, *The Early Civilisation of China*, Weidenfeld & Nicolson, London, 1975.

Xibin Yi, "Origin of Chinese rice cultivation according to new archaeological finds", *Agricultural Archaeology*, 2000, pp.61-67.

Hua Yu, Yingqian Xiong, Zhenxia Liu, Serge Berné, Chi-Yue Huang and Guodong Jia, "Evidence for the 8200aBP cooling event in the middle Okinawa trench", *Geo-Marine Letters*, Vol.28, No.3, 2008.

Melinda Zeder, "New perspectives on livestock domestication in the fertile crescent as viewed from the Zagros mountains", in J-D. Vigne, J. Peters and D. Helmer (editors), *The First Steps of Animal Domestication: new Archaeozoological Approaches*, Oxbow Press, Oxford, UK, 2005.

L.A. Zenkevitch (1963), "The biology of the USSR seas", in N. Aladin and I. Plotnikov (editors), *The Caspian Sea*, Lake basin management initiative, 2004.

Z.Q. Zhao, I.T. Riley and A.L. Lush, "Effect of temperature and antibiotics on the hatching of *Microxeromagna armillata* (*Mollusca hygromiidae*) eggs: developing an in-vitro bioassay for fungal egg parasites", *Molluscan Research*, No.24, 2004, pp.1-5.

G.A. Zielinski, P.A. Mayewski, L.D. Meeker, S. Whitlow, M.S. Twickler, M. Morrison, D.A. Meese, A.J. Gow and R.B. Alley, "Record of volcanism since 7000BC from GISP2 Greenland ice core and implications for the volcano-climate system", *Science*, Vol.264, No.5161, 1994, pp.948-952.

By the same author and also published by Grosvenor House Publishing:

The Origin of Tongues

This is the story of the spread of human civilisation across the face of the earth – told from the evidence of relationships between languages. It is a story which has never been told before, a story which challenges accepted wisdom and throws a totally new light on prehistory. If you want to know the truth about issues such as the peopling of America, the root of Chinese civilisation or the origin of Basque, even the true ancestry of English, then this book is a 'must'!
ISBN: 978-1-906210-32-8

History Rewritten

In this highly readable work, Nick Thom re-examines the evidence for dating of the ancient Middle East – and proceeds to retell history as it has never been told before. The founding of ancient Egypt in around 3000BC marks the start of a voyage of historical discovery, fascinating for those for whom the subject is new – surprising for those who think they know it already. Most surprising of all for some will be the new light shed on Bible characters such as David, Samson, Moses and Joseph, once they are assigned their true place in the history of the region.
ISBN: 978-1-906645-02-1

Lightning Source UK Ltd.
Milton Keynes UK
19 November 2009

146468UK00001B/45/P

9 781906 645922